EGO PSYCHOLOGY
and
CLINICAL PRACTICE

EGO PSYCHOLOGY
and
CLINICAL PRACTICE

RICHARD A. MACKEY, D.S.W.

GARDNER PRESS, INC.
New York & London

GARDNER PRESS, INC.
19 Union Square West
New York 10003

All foreign orders except Canada and South America to:
Afterhurst Limited
Chancery House
319 City Road
London N1, United Kingdom

Library of Congress Cataloging in Publication Data

Mackey, Richard A.
  Ego psychology and clinical practice.

  Bibliography: p.
  Includes index, tables, and figures.
  1. Ego (Psychology)   2. Psychotherapy.   3. Psychiatric
social work.   I. Title.
BF175.M263 1984   616.89'14   84-1575
ISBN 0-89876-101-8

Design by Publishers Creative Services Inc.

Printed in The United States of America

FOR MY FAMILY

CONTENTS

PREFACE

This book presents a theory of Ego Psychology from a structural and developmental perspective, and relates that perspective to the practice of Clinical Social Work. It focuses on and is circumscribed to a model of psychotherapy with people who are experiencing intrapersonal and/or interpersonal conflicts in their psychosocial functioning.

In organizing my ideas, I proceeded from several assumptions, the first of which is that therapy by a clinical social worker deals primarily with the effects, rather than with the causes, of biological, psychological and/or social impairments in the psychosocial functioning of human beings. Indeed, the causes of most ego impairments with which we are confronted in practice are still not understood clearly, and probably result most often from the interaction of biopsychosocial forces rather than from unidimensional or genetic factors alone. I also assume that psychic structures evolve continuously throughout life within the context of human relationships including the therapeutic relationship. The state of psychosocial organization of the ego is a reflection not only of today's realities, but of yesterday's human experiences interacting with current threats and challenges. Despite the many mysteries with which we are confronted, I believe in the value and power of the therapeutic relationship as an empathic vehicle through which ego functioning may be restored and psychosocial conflict ameliorated–this is the third assumption underlying my approach to this subject. Within that perspective, I view therapy as an opportunity offered to a client by a clinical social worker who makes her self and her skills available as resources in the human struggle to transcend past and present sufferings toward a future that is less conflictive and more fulfilling.

In my practice and teaching over the last several years, I have been confronted continuously with the need to develop a theoretical perspective on ego psychology that is responsive to the needs of the contemporary practitioner. This book represents an attempt to synthesize ego psychological theory and to integrate that synthesis with clinical skills. Because of the synthetic nature of the book, particularly its earlier chapters, readers will need to be familiar with the original sources upon which my concept of ego psychology is grounded. In that respect, the readings included in the references at the end of each chapter, as well as those in the bibliography, may be of value. I do not view this book as an introduction to ego psychology nor as an introduction to the psychotherapeutic aspects of clinical practice. It is addressed to students and pratitioners who have a serious commitment to clinical work. Because of the generic nature of concepts which contribute to the synthesis, the book will be of use not only to clinical social workers but to other disciplines engaged in dynamic counselling and psychotherapy.

The book begins with a discussion of the historical development of theory in the clinical aspects of social work practice. That chapter comes first because I believe it is important to acknowledge our indebtedness to others who have struggled with similar challenges in the past. Given the parameters of this book, I also believe that it is important to place my ideas within the broader historical context of theory building in clinical social work. The next four chapters are primarily theoretical and emphasize structural and developmental aspects of ego psychology. Chapter two deals with the notion of ego structures, while chapter three examines how these structures evolve over time through processes of internalization. In chapter four the primary themes in the second and third chapters are related to the classic conceptualization by Erickson of psychosocial stages of human development. Chapter five examines the idea of ego states and inter-systemic equilibrium. Clinical vignettes are introduced gradually in these chapters to illustrate my ideas. Subsequent chapters are progressively more clinical in their foci and emphasize the application of ego psychological theory to practice. That aspect of ego psychology referred to as object relations becomes a nodal concept for integrating theory with clinical skills in the last three chapters. Chapter six offers an overview of clinical practice, while chapters seven and eight develop my ideas about clinical skills of exploration, evaluation and therapeutic responsiveness in greater depth and relates these ideas to practice by use of clinical illustrations.

In selecting clinical vignettes, I have used my own material and that of colleagues. Identifying information has been changed in such a way that confidentiality has been protected. Examples were selected because they fit with concepts that are presented in the theoretical sections. However, I have not labored to find ideal cases to illustrate my ideas, nor have I tried to analyze comprehensively all of the dimensions of each vignette. Rather, I have been parsimonious in discussing clinical examples by limiting my observations to ideas that are compatible with the ego psychological paradigm. I have also selected clinical materials that reflect the realities of clinical social work practice today. The reader will find, for example, several references to people of color, single parent families, clients of middle as well as lower and marginal economic circumstances. I have tried to relate specific examples of practice to those theoretical concepts that have generic significance without doing an injustice to the differential aspects. In writing about practice, I have generally used the feminine pronoun in referring to the clinical social worker and the masculine pronoun for clients.

Finally, I write as a person whose identification has been with the profession of social work which is characterized by a wide variety of practice roles not easily defined by its constituents or those outside its borders. Social work is a profession that has searched historically and is searching today for its identity among human service disciplines. I believe that the strength of our profession lies in the complexity of its interventive orientations, the variety of its theoretical approaches to practice, and the wide range of methods which it has developed for dealing with the conditions of humankind. What holds us together as social workers is a value system and a thread of beliefs about people: their potential for fulfillment; their rights for privacy, confidentiality and self-determination; and their human claims for a life of dignity, social acceptance and self respect. My competence and expertise as a social worker has always been in the clinical and psychotherapeutic dimensions of the profession, and it is from that orientation that I approach the challenge of writing this book on Ego Psychology and Clinical Practice.

ACKNOWLEDGMENTS

Although it is impossible to acknowledge everyone—teachers, colleagues, students and clients—who may have contributed to my theoretical perspective on clinical social work practice, I would like to express my appreciation here to some of them. Colleagues at Boston College who read and shared their reactions to the manuscript include: Professors Bernard O'Brien, Anne Freed, Ann Sheingold, Robert Castagnola, Esther Urdang and Carolyn Thomas. They were most generous and helpful. I also wish to thank the President of Boston College, Rev. J. Donald Monan, S. J., the former Dean of Faculties, Rev. Joseph A. Panuska, S. J., the present Dean of Faculties, Rev. Joseph R. Fahey, S. J., and most especially, the Dean of the Graduate School of Social Work, June Gary Hopps, who made it possible for me to take sabbatical leave during the spring semester in 1982 when the manuscript was written.

In preparing the manuscript I am indebted to two people, May Benoit and Mary McManus, who typed my hand-written drafts with their usual care and dedication.

For those students too numerous to mention and those clients who would be inappropriate to identify, I wish to express my gratitude. They contributed more than they will ever know to my development as a teacher and as a clinical social worker.

To my family—Eileen, Greg, Lynn and John—who tolerated the demands on my time and energy, I will be forever grateful. My wife, Eileen, was the first person to read the manuscript. She has always been my most empathic critic. Lynn helped with the typing. Greg, an art student, did all of the illustrations for the book.

The contributions of Gardner Press to the fine tuning of the manuscript were not only indispensable but always constructive. In particular, I wish to thank Gardner M. Spungin, publisher, and Alyce Collier, editor.

Finally, I wish to acknowledge the following publishers for permitting me to use previously published materials:

Chapter Six is a development of my ideas about clinical practice which originally was published in *Social Casework,* December, 1976, by the Family Service Association of America;

The case study in Chapter Five appeared originally in *The Family Coordinator,* July, 1968, published by the National Council on Family Relations;

Harper and Row Publishers, Inc. gave me permission to quote from Alan Wheelis' "How People Change," which originally was published by *Commentary* in May 1969.

EGO PSYCHOLOGY
and
CLINICAL PRACTICE

1

CLINICAL SOCIAL WORK:

HISTORICAL AND CURRENT PERSPECTIVES ON THEORY BUILDING

Any attempt to conceptualize a model of practice must be assessed within the perspective of history. In ways often obscure to consciousness, the history of one's profession and those aspects that have become part of one's self, professionally and personally, shape the struggle to make sense of clinical work. To understand that struggle is first to appreciate its historical origins and present context. This discussion of clinical practice begins, therefore, with a review of salient events and trends in the development of theory in clinical social work.

I recognize the developmental metaphor in this approach. Indeed, we are a young profession struggling to gain respect for what we have to offer society. Our history (although tarnished in some respects) is a testimony to those who struggled with similar issues in professional development at different periods. It is, in so many respects, a history of which the profession can be proud and, as practitioners, we need to view our current efforts to conceptualize practice in the context of that history.

The first part of this chapter will present a historical perspective. The second part will examine the current state of theory-building ef-

1

forts in clinical social work by commenting on important aspects of these efforts to make sense of what is currently referred to as clinical social work.

HISTORICAL PERSPECTIVE

Social Work is the heir of the efforts of previous generations to counter-act tendencies toward dehumanization of certain types of individuals, groups or classes, which seems to be a recurring aspect of practically all societies and cultures (Laurie, 1957, 18-45).

In the United States social work emerged from the nineteenth-century American "relief" system which reflected the moral harshness and pu-nitiveness of prevailing social and economic beliefs about poverty. The most accessible model for contending with the problems of "pauperism" had been found in the provisions of the English Poor Law System which served as the basis for care of the poor in this country. Permeating that system were the morally oriented values of a grow-ing republic which considered hard work, industry, initiative and self-control as absolute virtues. Survival of the young nation depended upon these virtues in the seventeen hundreds; economic prosperity de-pended upon them in the eighteen hundreds.

As industrial America flourished on the abuses and exploitation of labor, a liberal movement in social humanitarianism was beginning among three small groups in society during the mid-nineteenth cen-tury: the state welfare organizations, the charity organization move-ment, and the social settlement movement. By the latter part of that century, individuals who were involved in these movements were emerging as an organized group although their work was almost ex-clusively characterized by local relief efforts in behalf of impoverished families in a community. In a sense, the profession of social work was born during that era out of the union of poverty and humanitarianism.

There was an emphasis in those times on affecting the behavior of the poor, who were generally considered to be morally inferior to the non-poor, through "personal influence and neighborly intercourse" (Cohen, N., 1958, 107). The social worker was expected to fulfill a role which was very different from our concept of the professional role to-day. She was acknowledged to be morally superior to her poor cou-sins and was expected to guide them on the road of improved social functioning, a road paved on a foundation of moral superiority. The worker was representative of a society which held that the cause of poverty was to be found in the faults of the individual and not in those of society. Because social work had not yet accumulated a substantial body of knowledge about its practice and had not yet reached even an initial stage of professional status, it was highly dependent on the norms of society for guiding its work with the poor and relied heavily on the notion of the worker as a model to be emulated by the poor client. Within that moral context, some assumed that the poor had to be "forced to endure deprivation in order to keep them at work" (Lowell, 1890, 81-91).

While that point of view was accepted by a large segment of humanitarians before the turn of the century, other perspectives began to evolve around that time and heralded the beginning of a new era in social reform. Progressive thinkers such as Robert Paine, first president of the Boston Associated Charities, wrote that the causes of poverty were to be found in "foul homes, intoxicating drink, neglect of child life, and indiscriminate almsgiving" (Paine, 1895, 23-52). Zelpha Smith, general secretary of the Boston Associated Charities, suggested that the poor were no different from others; she said, further, that "all human beings craved and could benefit from intimate family living and steadfast friendships" (Smith, 1888, 640-646).

Although the thinking of individuals such as Lowell was reflected in many aspects of relief programs after the turn of the century, the new and progressive philosophy of the Smiths and Paines was developing. Its implementation was enhanced by the introduction of a new breed of social humanitarian, the full-time paid staff members of private agencies whose approach to the problem of poverty was embodied in the concept of "scientific charity" (Briggs, 1910, 90). Recognition of the need for special training in the technique of scientific charity soon led to the establishment of summer training institutes and, eventually, of full-time schools of social work. Before the 1920s, the trend toward professionalization of social work was well established.

After Abraham Flexner addressed the National Conference of Charities and Corrections in 1915 and found social work wanting as a profession, there was a movement toward developing a methodology, which culminated in the publication of the casework classic, *Social Diagnosis* (Richmond, 1917). From its birth in poverty only a few years before, social work was now rapidly progressing from the hesitating steps of its infancy and eagerly attempting to formulate a *modus operandi* for its practice. Although the Milford Conference of 1923, at which a group of social workers met to define the generic aspects of casework, was not able to formulate a general definition of casework applicable to all fields of practice, the conference did conclude that the development of a method would be dependent on the "scientific attitude of social caseworkers toward their own problems and. . .of increasingly scientific adaptations from the subject matter of other services" (Report of The Milford Conference, 1929, as quoted in Kasius, 1950, 121).

Except for *Social Diagnosis* and a few other works, however, there was a void of substantive theory that would fit with the behavioral complexities with which workers were confronted. As social work encountered people who were not responsive to its approaches and as it expanded into other areas, such as the child guidance and mental hygiene movements, a knowledge of psychology became increasingly important for understanding and working with clients. In its search for a theoretical framework within which techniques for helping could be grounded, the young profession began to incorporate psychoanalytic concepts into its training programs and practice methods.

The one major exception to this trend was the School of Social Work at the University of Pennsylvania which adopted a Rankian framework. A split developed between the "Freudian/Diagnostic" and the "Rankian/Functional" schools which tended to obscure efforts to define the raison d'étre of casework and the valuable contributions which each perspective had to offer the other. Because of its dominance in the field, the diagnostic school had a more significant impact on practice and only gradually came to acknowledge the value of functional ideas to dynamic practice such as process, time, structure and the fundamental importance of the casework relationship (Robinson, 1930 and Aptekar, 1941). As practitioners began to adopt a more ego-oriented approach to practice, a perspective on human psychology which evolved out of psycholanalytic theory in the late 1930s, many of these functional ideas were integrated into diagnostic practice although their source was not often attributed to the functional school of thought. As we shall see later, the "functionalists" have had a significant, although obscure, impact on contemporary practice, the roots of which may be traced to these early years in the professionalization of social work.

By the 1940s, practice had become more complex and social workers were involved with a more heterogenous clientele in a variety of settings. A search was underway to consolidate the generic aspects of practice which would define a stable method (of practice) despite the specialized and varied settings within which social workers were employed. Hamilton in 1940 observed that . . .

> ...the case work idea [was] no longer circumscribed by the practice of relief giving [but was] utilized whenever people have impaired capacity to organize the ordinary affairs of life or lack satisfactions in their ordinary relationships...(Hamilton, 1940, 26).

She observed further that each case involved both individual and social aspects, "a complex of inner and outer factors" which were studied, diagnosed and treated within a relationship characterized by respect for the individuality of the client. In its search for a generic method, social work had adopted the "medical model" of study, diagnosis and treatment and adapted that model to the unique characteristics of casework practice. In expanding upon her earlier notions, conceptualized in the first edition of her book, Hamilton, in her second edition (1951), introduced the idea of casework as a "psychosocial process" or a "living event" within which there were always economic, physical, mental, emotional, and social factors in varying proportions" (Hamilton, 1951, 3-4).

Theory building during the 1930s and 40s reflected several themes, not the least important of which was that the method of helping must be responsive to the realities of the client's life. As a consequence, the social worker was to focus differentially on varying aspects of the "person-in-situation configuration" without losing perspective of the bio-psycho-social gestalt of life for an individual client. The notion of parsimony began to creep into the professional literature in relation to the focus and length of treatment as well as to the nature of "data" necessary to treat a particular problem. Although the functional school had always emphasized the importance of horizontal rather than vertical dynamics, the diagnostic practitioner was beginning to appreciate that the worker-client relationship was potentially an adaptive experience in which the client could be helped to endure or master the experiences of his present life without necessarily understanding their linkage to the past (Rank, 1936, paraphrased from Kasius, 1950). In addition to these themes, social work was beginning to recognize the cultural relativity of attempting to define norms for healthy development. Although the psychological axis of the psychosocial approach to casework had been in ascendency for three decades, practitioners and educators were now questioning the applicability of psychological measures of "normalcy" apart from the context of the sociocultural milieu.

By the 1950s, casework was increasingly identified with its clinical aspects although the distinctions between casework and psychotherapy remained unresolved. For example, Virginia Robinson in

1930 had defined casework as "individual therapy through a treatment relationship" (Robinson, 1930, 187). In 1932, Bertha Reynolds discussed casework as a "process of counseling" with a person who is experiencing "difficulty in...social relationships" (Reynolds, 1932, 9). In 1946, Wilsnack referred specifically to casework as a "therapeutic discipline for encouraging ego development" (Wilsnack, as quoted in Kasius, 1950, 103). In spite of the blurring of therapeutic functions between casework and psychiatry as well as psychology in dynamically-oriented treatment, the social worker tended to bring more of a psychosocial perspective to her work which included an appreciation, not only of inner forces but of the social contexts within which clients lived and their effects on the client. In addition, the awareness of community resources and an ability to utilize those resources in behalf of a client was also considered a unique characteristic of the social work role. Two other attributes of the social work perspective also tended qualitatively to differentiate psychotherapeutic practice by a social worker from that of her colleagues: the importance which social workers placed on the empathically supportive relationship with a client and the humanistic values of individuation, acceptance, self-determination and respect for the dignity of the human being.

During this period, the profession continued to struggle with refinement of the casework method which was increasingly referred to as the helping process, a concept derived from the functional school. Elements of study, diagnosis and treatment which made up the casework method were viewed as organizers of practice which merged in the relationship between worker and client during the helping process. That is, study, diagnosis and treatment were dynamically present in the beginning, middle and end of the process although each (element) was instrumental in helping the client at particular phases (of the process). Thus, study was more characteristic of the beginning phase as worker and applicant explored the nature of the problem(s) with which the applicant was seeking help. While diagnostic questioning and thinking occurred thoughout the process, it was largely characteristic in later stages of the beginning phase–after the social worker had accumulated enough data about the nature of the applicant's problem(s) to think through the meaning of the problem(s) in relation to the client's assets and liabilities, the effects of the problem(s) on psychosocial functioning and the etiological factors (past and present) that may have contributed to the problem(s). Treatment was a focus in the process once the worker and applicant arrived at a mutual decision about the means through which the problem could be resolved. In treatment, the worker and client also restudied and rethought the psychosocial dynamics and etiological aspects of the problem as they worked together to help the client cope more effectively with his life. Study was essentially applicant-centered: the worker attempted to explore how the person thought and felt about the problem(s) with which he wanted help; diagnosis was perceived as worker-centered: she thought about the nature of the problem(s) and struggled to understand the client within a psychosocial context. Treatment, although a part of the process, that began in the intake interview, was a joint endeavor of seeking a solution to the problem(s) with which the client was confronted. Putting the method to work effectively within the parameters of the function of the agency in which the social worker was employed was the artistic task of the worker. Social and psychological theories provided the knowledge base through which the worker carried out that task.

Toward the end of this decade, Perlman conceptualized casework as a problem-solving process (Perlman, 1957). Her model for practice provided continuity with preceding efforts to organize practice methods according to the state-of-the-art of the social and behavioral sciences at a given time. In that respect, Perlman based her concept of practice on ego psychology and social role theory which had emerged in the 1930s, 40s and 50s. She valued the wholeness of the human person, viewing him as a being-in-process whose life was shaped by "his constitutional makeup, his physical and social environment, his past experience, his present perceptions and reactions, and even his future aspirations" (Perlman, 1957, 5-7). An applicant for casework services typically was a person who was experiencing difficulty in a critical life role because his ego was unable to cope with the stresses of mediating internal needs with expectations by those around him. Although she did not address techniques of ongoing treatment in that book, Perlman did suggest that "the casework process sustains, supplements and fortifies the functions of the client's ego" (Perlman, 1957, 86). The problem-solving model fit well with the social work tradition of ego supportive treatment within a purposive and growth enhancing relationship. Many concepts from the functional school were also compatible with and integrated into the model, such as a primary focus on the present, the parsimonious use of time and structure as well as the ego-adaptive orientation of interventive goals.

During this same period there were attempts to integrate ego psychology theory with casework practice but, for the most part, our preoccupation was with the methodological aspects of practice rather than with its theory base (see Parad, 1958 and Parad, 1963). There was also an emphasis on "putting the social back into social casework" which reflected a concern about:

—the skew in the psychosocial orientation over the previous decades toward the psychological aspects of practice;
—the importance of social and cultural forces on one's internal sense of wellbeing;
—the unique attributes of social work practice, particularly in clinical settings where there was considerable overlap and similarity among various disciplines in the practice of dynamic psychotherapy; and
—the impact of the worker's value orientations, based on her professional as well as personal identifications, on the client and on the casework relationship.

In relation to the last point, social work practice as well as that of other helping professions reflected to a considerable extent the individualism of white, middle class American (CSWE, 1955). Many clients with whom social workers were involved did not share in all the cultural values of the middle class, a disparity which had a significant effect on clinical practice in social work as well as on psychiatry and psychology. For example, the Joint Commission on Mental Illness and Health had concluded that those Americans who sought professional help for major personal problems were usually people with better educations and higher incomes (Final Report, 1961). Their findings conformed to those of Hollingshead and Redlich who had found that noninstitutional psychiatric facilities were used primarily by higher socioeconomic groups; patients from lower economic groups were more often diagnosed schizophrenic and hospitalized in State institutions. Their study concluded that psychotherapists frequently disliked poor patients, did not understand their values, and often had difficulty in understanding them as persons. Reciprocally, poor patients were less likely to understand what their psychotherapists were driving at although they sought relief from misery (Redlich, et al, 1955, 143-144). In another study, Coleman and his associates found that poor patients tended to receive less favorable consideration for continued treatment (regardless of diagnosis) in a psychiatric clinic and family service agency; Coleman's study suggested that the attitudes of therapists toward poor patients may have contributed to this finding since such people may never have met certain criteria before their acceptance as patients: acceptance of their problem, concern about it, wanting help and recognition of the authority of the therapist (Coleman, et al, 1957).

Another manifestation of the trend toward integration of the social dimension in psychosocial casework was the development of family therapy as a legitimate mode of intervention. Ackerman's book *The Psychodynamics of Family Life,* was a nodal point in the development of techniques for treating impaired family relationships and in the conceptualization of the family as the environment within which problems began and were perpetuated. Because of their historical identification in practice with the family and their treatment focus on familial relationships, social workers assumed a significant role in the early development of theory and techniques of family therapy (e.g.: Ackerman, et al. 1961 and 1967; Satir 1964; Bardill and Ryan 1964).

Concurrent with the reemergence of the family as a focus of service was the emphasis within the profession on "the enhancement of social functioning" as the goal of social work practice (Boehm, 1959, 46-50). Casework was conceptualized as a method through which social roles and relationships could be restored, maintained or enhanced. Later, Gordon was to reinforce and amplify upon this primary focus of [social work] practice which he conceptualized as:

the matching of people's coping patterns with the qualities of impinging environment for the purpose of producing growth-inducing and environment-ameliorating transactions (Gordon, 1969, 10).

Throughout the 1960s and 1970s increasing concern evolved about the social dimension of the psychosocial approach to practice, a trend accelerated by renewed interest in social reform as a result of the War on Poverty, the Civil Rights Movement, the protests against the war in Vietnam and the Women's Movement. Distrust of social institutions prevailed, particularly among young people, women and ethnic minorities which, within the profession, was often directed at casework practice. Questions arose as to its empirical validity as a method of helping people and whether the profession should move away from the individual clinical approach to concentrate professional resources on larger issues related to social change. The general disenchantment with "traditional clinical work" was also shared by many clinical practitioners within the profession who began to search for and to adopt, in addition to family therapy, other approaches grounded in a variety of theoretical perspectives. When Francis Turner published a collection of essays on social work treatment in the 1970s, nineteen different modes of clinical practice were included in the book, most of which had emerged in the [social work] literature during the preceding fifteen years (Turner, 1979).

It was a time of theoretical turbulence in which many of the assumptions, traditions and commitments underlying casework (increasingly referred to as clinical social work) were questioned, challenged and, in some instances, devalued (see: Fisher, 1976). It was also a time of concern about accountability and need to demonstrate the worth of clinical services funded by public and private resources within an economy beset by inflationary pressures and managed increasingly by conservative monetary and fiscal policies. In contrast to the expanding nature of the profession from the 1930s through the 1960s, social work was now confronted with challenges to its credibility, both within and outside of its boundaries.

This atmosphere notwithstanding, there were significant developments in building upon the theoretical traditions of the psychosocial approach to practice. Hollis, who had been a major contributor to theory building efforts since the 1930s, published her first edition of *Casework: A Psychosocial Therapy* in 1964, and subsequently published a second and third edition in 1972 and 1981 (Hollis and Woods, 1981). Each of these editions reflected the changing nature of practice during the 1960s and 1970s. In addition, each acknowledged the contributions of social and behavioral research and theory to the psychosocial approach. In many respects, Hollis was attempting to accommodate to the shifting focus of social work practice, as articulated by Gordon in 1969, by incorporating into psychosocial therapy ideas generated from systems theory, role theory, communication theory and ecological theory. By 1981, she had defined psychosocial therapy as a form of intervention:

> in which social and psychological means are used to enable troubled individuals (singly or in family or formed groups) to cope with environmental, and/or intra-psychic dilemmas that are causing personal distress (Hollis, 1981, 5).

According to the model, the focus of the worker's efforts was the "person-situation gestalt" which referred to the "interacting balance of forces between the needs of the person and the influence upon him or her of the environment" (Hollis, 1981, 50). This work represented the most significant effort within the profession to remain faithful to the psychosocial traditions of clinical practice while at the same time trying to integrate more contemporary theory and research into that tradition.

Although several other contributions are evident in the clinical dimension of practice during this period, three of the more significant ones were by Gertrude and Rubin Blanck, Carel Germain and Alex Gitterman, William Reid and Laura Epstein. Among the contributions made by others were Fischer (1976), Krill (1978), Turner (1978), Strean (1978) and Schwartz (1981). The work of the Blancks might be plotted at one end of the psychosocial continuum with that of Germain and Reid at the other end. In many respects, the Blancks did not fit within the parameters of the psychosocial perspective since their efforts had been to synthesize the contributions of ego psychologists with their own concept of psychoanalytic developmental psychology in order to build a model of analytically oriented psychotherapy. Both were social workers who had devoted their professional lives to the study, synthesis and application of ego psychology to clinical practice (Blanck, 1974, and Blanck, 1979). Their contribution was to reformulate theory about the inner life of the human being which they thought emerged from interactions with significant figures in the external world. They conceptualized the ego as an organizing process which continues throughout life. In their model for understanding the individual, the Blancks clarified the progressive nature of drive theory and, while not discarding the dual drive hypothesis of Freud, they recast his notions into contemporary hypothesis that fit with their idea of ego as a continual organizing process. In their writings they clarified important dynamics, such as object replication and transference, and reminded us that the thrust of treatment was ultimately to facilitate the organizational potentialities of the ego, especially in those persons who had not reached or only partially reached a neurotic level of development.

In contrast, Germain/Gitterman and Reid/Epstein focused at the social end of the continuum. The "life model" assumed that problems in social functioning occurred as a result of discrepancies between the inner needs of people and environmental resources, the locus of which, they suggested, was the "interface" between the two (Germain, 1980). Professional intervention was oriented to what we will subsequently refer to as the adaptive system of the individual, to the reciprocal transactions of person and milieu and to the environment itself. Whereas the Blancks were concerned primarily with the organizational processes of inner reality, Germain was concerned with social/transactional realities. Her methods of intervention were designed to strengthen more adaptive interchanges with the environment, a highly supportive approach to problem-solving grounded in ecological theory. Reid also developed a socially oriented but highly structured approach to practice which included specific rules and procedures that were implemented in a prescribed sequence of steps (Reid, 1972). The goal of the "task-centered" approach was to alleviate problems through a constructive problem-solving experience. It was an action oriented technology for engaging clients in adaptive efforts toward mastery of specific problem-solving tasks. An important feature of the task-centered approach was its time-limited nature. In fact, Reid/Epstein argued that "planned short-term treatment should be the dominant focus of casework," and offered their interventive model as a mode of realizing that goal (Reid, 1972, 5).

During the 1960s and 1970s, there was a general interest in time-limited modalities, such as crisis intervention and short-term treatment. That interest was related to:

—disenchantment with the viability of open-ended, long-term treatment;
—empirical evidence that time-limited approaches produced positive and lasting effects; and
—economic pressures to make therapy more cost-effective and measurable, especially from third party payers of service.

The task-centered model was one attempt to respond to those trends.

By the late 1970s, the phrase *clinical social work* was used generally to refer to social work practice of a therapeutic nature with individuals, families and groups. The setting within which that practice took place was becoming less important than the principles, methods and techniques upon which it was based. To develop a definition of clinical social work that captured its generic attributes was important to the profession. Three trends had become evident:

—the proliferation of interventive modes in the 1960s and '70s;
—the movement toward private practice; and
—the overlapping nature of clinical practice by social workers vis-à-vis other disciplines.

In 1979 the National Association of Social Workers sponsored a forum on clinical practice to offer practitioners and educators an opportunity to explore the goals, competencies and knowledge base of clinical social work and to formulate a definition of that method of social work practice (Ewalt, 1980, III). As part of the forum proceedings, Cohen presented a paper (based on the work of a task force) which outlined the generic properties of clinical practice. While recognizing that variability among practitioners was not only inevitable but desirable, the task force identified the generic purpose of clinical social work as:

the maintenance and enhancement of psychosocial functioning of individuals, families, and small groups by maximizing the availability of needed intrapersonal, interpersonal, and societal resources (Ewalt, 1980, 30).

The process of clinical work was to be guided by a number of principles:

—holistic assessment of the biological, psychological and social dimension of a client's life and their interrelationship;
—a plan of intervention based on that assessment;
—a contractual understanding between worker and client;
—the incorporation of assessment as an ongoing aspect of the interventive process so that the worker would be responsive to the changing needs of the client;
—integration of evaluation of the effectiveness of clinical work;
—the need for clinicians to be sensitive to negative environmental conditions which could affect the wellbeing of clients; and
—taking action [as part of the helping process or outside of that process] to support social change.

These parameters were intended to serve as methodological norms for the practice of clinical social work which had become highly variable and specialized in terms of its theoretical base, its technology and its modes of intervention. In sixty years, practice had evolved from a rather simple notion of influencing people within a dyadic relationship to a complex process of working with individuals, families and groups. The forum was an attempt to bring order to the diversity of contemporary practice by identification of its generic principles, a task with which the Milford Conference had struggled in a different context fifty years ago.

CURRENT PERSPECTIVE

If clinical social work is partly "the heir of the efforts of previous generations to counteract tendencies toward dehumanization," it is also the heir to the efforts of its theoreticians and practitioners to conceptualize its important work. As those efforts are carried forward, we rely on the findings of colleagues in the past and in the present to guide this work. Although new knowledge pushes back the mystery and ambiguity of clinical social work, that knowledge also has a way of creating its own problems. One may become less certain of traditional beliefs and practices as one seriously entertains new hypotheses about clinical theory and practice. On the one hand, practitioners may become so eclectic about theory that practice becomes a pragmatic technology (as the worker attempts to "do" things to people without connecting these techniques to a meaningful theoretical base). On the other hand, the clinician may become so dogmatic about theory that practice becomes a way of verifying or confirming traditional assumptions; the consequent resistance to serious consideration of the value of new ideas to contemporary practice may be counterproductive. Fortunately, most practice lies somewhere between these extremes. Considering the complexity of the professional scene today, the clinical practitioner is confronted with a need to preserve traditional knowledge–which is humanistically of value in her work–while adapting new ideas and techniques to enhance her clinical skills.

Throughout social work history, there has been a loose connection between human behavior theory and the practice of clinical social work. Rather than a prescriptive structure, theory has offered a conceptual framework within which to develop practice skills. Because dynamic and developmental theories which are responsive to the needs of clinical practice are based on inference, they are often not compatible with precise quantitative verification. One may measure blood pressure, for example, but how does one measure an ego? To a considerable extent we rely on human judgment to build theory and, as a consequence, must contend with the inherent effect of subjectivity on inferential conclusions. In contrast, one of the reasons for the stability of behavioral therapy is that the gap between inferences about behavior and techniques of treament are mitigated by the empirical nature of that relationship; in dynamic therapy the gap may be more ambiguous and the therapeutic effects less quantifiable. For example, is it technique or relationship or a combination of the two that is instrumental to change within the client in dynamic psychotherapy? While theory may contribute to an empathic and more complete understanding of behavior even when that understanding is of an inferential nature, the actual practice of clinical social work remains more of an art than a science. One's hope is that the art of practice may become more orderly and responsive to the needs of clients as a result of theory building efforts.

The gap between theory and technique in clinical social work has a unique property. Attempts to narrow the gap have often been directed primarily to methods of practice rather than to theory building and research. With few exceptions, the literature cited in the historical perspective has been concerned with techniques of intervention. Whenever social work theorists write about the theoretical base of clinical practice, their discussion of that base is almost inevitably secondary to the primary focus on methods. Clinical social work has looked to other disciplines for its theoretical base, which means that the profession had to adapt those perspectives on human behavior to the needs of clinical social work practice. No doubt the profession's historical identification with service has contributed to that imbalance. To consolidate the identity of clinical social work today, the need is to adapt and synthesize dynamic perspectives on human behavior rather than continue to borrow the theoretical perspectives of others.

In adopting such a stance, one faces the broad scope of only partially charted territory within which the profession operates in trying to understand the complex biopsychosocial dimensions of human nature. In practice one learns to accept the unknowns of causality, in an absolute sense, and to work with correlations that contribute to understanding but never fully resolve the question of ultimate etiology. If these realities of contemporary knowledge are ignored, the tendency is to attribute certainty to theoretical constructs that are almost always derived from highly circumscribed and limited sources of data. Theory then becomes dogma rather than a catalyst for opening new doors and exploring new horizons. If viewed as a catalytic tool both in theory building efforts and in the clinical process itself, theory offers opportunities to question, explore, test, evaluate, reaffirm or modify existing values and ideas. As with the ego, theory about ego psychology is in a continual process of evolution toward more complete understanding of the structural and developmental aspects of human behavior.

Theory building is as much a responsibility of the clinical practitioner as it is of the researcher or the academician. In the tradition of social casework and more recently of clinical social work, clinical practitioners have not been inclined to incorporate theory building into clinical practice. Too often the preoccupation has been with the impossible task of disproving general null hypotheses rather than cultivating an inquisitive, exploratory attitude. Moreover, we have tended toward compartmentalization of research and clinical practice which has often precluded "the possibility for exchange of information necessary for research to be addressed to relevant clinical problems" (Wodarski, 1981, 187). Although professionals need quantitative research to measure the effect on clients of clinical intervention, we also must encourage clinical practitioners to share their thoughts about theory and its effects on their therapeutic intervention. Qualitative research of that nature is as critical to the viability of the profession as is empirical research. We need not apologize for that form of research nor need we discourage the efforts of those who would make a contribution by accepting that responsibility.

Qualitative contributions to the knowledge base of clinical practice should be tempered by quantitative research focused on attempts to measure the effectiveness of clinical work. Over the past two decades questions about the relationship of theory to practice as well as about the efficacy of clinical practice in general has provoked heightened concern about measuring the results of psychotherapy and social casework. The results of these quantitative studies have been ambiguous partly because of methodological and ethical constraints in the design of clinical research. Major limitations have been related to problems in specifying norms by which positive change may be measured (Hollis, 1976, 204-222); to developing appropriate methods, including experimental and control groups, to scientifically support results; and to the dilemma of accounting for intervening variables in devising general standards of success (Sloan, 1975, 18).

In spite of the mixed picture of results in quantitative studies, some general observations are valid about the effects of psychotherapy. We know, for example, that a significant gap in social status between the middle class clinician and the poor client may lead to negative results unless the therapist is able to adapt her skills to the needs and problem-solving perspectives of the poor client (Redlich, 1955; Coleman, 1957; Timms, 1970). We know also that certain modes of therapy tend to be more effective with some clients than with others. For example, males appear more responsive to structured, planned short-term treatment, conjoint marital therapy and family therapy. Women, on the other hand, seem more responsive to open-ended therapy (Beck, 1973; Reid, 1969). Young, attractive, verbal, intelligent and resourceful people (YAVIS Syndrome) troubled by ego-dystonic conflict and coping with their lives with a flexible range of defensive and adaptive mechanisms seem more responsive to therapy than are others without comparable inner resources. No doubt their responsiveness is reciprocal, for therapists like to work with that population rather than with clients whose conflicts are ego-syntonic and whose motivations may not coincide with the intent of the therapist (Schofield, 1964).

Although dynamic psychotherapy tends to involve clients in more lengthy therapeutic relationships, there is no substantive evidence that lengthy therapy is a valid measure of its effectiveness. To the contrary, short-term gains seem to be of lasting value to many clients and may not be contaminated by or undone by symptom substitution which had historically been a criticism of behavioral and planned short-term methods of therapy (Reid, 1969; Weismann, 1974). As we have noted earlier, behavioral therapy has traditionally been the object of empirical evaluation, the results of which have supported its efficacy with specific behavioral disorder such as phobias. Recent research suggests that behaviorally oriented therapy is effective not only with simple, symptomatic complaints but with more complex and severe conflicts as well (Sloane, 1975).

Research which has included feedback from clients about their reaction to therapy suggests that relationship factors between therapists and clients, rather than specific technical interventions, appear highly instrumental in promoting change in significant social roles and relationships and in enhancing self-esteem (Epstein, 1981; Weissman, 1974; Strupp, 1969; Sloane, 1975). The corrective experience of a supportive, respectful and empathic therapeutic relationship seems not only instrumental to the effectiveness of technique but may be a critical factor itself in promoting change (Strupp, 1969; Strupp, 1973; Malucci, 1979; Beck, 1973).

Our theory-building efforts occur inevitably within complex sociocultural contexts which have profound effects on models of intervention. The struggle to humanize clinical practice may be compromised by personal, theoretical or situational lacunae which get in the way of genuine attempts to empathically connect with and to accurately understand the other person(s) whom we call client (Truax and Carkhuff, 1967). Any theoretical perspective may also have limited applicability when its conceptual formulations are derived from the observations of a particular population; this has been generally true of the theories underlying dynamic psychotherapy, the empirical evaluation of which is difficult. Nevertheless, any contemporary model of dynamic therapy must be tempered by the empirical data which is available–notwithstanding the limitations of that data.

While we strive for congruence between what Argyris and Schon have referred to as "espoused theory" and "theory-in-use," there is rarely an exact compatibility between our inner conceptualizations of what we believe and what we actually do in practice (Argyris and Schon, 1974). The actual practice of clinical social work is highly individualized. Even when clinicians share a similar theoretical orientation, their mode of carrying out that orientation may be affected by a number of intervening variables idiosyncratic to the personalities of therapist and client and unique to the transactional effects of differing therapeutic relationships.

To function effectively within the parameters of that special relationship, the clinician must become conversant with and accepting of his/her own assets and liabilities in working with different individuals; the consequence of this may be an enhancement of one's effectiveness with those people with whom one can work and an opportunity to offer other options for those people with whom one cannot work. No one person can be all things to all people and to work at being humble enough to realize and accept that reality has the potential for freeing one to be better at those aspects of clinical work and theory building with which one may be most effective. Acceptance of limitations holds the promise that clinical practitioners may be more ready to lend their support to others in the profession who can do other aspects of the job better than they. In effect, practitioners need to give as much attention to their own individuality–and training centers must pay as much attention to the uniqueness of each worker–as clinicians now give to the individuality of their clients. We need to acknowledge that our contribution to the wellbeing of clients and of the profession is contingent upon the freedom to translate a theoretical orientation into a unique practice style (Mackey, 1976, 620).

CONCLUSION

The history of theory building in social casework and clinical social work is testimony to the evolving nature of practice. In early years, models were rather simple and focused on ways in which workers could influence the poor to adopt more acceptable modes of behavior. As the profession grew and became aware of the complexities which affect people's behavior, both within and outside the helping relationship, the notions of practice changed. Because of the historical identification with service, models of practice have focused on methods and techniques of helping people and have relied on the contributions of other disciplines for a theoretical base. In recent decades we have come to acknowledge the important relationship between theory and practice and have focused a larger share of our resources to develop theoretical paradigms and practice models. Today, clinical social work remains essentially an art shaped by the individual creativity and resourcefulness of its practitioners, tempered by the humanistic values of the profession, and informed by a theoretical framework that encourages understanding of the dynamic nature of the human being.

REFERENCES

Ackerman, N. *The Psychodynamics of Family Life.* New York: Basic Books, 1958.

Ackerman, N., et al. (eds.) *Exploring the Base For Family Therapy.* New York: FSAA 1961.

Ackerman, N., et al. (eds.) *Expanding Theory and Practice in Family Therapy.* New York: FSAA, 1967.

Aptekar, H. *Basic Concepts of Social Casework.* Chapel Hill: University of North Carolina Press, 1941.

Argyris, C., and Schon, D. *Theory in Practice: Increasing Professional Effectiveness.* San Francisco: Jossey-Bass, 1974.

Bardill, D., and Ryan, F. *Family Group Casework.* Washington, D.C.: Catholic University Press, 1964.

Beck, D., and Jones, A. *Progress on Family Problems: A Nationwide Study of Clients and Counselors' Views on Family Agency Services.* New York: FSAA, 1973.

Blanck, G., and Blanck, R. *Ego Psychology: Theory and Practice.* New York: Columbia University Press, 1974.

——. *Ego Psychology II: Psychoanalytic Developmental Psychology.* New York: Columbia University Press, 1979.

Boehm, W. *Objectives of the Social Work Curriculum of the Future.* New York: Council on Social Work Education, 1959.

Briggs, R. "The Problem of Dependency," City: *Proceedings, First National Conference of Catholic Charities,* 1910.

Cohen, N. *Social Work in the American Tradition.* Hinsdale: Dryden Press, 1958.

Coleman, J., et al. "A Comparative Study of a Psychiatric Clinic and a Family Agency," *Social Casework,* XXXIII: 1, 2 (January-February 1957).

Council on Social Work Education. *Socio-cultural Elements in Casework,* 1955.

Epstein, N., and Vlok, L. "Research on the Results of Psychotherapy: A Summary of Evidence," *American Journal of Psychiatry,* 138:8, August 1981.

Ewalt, P. (ed.) *Toward a Definition of Clinical Social Work.* Washington, D.C.: National Association of Social Workers, 1980.

Fischer, J. *The Effectiveness of Social Casework,* Springfield, Ill.: Charles C. Thomas, 1976.

Germain, C., and Gitterman, A. *The Life Model of Social Work Practice.* New York: Columbia University Press, 1980.

Gordon, W. "Basic Constructs for an Integrative and Generative Conception of Social Work," *The General Systems Approach: Contributions Toward an Holistic Conception of Social Work.* Edited by G. Hearn. New York: Council on Social Work Education, 1969.

Hamilton, G. *Theory and Practice of Social Casework.* New York: Columbia University Press, 1940.

——. *Theory and Practice of Social Casework.* (2nd Edition, Revised). New York: Columbia University Press, 1951.

Hollingshead, A. B., and Redlich, F. K. *Social Class and Mental Illness.* New York: John Wiley and Sons, 1958.

Hollis, F. "Evaluation: Clinical Results and Research Methodology," *Clinical Social Work Journal.* 4:3 (Fall 1976) 204-222.

——, and Woods, M. *Casework: A Psychosocial Therapy* (Third Edition). New York: Random House, 1981.

Joint Commission on Mental Illness and Health. *Action for Mental Health.* New York: Basic Books, 1961.

Kasius, C. (ed.) *Principles and Techniques in Social Casework: Selected Articles, 1940-1950.* New York: Family Service Association of America, 1950.

Krill, D. *Existential Social Work.* New York: The Free Press, 1978.

Laurie, H. "The Development of Social Welfare Programs in the United States," *Social Work Year Book,* 1957, 19-45.

Lowell, C. "The Economic and Moral Effects of Public Outdoor Relief," *National Conference on Charities and Corrections,* 1980, 81-91.

Mackey, R. "Generic Aspects of Clinical Social Work Practice," *Social Casework.* 57:10 (December 1976) 619-624.

Malucci, A. *Learning from Clients: Interpersonal Helping as Viewed by Clients and Social Workers.* New York: The Free Press, 1979.

Paine, R. "Pauperism in Great Cities: Its Four Chief Causes," *Proceedings, International Congress of Charities* I:II. Chicago: 1895.

Parad, H. *Ego Psychology and Dynamic Casework.* New York: FSAA, 1958.

———, and Miller, R. *Ego-oriented Casework: Problems and Perspectives.* New York: FSAA, 1963.

Perlman, H. *Social Casework: A Problem-solving Process.* Chicago: University of Chicago Press, 1957.

Redlich, F., et al. "Social Class Differences in Attitudes Toward Psychiatry," *The American Journal of Orthopsychiatry* XXV; 1. (1955) 60-70.

Reid, W., and Shyne, A. *Brief and Extended Casework.* New York: Columbia University Press, 1969.

———, and Epstein L. *Task-Centered Casework.* New York: Columbia University Press, 1972.

Reynolds, B. "An Experiment in Short Contact Interviewing," *Smith College Studies in Social Work* III:1 (1932) 3-101.

Richmond, M. *Social Diagnosis.* New York: Russell Sage Foundation, 1917.

———. *What is Social Casework: An Introductory Description.* New York: Russell Sage Foundation, 1922.

Robinson, V. *A Changing Psychology in Social Casework.* Chapel Hill: University of North Carolina Press, 1930.

Satir, V. *Conjoint Family Therapy.* Palo Alto: Science and Behavior Books, 1964.

Schofield, W. *Psychotherapy: The Purchase of Friendship.* Englewood Cliffs: Prentice-Hall, 1964.

Schwartz, A. *The Behavior Therapies: Theory and Application.* New York: The Free Press, 1981.

Sloane, et al. *PLsychotherapy versus Behavior Therapy.* Cambridge: Harvard University Press, 1975.

Smith, Z. "Country Help for City Charities," *Lend a Hand,* III. City: Publ., 1888.

Strean, H. *Clinical Social Work: Theory and Practice.* New York: The Free Press, 1978.

Strupp, H. *Patients View Their Psychotherapy.* Baltimore: John Hopkins Press, 1969.

———. *Psychotherapy: Clinical, Research, and Theoretical Issues.* New York: Jason Aronson, 1973.

Timms, N., and Mayer, J. *The Client Speaks: Working Class Impressions of Casework.* Atherton Press, 1970.

Truax, C., and Carkhuff, R. *Toward Effective Counseling and Psychotherapy.* Chicago: Aldine Publishing Company, 1967.

Turner, F. *Psychosocial Therapy: A Social Work Perspective.* New York: The Free Press, 1979.

———. (Editor) *Social Work Treatment: Interlocking Theoretical Approaches.* (Second Edition). New York: The Free Press, 1979.

Weissman, M., and Paykel, E. *The Depressed Woman.* Chicago: University of Chicago Press, 1974.

Wodarski, J. *The Role of Research in Clinical Practice.* Baltimore: University Park Press, 1981.

2

TOWARD A
STRUCTURAL UNDERSTANDING OF EGO

The concept of Ego has been utilized extensively in theory related to understanding the human psyche and in the development of techniques for treating dysfunctional states. No other concept has been employed more extensively and used with less precision than that of "EGO."

The need for conceptual clarity is particularly important when one attempts to integrate understanding of human behavior with interventive skills. Whether the conceptual model is made explicit or remains implicit, it will, nevertheless, have a significant impact on the formulation of interventive skills and on modes of therapy (Lazare, 1973).

We begin, therefore, with a discussion of the psychological organization of the human person, the most uniquely human part of which is the structure known as the Ego. Because the ego never functions in isolation from other parts of life, it must be conceptualized with a context that includes biological, psychological and social dimensions. The primary questions here are:

—what role does the ego play in human affairs?
—what are its characteristics or properties?

—how may a more precise understanding of the ego be useful in the development of a model of clinical intervention?

My approach will be first to explore the evolving nature of the conceptualization of ego over time. Second, to present a model for organizing the complex nature of the ego within a social context. And, third, to suggest some relationships between the model and clinical practice.

BACKGROUND

To understand the concept, one must appreciate the original formulation of the ego in Freud's work and the modifications that have taken place in the meaning of the concept in recent times. Freud was clear and unequivocal about the ego which he viewed as a part of the psychic apparatus that emerged as a result of conflict between the id of the child which operates on the pleasure principle and the expectations of the human environment which introduces the child to the reality principle (Freud, 1966, 356-357). That conflictual relationship and the resulting intrapsychic structures are shown in Figure 1. He assumed that no structure of the psychic apparatus was present at birth other than the id which consisted of constitutional forces known as instincts.

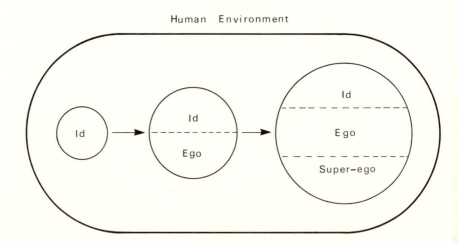

Figure 1   Freud's Structural Hypothesis

The ego became a reality only as a result of the inherent conflict between the primordial imperatives of the id and the constraints of the human environment which made demands upon the individual for conformity with cultural norms and mores, which once internalized through mechanisms of identification and introjection, became the third structural component of the psyche, the superego.

Hartmann departed from Freud's original formulations about the nature of the ego by suggesting that all pieces of the psychic apparatus were present in the organism at birth and evolved together as a result of the interaction between the individual and the caretaking world (Hartmann, 1964). His formulations of the undifferentiated matrix and the average expectable environment convey the essence of his ideas, which have generally been accepted by more recent theory builders in Ego Psychology such as Spitz, Jacobson, Mahler, and the Blancks. His conceptualization of ego departed from Freud's original notion in one significant respect. Hartmann argued that the ego has a life of its own which includes conflict-free spheres and was not necessarily a structure which emerged as a result of strife between the id and the human environment (Hartmann, 1964, 114). It was a more positive and potentially more freeing idea than the deterministic position of Freud.

The contemporary school also places greater emphasis on the social aspects of ego development compared to the Freudian school,

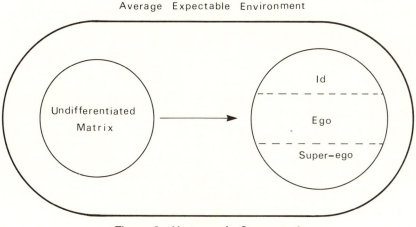

Average Expectable Environment

Undifferentiated
Matrix

Id

Ego

Super–ego

Figure 2 Hartmann's Concept of
Structural Development

which was primarily biopsychologically oriented. Current theory builders view the human being holistically or within a biopsychosocial framework. In that framework an understanding of the ego is, first of all, predicated on a set of constitutional "givens" inbred at birth which may include biological predispositions in temperament and intelligence as well as other endowed characteristics such as physical appearance. Second, these predispositions can be understood only within the context of a human environment which exerts enormous influence on the individual through processes such as emotional attachment, nurturance, psychological stimulation, reinforcement, and identification. Third, no dimension of the psychic structure or the human context within which the parts evolve are entities unto themselves, and to view any aspect as separate and distinct from the whole leads to a skewed and distorted understanding of the complex nature of human development.

To understand the organizational aspects of the ego, one must understand the relationship, interdependence and connectedness of that psychic structure to the internal world of instincts, needs, and affects and to the external world of cultural norms, values, social roles and relationships. That aspect of self referred to as the internal world consists of the id, with some modifications as discussed below. The internal world also is the home or repository of thoughts and feelings which at one point were available to the conscious ego but subsequently relegated to a level of non-awareness by the defensive system as a result of the censoring function of the super-ego.

The traditional notion of instincts as dualistic in nature has been modified recently to reflect the complexity and inter-relatedness of instincts with the social world within which an individual exists. Breger has suggested, for example, that human instincts are highly complex and varied (Breger, 1974). He also believes that instincts cannot be understood within an intra-psychic perspective alone but must be viewed in relation to the social context of the individual. His model for understanding instinctual life departs from Freud's in that respect but also in hypothesizing a "group of primary instinctual areas, each with its characteristic emotion" rather than one or two primary instincts (Breger, 1974, 27). These observations are important to the development of our understanding of instincts, both in lower animals and in humans; they also introduce the need for clarification of terms and processes at that level of human existence. As the Blancks have suggested, it is important to be as precise as possible about the meaning and significance of terms used in reaching for a better understanding of human behavior (Blanck, 1979). Before moving on, it is necessary, then, to clarify three concepts: instinct, need and affect.

At the innermost core, humans inherit what Breger has called a "primate heritage" (Breger, 1974, 18-99). Instincts originate in our evolutionary heritage, as members of the animal kingdom, even though we are distinguishable from the rest of that kingdom by our capacity for abstract thinking and by the potential of our egos to act more or less autonomously from our instinctual heritage. Although instincts in humans retain their imperative quality, they do not necessarily impel us to act out of purely instinctual motives. Unlike other animals, human beings possess the potential to transcend their instinctual heritage and to become masters of those forces rather than their servants.

Instincts predispose one to act "impulsively" toward the physical and social environment and to react to environmental stimuli in stereotypical and spontaneous ways. The most basic of instincts from which all others evolve is that of survival. The force to survive is an inborn part of infantile makeup which persists, albeit in modified form, throughout life. It is manifested initially at the biological level, then at the psychological and, eventually, at the social level. Thus, the infant cries for food, essential for physical survival, but soon the cry is a demand for love and security and, later, for social contact and attachment to a loving object to nurture and care for biopsychosocial well being. Beginning early and extending through life, the three levels of instinctual expression occur concurrently and are so interdependent that deprivation at any level may lead to serious consequences in ego development.

There are two other aspects of our heritage which need clarification. These are the concepts of need and affect. As instincts demand expression, powerful needs are created which may be gratified and fulfilled only through interpersonal contact. While the instincts *push* for expression, needs *pull* at the human world and create demands on it for biological, psychological and social supplies. Although physical survival may be assured, at least temporarily, by food provided by a caretaker, survival and fulfillment in a fully human way may be realized only through meaningful contact with another human being who is responsive, not only to the biological needs of the infant for food, but to the equally important need for psychological wellbeing, self esteem, and human contact. As a consequence, the developing person begins to associate emotions with internal representations of self and other(s).

Affect refers to the emotional response within us as a result of the manner in which our needs are met or not met at age-appropriate times throughout the life cycle. We react with feelings along a continuum from positive (loving) to negative (aggressive) poles both to ourselves and to people in the environment as a consequence of their responsiveness to us and to our needs. These interpersonal experiences determine the affective development of the individual, which begins at an early age. The precursors of affect (or feelings) are found at the need-gratifying level of ego development before separation/individuation becomes a nodal developmental issue. During the latter phases, once the ability to differentiate self from other(s) becomes a reality which is inherently linked with the cognitive capacity for representational intelligence, the organization of affect becomes a viable developmental line. If rudimentary experiences, oriented to survival and need gratification, have been successfully negotiated, the differentiated person will then be motivated by affective associations to human events which will henceforth, shape and color his esteem for self and his esteem for internal representations of significant human figures in the external environment. As these affective reactions are internalized over time, they become important sources of self esteem which form and reinforce the value which we associated with our very existence as biopsychosocial beings.

Clinical observations of behavior may be conceptualized within the instinct-need-affect framework. For the severely impaired patient whose ego may be functioning at a primitive level of biopsychosocial development, we hypothesize that the nodal issue is instinctual and that psychosis represents a critical preoccupation with psychological survival. For the severely to moderately impaired patient arrested at a need-satisfying level of development (prior to separation/individuation) clinical diagnoses are represented by the narcissistic disorders. For the severely to moderately impaired patient with arrest partially at the need-satisfying level, but also at the differentiated yet non-integrated level of object relations, diagnoses are conceptualized along a continuum of borderline states from low to high, depending on the severity of arrest in need-satisfying relations and on the extensiveness of divorce of internal representations of self and others. For the moderately impaired client who has successfully experienced and negotiated earlier survival and need-satisfying stages, affect may play a more central role in conflict and influence biopsychosocial functioning in specific interpersonal relationships. While influencing functioning at any level of ego impairment, affect will have a more balanced and integrated quality in the more highly organized ego. Positive and negative feeling will then be represented by degrees of "goodness" and "badness" even within the same interpersonal event rather than in polarized fixations of "good" and "bad."

In summary, then, at its innermost core, the internal world consists of instincts, the most important of which is survival. Instincts create needs which draw on the human environment for biological, psychological and social supplies. The manner in which the human world responds to these needs—from gratifying to frustrating them—elicits emotions. Unlike the ego, the internal world of the human psyche retains its undifferentiated nature throughout life although that world may be manifested in varied forms depending on constitutional factors and socialization experiences. The latter shape the differentiated and individualistic quality of affects, particularly as they become associated with functions and functioning of the ego.

A CONCEPT OF EGO

With these notions in mind, we now move to a consideration of the nature of the ego. The ego is that part of self which mediates between the "push" of forces from the internal world and the "pull" of forces from the external world (as the latter have been internalized into the structure known as the superego). That conceptualization of the ego is not sufficient: it is too abstract and fails to identify more specific characteristics which may be inferred by observation of concrete behaviors.

This second level of understanding may be realized by examining the specific manifestations of the mediating role, which is another way of stating that the ego is defined by its functions (Hartmann, 1964, 329). Ego functions may be understood by studying the ways in which functions serve the individual and by clarifying when these functions emerge and become operative in the biopsychosocial process of human development. Ego functions serve the needs of the individual only when they contribute to the mediating role of the ego and only when they facilitate the integration of new learning with previously internalized learning. Within that framework, the ego may now be viewed as a part of the psychic apparatus, which consists of three primary subsystems:

—the defensive system
—the executive system
—the adaptive system

Each of these systems contains specific ego functions which emerge at different points in the early years of life. Once established, these systems become dynamic and progressively complex parts of the organization of the ego, a structural concept illustrated in Figure 3. The inner boundary of the ego is defined by the defensive system and the outer boundary by the adaptive system. In the middle, looking inward and outward, is the executive system with functions such as cognitive mastery, emotional sensitivity, object relations and reality testing. Although all three systems are so interrelated that all must be understood as a gestalt to appreciate the importance of any one, the executive ego has a special role in integrating and synthesizing experiences and in maintaining a sense of equilibrium or balance with the social environment.

EGO FUNCTIONS

The Defensive System

The defensive system of the ego serves as a foundation upon which all other functions evolve and are organized. Structuralization of the ego cannot proceed unless a viable defensive system is established. That system serves as a check on the uninhibited expression of primary processes which in their uncensored state characterize instincts, needs and emotions. The defenses bind or redirect the spontaneous expression of emotion into modes that are acceptable to significant figures such as parents, peers and teachers. In that sense, the defensive system of an individual is acquired through a learning process which (unlike higher forms of learning that we will examine later) occurs primarily at an unconscious level. Defenses look to the internal world and have the primary function of protecting the ego from perceived threat or danger. As an unconscious set of mechanisms acquired through a learning process with significant others, defenses tend to reflect identification with defensive as well as other characteristics of people who have a powerful role to play in our psychosocial development. Internalization of these mechanisms is reinforced through persistent patterns of relationships across specific developmental phases.

They are established and maintained only through a process which exposes the individual to repetitious and persistent series of interpersonal encounters and cannot be attributed only to isolated events.

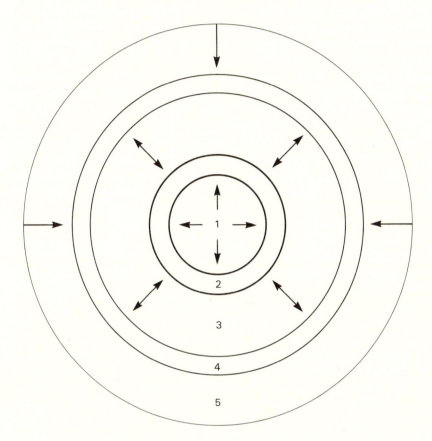

1. Internal world of Instincts and Bio-psycho-social Needs.

2. Defensive System; Inner Boundary of Ego.

3. Executive Ego including Functions of Cognition, Emotional Sensitivity, Reality Testing and Object Relations.

4. Adaptive System; Outer Boundary of Ego.

5. External World of Socio-cultural Expectations.

Figure 3   Structural Aspects of Self

As a primary system, defenses tend to be laid down early in the life cycle and perhaps remain more immune to modification than other ego systems. That is true not only because of their unconscious quality but also because, as noted, they serve as the foundation for other systems. Thus the premise that clinicians do not (or should not) tear down defenses is not only an essential component of effective intervention but often a crucial resource of psychological well-being for the individual.

The most generic of all defenses is repression, which Freud discussed extensively in his writings. Repression is generic in that it is the most basic of all defense mechanisms, one that is employed throughout the life cycle to bind the uncensored expression of instinctual discharge; repression is more immune to change (and necessarily so) than any other defense. Freud thought that psychoanalysis was successful when unconscious material was raised to consciousness through the relaxation of repression. Based on theoretical and empirical developments in ego psychology since Freud, we know that this hypothesis cannot be generally applied to clinical work today and must be carefully evaluated in relation to understanding any individual's capacity for containing the threat to well-being which is associated with uncovering work. The developmental level of the ego and the needs of the patient determine the type and degree of clinical intervention rather than an assumed proposition. In fact, we rarely meet a prospective client in typical outpatient settings today who might be appropriate for the level of therapeutic work to which Freud was referring. When we do encounter such people, the level of work may be determined by other factors such as motivation, availability of the client for long-term therapy, competing modes of intervention which may also be appropriate and other conditions beyond the control of client or therapist.

Building on the work of her father, Anna Freud extended our understanding of other "modes of defense" while at the same time clarifying repression as "a special method of defense" (Freud, 1946). In addition to repression, she identified nine other mechanisms that protect the conscious ego from the dangers associated with awareness of "forbidden" instincts and feelings which at one time–even for a moment—may have been conscious. She also contributed to our understanding of the origins and structure of the defensive system by exploring the sources of motivation for that system:

—id anxiety (fear of engulfment or annihilation)
—object anxiety (fear of punishment)

—super-ego anxiety (guilt)
—ego anxiety (fear of disintegration of synthesis in the adult) (Freud, 1946, 58-70)

In all sources, anxiety is the catalyst which signals the ego to mobilize defensive measures for its protection. Anxiety is the psychological phenomenon of the ego which has the conscious and unconscious function of anticipating threat and of mobilizing inner resources in order to avoid the pain of guilt, punishment, annihilation or disintegration. For the most part this is a process which takes place outside of awareness and contains a level of irrational anticipation out of proportion to the real consequences that might incur to the ego if the affect were allowed to reach consciousness.

The defensive system evolves in accordance with the state of biological maturation and with the level of psychosocial development of the executive ego. As a primary structure upon which other systems of the ego are built and as a subsystem which evolves almost exclusively at an unconscious level, different defenses become operational at particular points in the life cycle, depending on the developmental state of the total organism. The trigger or catalyst for early or primordial defenses is survival anxiety. Defenses that organize as a consequence of that type of anxiety are referred to as primitive defenses; they protect the ego from anticipated engulfment of primordial instinctual forces. Examples include denial of reality, withdrawal into autistic states, gross dependency and helplessness inappropriate to one's development level. Generally, defenses at that level of ego development have an all-encompassing effect on the individual, and have a powerful narcissistic quality; they tend to distort reality in gross and persistent ways and may become ingrained as a syntonic part of one's character.

The second level of defense is triggered by anxiety from early need-gratifying relationships at a point when there is some recognition and rudimentary comprehension within the ego that human objects can not only reward but punish the individual. At this level the ego is defending against perceived pain at the hands of external objects such as parental figures. Defenses now take on a more interpersonal dimension which may manifest in a fight, flight or splitting quality. Examples include projection, displacement and identification with the aggressor.

The third level of defenses evolve later in development—after the individual has acquired the cognitive capacity for representational thinking and the capacity to reflect upon the rightness or wrongness of behavior. The catalyst is inner shame and then guilt, rather than fear of external figures. Unlike earlier mechanisms, these third level defenses (often referred to as higher level defenses) have a more fluid quality, take on an ego-dystonic character, and include a cognitive component. Examples include rationalization and intellectualization, reaction formation, and pervasive ambivalence. These third level defenses are more amenable to modification through psychotherapeutic intervention oriented to self-awareness, insight and intra-systemic reflection.

The fourth level of the defensive system evolves after integration and consolidation have taken place in all three systems of ego development. They may be triggered when an individual who has previously achieved considerable success in coping with conflict is confronted with an unusual and unexpected event that may stimulate feelings of loss, threat or challenge. Compared to other defenses, these mechanisms can be mobilized in specific, transitory situations that affect only a sector of one's life rather than one's general sense of well being. They also tend to have an adaptive quality by temporarily binding forces from the internal world which might interfere with the synthesizing capacity of the ego to cope with a period of upset. Although these fourth level defenses may include mechanisms from the other three levels, they are mobilized for limited periods of time and can be given up once the critical event(s) is negotiated by the executive ego. In other words, they never become a permanent part of the character and are functional only in relation to temporal, special and situational factors.

Although this discussion of the defensive system relies on an intrasystemic focus, the defenses, in fact, may be understood only from an inter-systemic perspective. Defensive behavior always involves more than one ego system and form of behavior such as cognition, reality testing and object relations. The initial process of organizing the defensive system always occurs within a human context in which the individual is reinforced by significant figures for acceptable and unacceptable behaviors. Moreover, the development of this system is part of the socialization process which consists of identification with and introjections of characteristics of important figures; these take place at levels of awareness beyond the influence of conscious and rational levels of the executive ego.

Finally, the identification and labeling of specific ego defenses is less important than understanding their raison d'etre and modus operandi. To distinguish various levels of defense and to understand their significance in the gestalt of biopsychosocial functioning is more critical to assessment of the ego than is categorization.

The Executive System

The executive ego, the second sub-system, sits between the defensive and adaptive sub-systems which form the inner and outer boundaries of the ego. In juxtaposition to defenses which look inward to the internal world and to adaptive mechanisms which look outward to the external world, the executive system looks both ways. It relies on the other two systems for resources to assist it in effecting a balance or sense of equilibrium between human needs and social supplies. Four functions make up the executive ego:

—cognitive mastery
—emotional sensitivity
—reality testing
—object relations

The structuralization of these executive functions occurs within the biopsychosocial process of human development. Although each can be identified by its unique contribution to the mediating role of the ego, none can be understood outside of an inter-systemic context. That is, the functional quality of each is interrelated with other executive functions and highly susceptible to the influence of the defensive and adaptive systems. Impairment in any function will invariably have an effect on other functions.

Cognitive mastery is a result of the interaction between genetic endowment and intellectual stimulation from the social environment. Although the potential for cognitive growth may be limited by neurological structures already in place at birth, that potential can be activated only by social resources that stimulate and nourish intellectual understanding of the external world. Biological endowment may determine the minimal and maximal capacities of the individual's ability to think and to learn but the environment controls the availability of opportunities for support of intellectual development. As Kagan has observed, "the differences between species are fundamentally hereditary...but as for the differences within a species...in man...it is not clear how much can be attributed to heredity." He attributes the same observation to other traits as well and concludes that "the evidence today for a genetic cause is not any better than the evidence 30 years ago for an environmental cause" (Yahraes, 1978, 5).

As the individual matures biologically and develops psychosocially, he acquires an increasingly sophisticated and complex apparatus for cognitive mastery of the world. That apparatus includes ego functions such as perception, memory, reasoning and judgment. While readiness for learning may be dependent upon the evolving neurological system within the individual, support for cognitive development is dependent upon the responsiveness of significant others to the child's physiological and psychological receptivity for intellectual mastery. Thus, the function of cognition is the result of the interaction among three spheres: biological readiness, psychological receptivity and social support. As with all evolving ego functions, this one cannot be understood without consideration of all three spheres.

Piaget suggests that this complex process may be classified into four principal stages (Piaget, 1973 and Maier, 1965). The first stage, the sensorimotor phase, lasts until age two (approximately) and is characterized by highly egocentric behavior. The ego evolves during this period from a simple state of development characterized by autism to a more complex state characterized by the beginnings of language. The cognitive operations of this stage lay the foundations for subsequent stages.

During the second phase—from two to six years—the child engages in continuing exploration of his world, including new experiences, relationships and an increasing capacity for intellectual recognition and representational understanding of different elements in the environment. The process is facilitated by greater motor activity and mobility, development of language, play and identification with significant adult models. The cognitive function in this preconceptual phase is characterized by subjectivity of reasoning and judgment in which reality is limited to that which is observed. The child cannot yet differentiate the more abstract meanings behind concrete events which he observes and internalizes as representational images. During this second phase, the individual no longer considers all actions as originating from within himself and begins to attribute unusual power over events to others in his environment, a feature of human development that has profound significance to the organization of the superego.

Around seven years of age the child enters a phase of concrete operations which lasts until adolescence. During this phase the child develops a concrete and formal system of thinking in which he becomes better able to understand conceptually the relationship between means and ends, a cognitive skill that contributes immeasurably to the consolidation of all ego systems prior to adolescence. He also develops systems for classifying objects and for seeing the relationships between parts and wholes. As a result, the ego of the child is, for the first time, able to employ a deductive, rather than inductive, mode of thought.

The fourth stage, the phase of formal operations, extends from adolescence through adulthood. Cognitive mastery reaches its optimal level during this period as the individual becomes ready (and receptive) to think abstractly, reason creatively, and to engage in systematic modes of problem-solving. Differentiation, integration and consolidation of the inner world again become nodal issues in development as the individual acquires the skills to reason by formulating and testing hypotheses and to derive knowledge through processes of implication and inference. The cognitive function, which has developed on a horizontal plane up to this period, now takes on a vertical character in which the person is able to think about the significance of past, present and future dimensions of life. This fourth level of cognitive development provides further intellectual resources for organization of the adoptive system which contributes to the generativity of the adult.

Given the availability of certain resources or supplies such as adequate diet, socio-emotional nourishment and intellectually stimulating environments, the individual will proceed through these stages in an orderly and sequential way. Each phase will build upon preceding phase(s) and lead to an adult ego with a highly integrated and differential capacity for cognitive mastery, limited only by the constraints of its endowed potential. The development of this function is interrelated with all other functions. To be free to learn, the ego must have developed the capacity to defend against emotions that would interfere with the learning process. It needs, as well, the sustenance of loving and caring relationships and humane systems that will realistically promote intellectual achievement through positive reinforcement, encouragement and psychosocial support.

Emotional sensitivity is a function which originates in the primary narcissism of the infant when the ego is oriented to the self-centered satisfaction of its primordial needs. These needs pull at the human environment for gratification and, depending on the quality of responsiveness of that environment, the individual will experience feelings of fulfillment or deprivation, extending along an emotional continuum from gratification to frustration. For optimal development of this ego function, there must be a combination of fulfilling and depriving responses from human caretakers appropriate to the developmental capacity of the child to tolerate increasing amounts of frustration. The process of helping the ego of the child to develop a tolerance for frustration and to move from self-centered to object-centered modes needs to be accomplished gradually and within a consistent relationship with important human figures. As this process unfolds, the ego begins to incorporate the capacity, once offered by others, to become aware of the feelings of others and, as a consequence, to be empathic with their emotional states. Later, the ego develops the capacity to reflect sensitivity upon itself and to become aware of intrapsychic, affective responses. In a real sense, the ego function of emotional sensitivity is founded on a narcissistic base which is transformed through sublimation, a high level ego defense, to the more altruistic behavior we call empathy. Empathy, then, is sublimated narcissism. No matter how altruistic an act may appear, however, it is never completely free of its narcissistic heritage.

Elsewhere, I have reported that

> ...empathy is the acceptance of our common humanity...the recognition that the helping person is fundamentally no different from those helped at one level of existence and the freedom to feel within ourselves a semblance of what clients experience because their needs and ours are linked in a common human existence...(Mackey, 1976, 623)

That notion of emotional sensitivity or empathy represents an optimal level of sublimation. As we grow and develop, not only may our capacity to engage in more altruistic behavior become real, but the nature of our needs change as well (Erikson, 1950).

For example, helplessness and the fulfillment of the accompanying need for basic trust insures well-being and is essential to survival in the infant. The cry is a narcissistic signal for food. The unconditional response of the empathic mother to the primary narcissistic needs of the infant lays the foundation for the internalization of a sense of trust which facilitates the establishment of emotional sensitivity as an ego function. The development of that function is contingent upon the experiences of the individual at each stage of psychosocial development, particularly in the quality of responsiveness of important caretakers to age appropriate needs. Too much gratification of primordial needs may lead to insensitivity and self-centeredness in the adult characterized by a sense of entitlement. Too much frustration, depending on the developmental level at which it occurs, may lead to feelings of apathy, self-degradation or alienation which may be manifested in helplessness, depression, sporadic violence, deviant behavior or psychosis. The core conflict in both situations is an underlying rage at having been cheated of essential supplies or opportunities by important human objects, fear of one's impulses to act on that rage, guilt for the intensity of one's emotional reactions and the persistent need to seek out and to replicate in current relationships the lost opportunities of earlier developmental stage(s).

Hoffman suggests that the development of a capacity for empathy is related to cognitive mastery. He proposes a model of empathic development which includes four stages:

1. Prior to differentiation of self from other(s), the infant responds to environmental stimuli by mirroring the distress of the other, such as an infant who cries in response to the crying of another infant.

2. A second stage emerges when the sub-phase of differentiation has been reached. During that period, the child assumes that the inner emotional state of another individual is a mirror of his own (inner state) and responds to the other as if the latter's experience(s) were the same as his inner state.

3. In optimal circumstances, the child begins to acquire a sense of object constancy between two and three years of age when he experiences himself as separate from other people, and experiences them as having feelings and thoughts distinct from his own inner state. With the development of representational intelligence, the child can identify internally with another person and can imagine himself in the place(s) of the other.

4. During the latter part of childhood, the child gradually expands his affective and cognitive recognition of the experiences of others. His empathic responsiveness goes beyond specific interpersonal situations involving pleasure or pain to include the "context of a larger pattern of life experiences", (Hoffman, 1977, 182-184).

Endowment, interacting with human opportunities, plays a critical role in the development or inhibition of this important ego function. The family into which one is born and the social context within which one is raised channel our innate needs into different defensive and adaptive modes. Where emotional expressiveness is accepted within reasonable limits, the profound power of human needs may become sublimated into adaptive human relationships characterized by sensitivity to and empathy for the feelings of others. Where that potential is stifled or permitted unlimited expression, it may become a disabling defense and lead to debilitating behaviors. In another context:

> . . .all people share the human condition which is undifferentiated in its primary core but which is manifested in various ways depending on the life experiences of each person as he first comes in contact with and is involved with the world of significant others, the family and the wider social milieu. Because there are no social statuses or pecking orders at this level of human existence, people are one: there are no teachers, no students, no caseworkers, no clients, no healthy people, no deviants. . . . Differentiation occurs at one level and results in manifest differences of ego states among people while the interior world of all remains constant

and is the repository of man's needs to be cared for, to grow and to become a somebody—a person of worth and dignity who needs the acceptance, respect and support of those around him (Mackey, 1976, 623).

All of us are exceptions to this "rule." No one escapes the developmental process unscathed. Most of us are a complex mixture of narcissism and altruism, struggling to escape the narcissistic entitlement to our egos of powerful residual child-centered needs, while at the same time reaching to become more compassionate, sensitive and accepting adults. In fact, one of the great mysteries of this ego function is the capacity for empathic behaviors which some people acquire despite overwhelming odds or absence of certain experiences. That reality is a reflection upon the resilience and adaptability of the human ego and its capacity to deal with impairment in function through compensation by other intact functions.

It is difficult to empathize with a reality that one has not known. To have experienced what another has experienced may, with appropriate constraints, facilitate empathic contact with the feelings of the other, but empathic contact can also be facilitated through other means. One does not have to be poor, for example, to appreciate the suffering that poverty inflicts upon an individual. Other examples related to race, ethnicity and sex may be found in contemporary life. In situations where basic differentials are obviously not subject to change, emotional sensitivity may be cultivated and enhanced by cognitive and emotional understanding of others. Perhaps there is no substitute for experience but a lack of experience may be ameliorated by genuine and responsible involvement in learning about other people who are "different." In the process, one may learn about one's self not only in relation to differentiation which promotes individuality but in relation to the collective needs of humans which facilitates a sense of empathic connectedness.

The idea of compensation is critical for many people who have experienced deprivations that cannot be "made up" by therapy or therapists. The medium of the empathic relationship as a compensating experience may be a significant source of affective, cognitive and behavioral change for these people but can never become a substitute for the lost opportunity. Of course, our own psychic house must be in order so that we may "permit" that type of growth to become a possibility for it is most difficult for clients to grow beyond the developmental level of their therapists.

Reality testing, as an ego function is intact when a fit exists between the subjective and objective aspects of a personal encounter with the external world. Congruence between executive skills of perception, evaluation and judgment on the one hand and the real properties of external world on the other hand is the distinguishing characteristic of this function. That observation implies an optimal state of reality testing and does not imply that a lack of fit is not experienced as real by an individual. For example, the auditory hallucinations of the person whose ego is impaired at a psychotic level is real for the person even though others may know that no voices exist outside of the individual's mind. Reality for the ego in that state is limited to interior processes which are damaged and reality testing for that person is impaired only because there is a lack of fit between subjective experience and objective fact.

The organization of this ego function is contingent on the processes of assimilation and accommodation identified by Piaget (Piaget, 1973). In the earliest stages of development the individual does not have the capacity to distinguish among environment inputs that tend to be absorbed in an undifferentiated way as long as they meet his egocentric needs. Maier suggests that "experiences are taken in only as far as the individual. . . can preserve and consolidate them in terms of his own subjective experience" (Maier, 1965, 88). The infant's "outlook" on the world during this early period is based on the pleasure principle which serves the process of assimilation. As development proceeds, the individual encounters increasing disparity between his ego-centered needs and the response(s) of the human environment to those needs. He then must learn to accommodate to the world as it really is or to act on the reality principle. The process of accommodation, which evolves from the process of assimilation, is the basis for reality testing. Although both processes continue to act together throughout the life cycle, accommodation becomes the master of assimilation as the individual learns to adapt to the realistic expectations of the external world.

As the individual travels through the life cycle, exposure to differing and expanding realities becomes a fact. The initial dyad becomes triadic and soon enough involves the individual with widening groups of people outside of the nuclear and extended families. While the basic skills for appraising reality are laid down within the primary group of the family, the individual is soon exposed to other realities. How open or closed the individual will be to these new situations is determined by the quality of the accommodating process cultivated in the primary group. If the child has internalized the outside world as a dangerous place, that perception will influence his readiness to risk involvement in secondary groups. He will consequently be more closed to cognitive, emotional and social opportunities for expanding his realistic horizons and for accommodating to new situations. Appraisal of the objective world as a reasonably safe place will facilitate his involvement in new social situations and, as a consequence, offer him new opportunities to learn about the unfamiliar world beyond the safe frontiers of his primary group. The function of reality testing is inherently linked with that of cognitive mastery since the appraisal of reality involves a significant accommodating aspect. It is contingent, as well, upon the development of a repertoire of defenses which permit the individual to cope with new situations in dynamic, nonstereotypical and progressively open modes of reality testing rather than in rigid projections of one's inner reality onto others.

Object relations in the adult—or more precisely, object relatedness—is the capacity to become involved in the world of human relationships without losing an internal sense of one's identity and individuality. The development of this ego function begins at birth when the infant is helpless and totally dependent on mother for survival. In response to that reality, mother and child become involved in a highly cathected and interdependent relationship that exists for many months and insures the child's survival and sense of psychological well-being. During this period, the mother or mothering figure is the most significant human object in the child's world. Gradually the child acquires a capacity to become more independent, not only as a result of physical maturation, but also because the security and constancy of the relationship with mother provides the required psychological supplies for eventual independence. The natural thrust toward growth and psychological independence is facilitated by adult caretakers, principally the mother, and then the father, whose own egos are able to connect initially with the primordial needs of the child for attachment and fusion, and later with his needs for differentiation and separateness. The process of that gradual development of internal representations of self and the object world is shown in the following table which summarizes the contributions of some principal investigators to object relations theory.

Development of a capacity for mature object relations takes several years; this process is repeated (at least thematically) throughout the life cycle whenever the individual is confronted with and becomes involved in new human relationships that he experiences as critical to his well-being. The original relationship(s) with primary figures, however, supplies the individual with the ego skills or functions which influence the quality of all future relations. The level and extent of "progressive internalizations" of consistent supplies from significant others and the capacity of significant others to become involved and

then to be able to let go (at appropriate stages of psycho-social development) is the vehicle through which ego autonomy is eventually realized. Constancy of love, responsiveness to age appropriate needs, sensitivity to individual differences and the quality of one's own
internalized images on the part of significant caregivers—these facilitate the child's journey toward "object constancy" or the internalization of a set of images that become consolidated in the mind of the
child through a consistent thread of positive regard, caring and love.
The ego function of object relations is thus developed within a reciprocal parent-child context which serves as a model for all subsequent
relationships. What the child receives in his generation will be
returned to the next generation in the form of new object offerings to
his child.

The ego capacity for object relations is functional or intact when
the individual is able to become involved in relationships without losing perspective on the boundaries and separate characteristics of subject and object. Because of the vicissitudes of forces beyond our control, no one ever reaches an optimal state of ego autonomy in all
relations. The unfinished business in the process of achieving object
constancy is manifested in various transferential reactions which, in
fact, belong to previous significant human objects in one's life. When
the function is intact, the individual is able to distinguish, cognitively
and emotionally, between what is real and what belongs elsewhere.
Mature object relations is "objective" in the sense that the interaction
between ego and alter is appropriate to the raison d'etre of this relationship and is not affected adversely by unfinished aspects of previous relationships. Internally, object relations become organized as
whole images of self and object(s) within interpersonal relationships.
These endopsychic representations are initially fused in the infant; as
symbiosis wanes and separation-individuation takes place, the internal representations become differentiated yet polarized; during
separation-individuation they become gradually integrated; with the
resolution of rapprochement the child is "on the road to object constancy" in which inner images of significant others are valued, emotionally and cognitively, for the continuity they provide in sustaining
"self-sameness" as one becomes involved in a widening array of new
relationships outside the secure boundaries of the primary group.

The ego function of object relations facilitates the journey toward
ego autonomy. As the child enters the social arena of the world outside the primary family group, his ego is subjected to new relationships
that contain their own agendas for him. At that development level, the
ego of the child can not only recognize human figures in the environ-

Table 1   Development of Object Relations

	Spitz (1965)	*Jacobson* (1954)	*Mahler* (1975)	*Kernberg* (1980)	*Kohut* (1977)
2 months	Objectless (smile response)	Undifferentiated Psychophysiological self	Autistic phase	Undifferentiated self/object	Primal Rudimentary self
	Pre-object	Fusion of self/object representations	Symbiotic phase	Consolidation of self/object image within libidinal attachment	Empathic merger with self/object via need-satisfying actions of self/object
6 months	Rudimentary Ego (stranger anxiety)				

Optimal failures in empathic responsiveness of self/object promote structuralization via transmuting internalizations

Differentiation of self from object Representations

Integration of self and object representations

Differentiation

Practicing

Rapproche-ment

Object Constancy

Differentiation

Without

Integration

Integration of self/object representations

Integration of self/object with super-ego (through latency) i.e. consolidation

Differentiation

(semantic communications)

10 months

18 months

36 months

36 months and beyond

ment, but can also differentiate among them. Differentiation within the self occurs as a result of the development and structuralization of other ego functions that enable the individual to experience himself as well as other people as more fully human. Carrying with him internalizations from primary dyadic relationship(s) (which serve as a foundation for future attachments), the child is then ready to become involved in increasingly varied and complex social networks. Identifications with and internalizations from relationships at new levels may add to and even modify earlier internalizations from the primary family group; but these secondary experiences will never have the impact on core identity and self-esteem of the original experiences. The latter point is particularly important for understanding the limits of any psychotherapeutic relationship with people who suffer from severe ego defects in object relationships. While the therapist may never make up for these deficits by "becoming" a substitute parent, although the power of the transference pushes the therapist to assume that role, she can provide a new experience with a real object who is available to join the intact executive ego in its journey toward greater autonomy. In this frame of reference, the ego of the therapist becomes a resource for restoring impaired ego functions in the client and for supporting the integration of new knowledge about current realities.

A final note about secondary objects and the contemporary emphasis on role theory and concrete behavioral change in therapy: Role theory accounts for the pull of social expectations on the human being. Conformity to specific social roles which are in accord with normative expectations pulls on our egos and shapes behavior but does not account for the internal push toward completing the gestalt of object incorporation about which we have been talking. That push is as important in assessing the intactness to impairment in ego functions as is an understanding of normative expectations about role behavior. The mature unimpaired ego will be capable of mediating most conflicts between the push of internalized representations and the pull of social expectations. In fact, one measure of the intactness of the ego is its capacity, as manifested in concrete situations, to adapt to such conflict.

The Adaptive System

The adaptive system is built upon both the defensive and executive systems. In contrast to the defenses, adaptation looks outward to the external world in more conscious, rational, task-oriented and problem-solving modes. While defenses face inward and help the executive ego avoid perceived threats, the adaptive mechanism engages the ego in constructive attempts to accommodate to reality. In this respect the individual may not only engage in behavior that will help him adjust to or fit in with the environment but may also manifest behavior that will change the environment so that it will support his needs for biological, psychological and social well-being.

The adaptive system relies on the defensive system to bind anxiety by preventing upsetting thoughts and feelings from reaching—or from remaining in—consciousness. As a consequence, the ego is freed to engage in purposive activities that will promote effective social roles, appropriate communication skills and mutually satisfying human relationships. The adaptive system also relies on the functional resources of the executive ego since all adaptive behavior, by definition, is dependent upon intact functions of cognition, sensitivity to others, reality testing and capacity for age appropriate relationships. As the defensive system forms the inner boundary of the ego, the adaptive system forms the outer boundary—the interface of the person with the environment.

Although the adaptive system is dependent upon the other two ego systems for resources and will remain incomplete without their contributions, adaptive functions begin very early in life before structuralization of these systems has proceeded beyond a rudimentary level. To be adaptive, behavior does not necessarily have to be based on higher level ego functions such as those which emerge during the phase of formal cognitive operations. Thus, the cry of the infant may be considered adaptive although it is based initially on primary rather than secondary processes of "thinking." Given social resources available to the individual at any point, and the inherent limitations imposed upon the ego as a result of maturation levels, the ego functions in an adaptive way whenever it acts to meet appropriate needs by way of age-realistic modes of behavior. That principle does not dismiss the notion of complex origins of behavior whose roots may stem from the pleasure principle which persists as a powerful source of motivation throughout life, although in modified form. Adaptive functions develop in accordance with the capabilities of the ego to accommodate to the reality principle at specific points throughout the life cycle. In the adult, adaptive behavior is shaped by the process of sublimation so that motivation is often influenced primarily by the needs of others or the circumstances of the social situation and, secondarily, by one's own needs.

The Blancks have observed that the ego develops secondary autonomy when defenses change in function and become adaptive (Blanck,

1974). As a result, the individual takes pleasure in the practice of adaptive skills themselves. That change is contingent upon the emergence of increasingly sophisticated functions of cognitive mastery and on the readiness for engagement in more complex social networks as a result of the attainment of internalized object constancy. The change in function is facilitated by the availability of timely and meaningful positive reinforcers from the human environment so that the individual experiences rewards from his successes and takes pleasure in their accomplishment. Although the adaptive system changes throughout the life cycle in accordance with the biopsychosocial needs and availability of human resources in a particular period, it reaches an optimal state of function during adulthood when the potential for ego autonomy is at its peak. A well developed adaptive system is a "sine qua non" in the pursuit of ego autonomy.

Clinical intervention, the effective practice of which is an example of a highly adaptive system in action, is always supportive of the client's adaptive functions. In fact, when we talk about supportive treatment we are usually referring to intervention on the part of the therapist to positively reinforce the adaptive system within the client. Since adaptive behavior is indicative of a relatively high level of ego development, this behavior is never the object of intervention designed to facilitate cognitive, affective or behavior modification that is characteristic of confrontive and interpretative intervention. On the contrary, the latter are usually directed at the defensive rather than the adaptive system. Within that framework, therapeutic intervention is supportive whenever it helps to promote or enhance adaptive functions.

A distinction must be made, however, between the principles of therapy as always supportive and the differential use of support as a clinical skill. Therapy is supportive when the ego of the therapist connects with the conflict-free ego of the client within a relationship of respect, acceptance and genuine regard for the well-being of the client(s). The therapist reinforces and promotes intact ego functions in order to enhance adaptive behavior and/or to enable intact functions to serve as a vehicle for restoring functions that are impaired. For example, cognitive insight coupled with emotional awareness of an ego alien feeling that was previously denied may lead to a greater sense of wholeness and integration within the client. Insight is a means for achieving a therapeutic objective and never an end in itself. It is one way among several for facilitating the restoration and/or enhancement of adaptive functions.

The adaptive system functions at an optimal level when all ego functions operate in an integrated way so that the three ego systems complement one another. The functions of the defensive and executive systems then serve the adaptive functions of problem-solving, human relationships and interpersonal communication. Inter-systemic equilibrium of ego systems is essential for effective involvement with the external world, which is the primary role of the adaptive system. Of course, we have explored only one dimension of a very complex equation which involves the reciprocal nature of human connectedness in a real world; this also has an effect on the ego. Before examining that dimension, we need to explore a final aspect of the person—the superego–which plays a powerful role in intrapersonal affairs.

THE SUPER-EGO

The traditional concept of *superego* identifies it as a separate structure in the tripartite organization of personality. Freud hypothesized that the superego became organized as a result of the resolution of the Oedipus complex. He was hypothesizing a dynamic model for understanding this psychological agency of morality, the roots of which he attributed to the process of early identifications with and internalizations of personal standards from significant human objects in the child's environment. These objects were the father and mother, and the environment consisted of the intimate relations of the nuclear family. According to Freud, the origins of the super-ego could be traced to the interplay of two critical factors: the prolonged period of dependency of the child on his parents and the emergence of the ego ideal as "the heir of the Oedipus complex" (Freud, 1962, 25-26). At times, Freud appeared to use the terms *super-ego* and *ego ideal* interchangeably and suggested that the latter was the result of a conflict that involved an expectation that the child should identify with characteristics of the parent of the same sex although the child was prohibited from assuming the prerogatives of that sexual role. In the ego ideal, Freud saw the genesis of religious beliefs which, he suggested, were based on a group of people with the same ego ideal (Freud, 1962, 27).

Since Freud's original formulation, there have been significant theoretical developments in understanding the super-ego aspect of the personality. In particular, we will examine the contributions of three people: Piaget, Kohlberg and Breger (Piaget, 1948; Kohlberg, 1964; and Breger, 1974). Piaget's views about moral development must be understood within his general theory of cognitive development. Based on his observations of decision-making among children in different types of situations—such as their responses to stories and games—Piaget proposed two broad forms of moral judgment which coincide with his stages of cognitive development. The first form of moral judgment is referred to as "heteronomous." It is characterized initially by fear of the physical power of adults and then by deference to their authority. This type of moral response occurs at the preoperational stage of cognitive development (2-6 years) when the child is still highly centered on himself and considers all actions as originating within himself. Significantly, the preoperational ego of the child attributes unusual power (of an omnipotent nature) to adults and, as a consequence, is highly susceptible to their influence. Object anxiety and then guilt characterize internal responses of a defensive and adaptive nature during that period. The heteronomous period lasts until early latency when the child enters an "autonomous" period of moral development which coincides with his third and fourth stages of cognitive development.

During the stage of concrete operations which occurs during latency, heteronomous moral reasoning declines as the child develops the capacity to understand the relationship between means and ends as well as the distinction between parts and wholes. In contrast to inductive processes of thinking noted in earlier phases, the child now acquires the ability to employ deductive processes. As the individual begins adolescence, he enters the stage of formal cognitive operations in which he acquires an ability to think more abstractly and conceptually, and, as a result, is able to engage in more independent and complex modes of problem solving. His cognitive processes now permit him to formulate and to test hypotheses, to think critically and to arrive at conclusions by use of inference and implication.Because of the availability of increasingly sophisticated cognitive skills during these third and fourth stages, the individual acquires a second or more "autonomous" approach to moral reasoning. His decision-making processes about issues of rightness and wrongness are influenced progressively by internalized norms rather than by the external power of authority figures. Moral issues become objects of systematic study and inner reflection. They are evaluated increasingly within the context of their social manifestations rather than resolved on the basis of a priori precepts.

Kohlberg extended the work of Piaget by using more sophisticated research methods and by studying more heterogeneous populations. On the basis of his findings, Kohlberg proposed a six-stage model for understanding the orientation of an individual with regard to moral reasoning at various developmental periods:

1. Obedience/punishment orientation
2. Instrumental exchange
3. Good boy/nice girl
4. System maintaining
5. Social contract
6. Universal ethical principles

The orientation to moral reasoning is contingent upon the intellectual capabilities and cognitive skills of the individual. Thus, Stages 1 and 2 occur during the preoperational period (2-6 years); States 3 and 4, during the period of concrete operations (7-12 years); and Stages 5 and 6, during the period of formal operations (adolescence and adulthood). Kohlberg classifies these six stages of moral reasoning into three levels.

Level I includes the first two stages and is referred to as a preconventional level; Level II, the conventional, includes Stages 3 and 4; and Level III, the post-conventional, includes the last two stages. The beginning levels of moral reasoning are oriented more heteronomously while the latter levels are progressively more autonomous in their orientation. Although the model suggests that every individual has the potential, given certain inner resources as well as external opportunities, to progress through all six stages, few people actually move beyond the conventional level. In fact, studies suggest that a majority of people reach and remain at that level of moral reasoning (Muson, 1979, 48-68 and 92).

Breger makes a significant contribution to a contemporary understanding of the superego by attempting to integrate several theoretical models of human behavior. He draws upon the research from ego psychology, cognitive development and moral reasoning and concludes that "all three are different facets of one general process" (Breger, 1974, 293). Although each approach to understanding moral development may begin from a different set of assumptions and proceed along separate and independent lines of investigation, each concludes that the development of a moral structure within the self is a highly complex and progressive process which takes place within a human context. The organization of that structure proceeds from an undifferentiated to a differentiated state, from simple generalizations of right and wrong to complex notions of rightness and wrongness, from reliance on external agents of control to internalized norms, and from dependency on others for direction of one's life to an inner directedness.

In contrast to the original formulation of the superego by Freud, subsequent trends in theory building have emphasized the importance of conscious aspects of moral development, the influence of interpersonal and societal factors, the longitudinal learning aspects rather than one critical phase such as the oedipal complex, and the differential aspects of socialization on expected or normative role behavior. Freud considered the superego and its development as an unconscious process and did not account for the more conscious aspects of that psychic structure which we identify with the conscience. Recent theorists, such as Kohlberg, have emphasized the rational and conscious aspects of moral development. To appreciate the complexity of this psychic agency of morality, it is important to recognize that conscious as well as unconscious processes are at play in its formation. People arrive at a sense of rightness and wrongness and learn to value or to devalue people (including themselves) both in conscious and unconscious ways.

The important point is that the organization of our superego takes place within an interpersonal context of learning with significant figures who also suffer from limitations related to their own awareness of what they may be communicating to us. The consequences of that reality are more profound for the highly vulnerable child during the preoperational period which coincides with the oedipal level of development when the nucleus of the superego is being organized. The contrast with superego development during adolescence, when formal cognitive operations are available to the ego, is so clear that it needs no further elaboration. The potentials and risks of each developmental period have a differential effect on the formation of the superego.

Reference has been made to the superego as a separate structure of the personality. The point of view here departs from that traditional notion by postulating that the quality of the superego makes it separate at one level of analysis, a conceptual level, but not at an operational level. Rather than a separate structure, the superego is an infrastructure which permeates the existing ego and interfaces with each of its functions. The interface introduces an element of value which is associated with ego functioning such that the individual, consciously and unconsciously, associates thoughts and feelings of worth or worthlessness with specific aspects of himself and his self-object representations. For example, an individual may value cognitive mastery but view emotional sensitivity as worthless. At a conscious level, the ego of the individual may be aware of the values attached to intellectual achievement and experience empathy with disdain but have no conscious awareness of the reason for that state of affairs. Someone else may consider himself inferior to others (object representations) as a human being but have no awareness of the connection between that conscious representation and its linkage to his ideal ego which may have become internalized within a harsh relationship to significant figures during the preoperational period. Still others may have gaps or lacunae in their superego and, as a consequence, never connect a sense of value with specific behavior that causes them pain or gets them into trouble with others.

The development of the superego is inherently linked with the process of ego development. The nucleus of the superego is laid down in early childhood after the individual has entered a period of development when he is cognitively ready to assimilate information at a concrete level; that also happens to be a period when the individual is emotionally most vulnerable to the influence of significant human objects. Although the process of organizing one's cognitive and emotional associations to matters of value begins at birth and extends throughout life, the basic structure of the superego is consolidated during the preoperational period, when the task of "initiative vs. guilt" is of central importance to the individual. During that period the process of internalization of norms is accelerated and the potential impact of significant others on moral development is at its optimal level. Although the process of internalization continues throughout life, it is influenced considerably during subsequent periods by new attachments to secondary human objects and to the peer group, each of which makes its own contribution to the development of the superego. During those periods, however, the individual is better equipped to accommodate to new inputs of a moral nature as a result of a higher level of differentiation and integration of ego functions such as cognition, object relations and defense.

The process of internalization, which is essential to superego development as well as to the organization of the ego, consists of several interrelated aspects which occur within an interpersonal context:

—attachment
—involvement
—identification
—introjection
—differentiation
—separation
—autonomy

We shall explore each of these aspects in the next chapter as the processes involved in ego development are discussed.

SUMMARY

The human being is a complex and dynamic organism—biologically, psychologically and socially—who has the potential to transcend his primitive heritage as a member of the animal kingdom. The primary agency of that transcendence is the human ego which serves as a mediator between the biopsychosocial needs of the individual and the cultural expectations of his human environment. Development of the ego takes place within a human context which serves as a resource for the building of ego functions and as a vehicle through which cultural mores are progressively internalized as part of the socialization process.

The concept of self is more encompassing than that of ego. It consists of three interrelated structures:

First level—the internal world of human needs as well as thoughts and feelings which may have been conscious at one time but then relegated to that level of self by the defensive system of the ego.

Second level—the ego, which consists of three sub-systems. The inner boundary of the ego is defined by its defensive system, the outer boundary by its adaptive system. The ego proper or executive system is defined by its functions, which include cognition, emotional sensitivity, object relations and reality testing.

Third level—the superego, concerned with the moral life of the individual. Containing conscious as well as unconscious aspects, this structure is integrated with the ego and its three sub-systems, associating with each function a sense of its worthiness. The superego also exerts inner control by censoring unacceptable thoughts and feelings and checking the social manifestation of selected behavior. Taken as a whole, it shapes the form and substance of our self-object representations and, consequently, regard for ourself as a person.

REFERENCES

Blanck, G. and Blanck, *Ego Psychology II: Psychoanalytic Developmental Psychology.* New York: Columbia University Press, 1979.

Blanck, G. and Blanck, R. *Ego Psychology: Theory and Practice.* New York: Columbia University Press, 1974.

Breger, L. *From Instinct to Identity: The Development of Personality.* Englewood Cliffs: Prentice-Hall, Inc., 1974.

Erikson, E. *Childhood and Society.* New York: W. W. Norton and Co., Inc., 1950.

Freud, A. *The Ego and the Mechanisms of Defense.* New York: International Universities Press, 1946.

Freud S. *The Ego and The Id* (Translated by Joan Riviere). New York: W. W. Norton & Co., Inc., 1962.

——. *The Complete Introductory Lectures on Psychoanalysis.* New York: W. W. Norton & Co., Inc., 1966.

Hartmann, H. *Ego Psychology and The Problem of Adaptation.* New York: International Universities Press, 1958.

——. *Essays on Ego Psychology.* New York: International Universities Press, 1964.

Hoffman, M. "Empathy, its Development and Prosocial Implications" in *Nebraska Symposium on Motivation, 1977: Social Cognitive Development.* Edited by C.B. Keasey, University of Nebraska Press, 1977.

Jacobson, E. "The Self and The Object World." *The Psychoanalytic Study of The Child,* Vol. IX. New York: International Universities Press, 1954, 75-127.

Kernberg, O. *Internal World and External Reality: Object Relations Theory Applied.* New York: Jason Aronson, 1980.

Kohlberg, L. "Development of Moral Character and Moral Ideology," in *Review of Child Development Research,* Edited by N. Hoffman and L. Hoffman. New York: Rossell Sage Foundation, 1964, 383-431.

Kohut, H. *The Restoration of the Self.* New York: International Universities Press, 1977.

Lazare, A. "Hidden Conceptual Models in Clinical Psychiatry," *New England Journal of Medicine.* (Fall, 1973) 345-351.

Mackey, R. "Generic Aspects of Clinical Social Work," *Social Casework.* (December, 1976) 619-624.

Mahler, M. et al. *The Psychological Birth of the Human Infant: Symbiosis and Individuation.* New York: Basic Books, Inc., 1975.

Maier, H. *Three Theories of Child Development.* New York: Harper and Row, 1965.

Muson, H. "Moral Thinking: Can it Be Taught?" *Psychology Today.* February, 1979.

Piaget, J. *The Moral Judgment of the Child.* Glencoe, Illinois: Free Press, 1948.

——. *The Child and Reality.* New York: Grossman Publishers, 1973.

Spitz, R. *The First Year of Life.* New York: International Universities Press, 1965.

Yahraes, H. *Childhood Environment and Mental Health: A Conversation with Dr. Jerome Kagan.* National Institute of Mental Health.

3

EGO DEVELOPMENT:
PROCESSES OF INTERNALIZATION

OVERVIEW

Having explored the structural aspects of the ego and its monitoring partner, the superego, we will now examine processes of internalization involved in ego development which consist of seven different aspects organized within three developmental levels:
Lower Level Processes
—attachment
—involvement
Mid-Level Processes
—identification
—introjection
—differentiation
Higher Level Processes
—separation
—autonomy

Internalization is the gradual process by which the individual incorporates within himself those attributes, values and functions that were previously available to him and carried out for him by significant figures in the human environment. Although internalization has traditionally been linked to processes of identification and introjection, this model for understanding ego development hypothesizes additional processes within a three-dimensional paradigm. In a sense, the mid-level dimension of identification, introjection and differentiation may be considered internalization proper while the lower-level dimension of attachment and involvement may be considered antecedent or preparatory to internalization proper. The third dimension may be considered the consequent state of ego development as a result of the resolution of lower and mid-level processes. The rationale for including these three levels within the paradigm and referring to them as dimensions of the internalization process is to show continuity of ego development from a dependent and unorganized state to an interdependent and increasingly autonomous state.

These processes occur in the context of social relationships that begin within the dyad with mother, and gradually extend to a widening array of encounters with other people. The evolution of the ego through the building of functions by way of the life-long processes of internalization always includes a dynamic interplay of endowed potentials with environmental opportunities. Within that matrix, certain events of a psychosocial nature which we have identified as processes are instrumental in promoting and reinforcing the natural thrust of the human being toward eventual self-sufficiency and ego autonomy.

While this approach subscribes to the notion that basic structures are activated and organized during the first few years of life, it also assumes that ego development is a life-long and dynamic affair. The processes to which we have been referring are manifested in more specific form during the early years of ego development and in more thematic form in subsequent years as the individual is exposed to new and more complex human relationships. In other words, the individual at higher levels of development is confronted with more conceptual and affective themes which may spring from unfinished or incomplete processes of an earlier level. Of course, the individual is also confronted with the human agenda of the developmental period of which he is then a part. As a consequence, except for the earliest levels of ego development, we are all confronted throughout the life cycle with the needs and demands of our current situation, as well as with the unfinished aspects of earlier levels. The agenda which confronts the individual in the "present" is always influenced by the past, since no one escapes any developmental level by fully resolving the needs of that level. In fact, the absence of an ideal or complete resolution of any developmental period is a powerful source of motivation for reworking the missing piece(s) in subsequent periods and for sustaining one in the pursuit of new opportunities for realization of the ego ideal.

The human processes which facilitate ego organization are open affairs which have relatively specific beginnings, but no discreet endings. The structures identified in chapter two emerge at phase specific points in the early years of life as a result of lower level processes which occur within the dynamic context of human relationships. Once established, ego functions continue to grow throughout life within the context of mid and higher level processes which also change in relation to the needs of particular developmental stages. Early processes persist in modified form and serve as essential building blocks for subsequent processes. For example, attachment and involvement, as the initial and most fundamental processes in ego development, are the principal components of interpersonal relationships in the earliest months of neonatal life. They continue as essential processes in later periods of development although in modified and more mature forms. Basic processes serve as a nucleus from which subsequent processes such as identification and differentation evolve and develop. These lower level processes do not disappear or atrophy. Rather, they serve to facilitate involvement in higher level processes —the vehicle by which ego autonomy is eventually realized.

As has been mentioned, an important aspect of these processes is that they take place within a human context. The interpersonal milieu and the responsiveness of significant figures in the social environment are critical to organization of the ego and the superego. To understand the individual and the unique characteristics of his personal world, one must understand the sociocultural context of human relationships within which the ego develops and within which the superego and conscience are formed. How we value ourselves and ascribe value to others is the result of the kinds of experiences that our egos have encountered with significant others throughout the socialization process. From a conceptual perspective, these processes may be thought of as generic in nature, but their manifestation in real life will be tempered by the values of the family and other significant reference groups. Some ethnic groups, for example, may value collaterality rather than individualism in family relationships; this may affect the values associated with different processes. The differential influence of sociocultural values on internalization will be most keenly felt in mid-level processes, particularly in relation to identification, a theme to which we will return later in this chapter.

The transactional nature of internal-external encounters, which occur at the interface of the ego and the social environment, contributes to the shaping of endopsychic representations of self and other which transcend the esoteric boundaries of ego and superego (Jacobson, 1954). In their earliest and most rudimentary form, representations of one's sense of self as subject and one's sense of others as objects are undifferentiated; with maturation of neurophysiological systems and age appropriate developmental experiences with the human environment, these inner images differentiate and are valued with a sense of goodness and badness, which marks the beginnings of superego functioning. Later, they become integrated and finally consolidated to offer one a sense of continuity as a whole human being, the biological, psychological and social dimensions of which exist in dynamic states of change that shift in a progressive yet circular fashion over time. Depending on one's inner needs and the quality of external resources, these shifts may be manifested in dependent, pseudo-dependent and/or interdependent relations with the human environment.

Within those contexts, fusion ensures survival; differentiation promotes separateness; integration provides continuity; and consolidation offers stability. Each of these aspects will be valued or devalued throughout life at conscious, preconscious and unconscious levels as a consequence of several factors not the least of which are their significance for enhancing self-esteem, their compatibility with the value system of the culture or subcultural group, and their appropriateness to the needs of the individual within various developmental stages. For example, the dependency of childhood provides the cognitive and emotional supplies which facilitate the pseudo-independence that characterizes latency and then becomes a focal conflict of adolescence when the individual struggles to surrender the known securities of his past for the anticipated gains of an unknown future.

The stereotypical concept of adulthood as a time of independence is, in its mature form, a period of interdependence characterized by integration of ego functions with a more stable set of values. The achievement of integration ensures the consolidation of an inner representation of self, which leads to stability and conservatism. In its more extreme manifestation, conservatism is a defense against losing the gains to which one feels entitled as a result of developmental achievements; conservatism may also be a reaction to anticipated loss as an inevitable result of impending old age. The confrontation in mid-life with a sense of one's own mortality is a distinguishing feature of the interdependence of adulthood in contrast to the pseudoindependence of adolescence.

The model depicted in Figure 4 hypothesizes that processes of attachment, involvement, identification, introjection, differentiation,

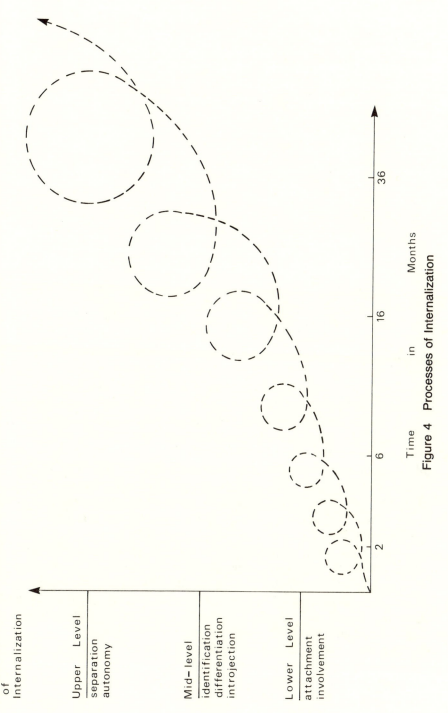

Figure 4 Processes of Internalization

separation and autonomy are activated in early childhood and are instrumental to biological, psychological and social well-being. Although
significant in human relationships within a variety of contexts throughout life, these processes are essential for ego development in the early
years when they serve as the interpersonal vehicles through which potential structures become organized out of the undifferentiated matrix.
During that period, there is distinct sequential movement from lower
to higher level processes for two reasons:

—biologically, neurophysiological maturation propels psychosocial development of the ego in a more linear direction and determines the readiness
for specific behavioral tasks more directly than in any subsequent phase;
—psychologically, the processes involved at upper levels are contingent
upon the quality of preceding processes

If the biopsychosocial supplies offered by significant figures have been
internalized in a reasonably integrated way within the context of lower
level processes, the individual will be prepared to engage in mid and
higher level processes without needing to spend considerable time and
energy in negotiating anew the most basic processes. Thus, the person who has experienced early attachments and involvements with significant figures in ego enhancing ways will be more ready to engage
in higher level processes than will a person who has developed a sense
of mistrust in attaching to and becoming involved in new relationships.

The foundation of each level is laid down during infancy and childhood and reworked, broadened and modified during subsequent stages
of development from adolescence through old age. Although change
is possible throughout life, earliest experiences with primary figures
become the internal representational prototypes for future relationships. These nuclei are generally beyond awareness of the conscious
ego. Because they have been internalized at a time of maximum structural plasticity, they have a profound and enduring effect on subsequent relationships. During adolescence and adulthood, the processes
are reworked but at a thematic level in which the individual is engaged
in adapting the processes to different and widening social relationships.
Many of the aspects occur concurrently during these periods of life
when there may be an amalgam of two or more aspects.

As a way of illustrating these ideas, consider the gradual change in
attachments, involvements and identifications during latency which
prepares the individual for confrontation with the more substantive

modifications in these processes during adolescence and adulthood. More intense relationships of a sexual and/or loving nature, characteristic of these later periods, require further adaptation of these processes, adaptations that are contingent upon the internalization of supplies offered in attachments to and involvement with primary figures who also supported gradual separateness and autonomy. The nature of one's identifications and the capacity to selectively introject values, ideas and other personal qualities of significant figures also change considerably from childhood to adolescence. A progressive sense of separateness and autonomy integrated with more sophisticated cognitive abilities promote more mature and egalitarian attachments to and involvements with friends and lovers during late adolescence and adulthood. While the processes may unfold in a linear fashion during childhood, they exist in a more circular and dynamic fashion in latency, adolescence and adulthood. During these latter periods, upper level processes temper lower level ones so that the attachments of mature friendships, for example, are characterized by respect for separateness and autonomy.

A different form of the manifestation of these processes may be found in clinical work which begins as the applicant forms a new attachment with a therapist and becomes involved in the role of client. Ultimately, the goal of therapy is to facilitate greater autonomy of the client's ego through identification with a method of change. In the treatment relationship, many of the aspects of ego development may be re-experienced, not in their original form, but in the transference. Depending on the assessment of the client and his situation, the therapist may choose to encourage specific processes and to discourage or benignly tolerate others in order to help the patient achieve greater independence in his daily life. Although the processes of ego development are never repeated in their original form with secondary objects such as therapists, they will, nevertheless, be present at least thematically in relationships, including the treatment relationship. Their presence is the basis for the concepts of transference and the "corrective emotional experience" (Alexander, F., 1963).

We will now examine the dynamics of each process. The method upon which this conceptualization evolved was based on a review of theory and research available on ego development, as well as a study of the experiences of clients with whom I have worked. The classification of these processes into levels is intended to clarify the relative importance of each to particular aspects of ego development and structuralization. No hierarchal ordering of processes is intended.

LOWER LEVEL PROCESSES:
ATTACHMENT AND INVOLVEMENT

Attachment begins during the prenatal period and extends into the neo-natal period. Initially, the fetus and then the infant is dependent on the mother for physical survival and is helpless without her. This bi-ological need for physical attachment to the mother becomes the ba-sis for psychological attachment to her and to other family members; this serves as the prototype of all future social attachments (Ainsworth, 1969).

As an aspect of ego development which begins at a primordial level, the process of attachment is motivated primarily by maturational needs and instinctual forces. The need to be connected with another person is initially an inherent condition for physical survival and soon enough for psychosocial well-being. Although the form and substance of hu-man attachments are shaped later by the capacity of the individual to use verbal symbols to communicate these needs, attachment—even at a highly developed level of ego organization—is influenced primarily by preverbal factors. The intuitive element in reaching out to another has its roots in early relationships, before development of the cogni-tive capacity to use symbols as a means of conceptualizing one's needs. That pre-verbal (as distinct from non-verbal) quality continues to play a critical role in all subsequent attachments.

Investigators who have studied ego development during the neona-tal period concur that the infant is in a state of transition from the in-ternal world of the womb to the external world of human relation-ships, which is negotiated through the dyadic contact with mother. Different concepts are employed to capture the essence of this transi-tory period. Mahler refers to it as the "normal autistic phase" in which "the infant makes no discernible distinction between inner and outer reality, nor does he seem to recognize any distinction between him-self and his inanimate surroundings" (Mahler, 1979, 160). Spitz iden-tifies coenesthetic sensing qualities of the infant which are primarily visceral and undifferentiated in nature (Spitz, 1965, 134-138). The coenesthetic sense is similar to Piaget's idea about assimilation dur-ing the autistic phase when reflexive behavior serves to satisfy organic needs (Piaget, 1973, 69-71). For Erikson, the process of attachment takes place at the beginning of the first developmental stage. As the neonate experiences a beginning sense of counting on the availability of a nurturing mother and on the constancy of her responsiveness to his biological needs, he begins the lifelong process of developing trust in the faithfulness of others. Again, the process of trusting in attachments is a very visceral matter as Erikson observes that "the first demonstration of social trust in the baby is the ease of his feeding, the depth of his sleep, the relaxation of his bowels" (Erikson, 1953, 247).

The early process of attachment lays the foundation for subsequent phases of ego development. A critical aspect of that process concerns the importance of the human context with which the individual may form a sense of connectedness to another person. That sense of making a connection with another and of being connected is primarily a pre-verbal phenomenon, more contingent upon the quality of non-verbal and meta-communication than on words. For the most part, this process takes place beyond the boundaries of awareness and is often represented by what we sense about another person which cannot be conceptualized neatly with precise verbal symbols.

A second aspect of the process of attachment is that it takes place initially in the life cycle at a time of maximum vulnerability and powerlessness. The infant is helpless and dependent on giants for survival. That sense of inequality is carried emotionally as a theme throughout life whenever the individual is confronted with new and unequal encounters with others. Even in human encounters in which there may be approximate equality in the developmental level of ego states, the individual is, more often than not, concerned initially with matters of perceived inequality and the corresponding threat to self-esteem and well-being. Trusting in new attachments is of concern to an individual whenever there is some aspect of the new relationship that stimulates a sense of biological, psychological or social vulnerability. These threats, real or fantasized, may generate corresponding emotional states related to personal survival, self-esteem and/or social acceptance which may interfere with the process of becoming involved in new relationships. The greater the psychosocial lesion in this aspect of the process of ego development, the greater will be the sense of risk in forming new attachments. As a consequence, the ego will mobilize primitive defenses in response to annihilation anxiety which may isolate the conscious ego from the threat of social connectedness. In situations where one is able to mobilize functions to compensate partially for the primary lesion, the individual may need to maintain very tentative attachment(s) for a long period of time before feeling ready to become more involved in the new relationship(s), an observation that has important implications for clinical practice with severely impaired people. (This will be explored later.)

The process of *involvement* with the human world begins at birth, although the formal process characterized by mutuality and reciprocity starts around two months and extends throughout the life cycle. As with attachment to others, involvement with others characterizes the interpersonal behavior of humans from birth to death; the manifestations of these processes change, however, depending on the developmental level of the ego. The foundation for subsequent attachments and involvements is laid down during the early years of life, the quality of which has a profound impact on the nature of all future human relationships (Fraiberg, 1977).

The ego is ready to become involved more fully in the interactive aspects of human relationships when rudimentary consolidation of the gains of the attachment process have been realized. Brazelton has found that the infant, shortly after birth, has the capacity to contribute, as well as to receive, in the dyadic relationship with mother. In other words, the neonate is capable, then, of involvement in a reciprocal relationship with the human environment. That responsiveness helps to promote attachment and to accelerate the involvement process in highly transactional ways (Brazelton, 1980). Complementing this gain in capacity to count on and to enjoy the experience of human connectedness is the maturation of biological structures which facilitate the development of certain ego functions such as cognition. Spitz observes, for example, that the first manifestation of the early organization of the psyche, the smile response, occurs at three months of age (Spitz, 1965). That maturational event suggests that the infant has developed a primordial capacity for perception even though he may, as yet, be unable fully to differentiate self from non-self. The smile response is an indication that the individual has acquired beginning skills in the ego function of cognitive mastery and the ability to recognize, perhaps only obscurely, a human object that will satisfy his needs. As a consequence, the child is now able to engage in a dyadic relationship that has rudimentary elements of mutuality and reciprocity.

Involvement, as a mutual and reciprocal process, is manifested during the symbiotic phase of ego development, from two to six months, and extends into the sub-phases of separation-individuation (Mahler, 1975). The symbiotic period, which coincides with Freud's phase of primary narcissism, is characterized by psychological coalescence of the infant with mother, which grows in intensity through the first half year of life. During that time, Mahler observes that "fusion with the representation of the mother...occurs...within the delusion of a common boundary of two...separate individuals" (Mahler, 1975, 45). The process is, by nature, a mutually satisfying one that requires the mother or mothering figure to relax her adult capacity for relatedness which is characterized essentially by constant awareness of biopsychosocial separateness, so that she may meet the needs of the infant

for psychic fusion. Within that intimate involvement of one human being with another, the infant also begins to develop a capacity for distinguishing between "goodness" and "badness" which initially become
associated with pleasurable and unpleasurable sensations as a result
of the mother's ministrations.

Mahler observes that highly transactional process characterizes the
dyadic relationship during this period, as the infant and the mother
develop individual capacities to "read" each other's signs and
signals—the beginnings of the ego function of emotional sensitivity.
Empathic responsiveness originates at this time and is primarily of a
non-verbal or intuitive nature. The beginnings of that function are enhanced when the responsiveness of the mother figure is focused accurately on the individual needs of the child through the symbiotic
phase into separation-individuation (Mahler, 1979). It may be impaired
when there is a significant mismatching of cues. The mismatching may
be the result of constitutional impairment in the child which interferes
with age appropriate response (see below) or may be the result of severe impairment in the mother's ability to connect empathically with
the needs of the child.

If, as Spitz observes, the involvement of the infant ego with the
mothering ego is experienced by the former within a relationship that
is primarily gratifying and loving, the child will grow in capacity to
trust the human world and to risk subsequent involvements with other
people. During the process of early involvement, however, the infant
who is still totally dependent on mother for physical survival is not
able to recognize the reality of psychic boundaries and, as a consequence, fuses his sense of ego with that of mother. When the fusion,
as represented in the bond between them, is experienced as pleasurable, any disappointments or frustrations may be experienced by the
infant as separate from the gratifying dyad. That rudimentary capacity for defensive splitting enables the infant to cope with the impact
of external stimuli in a world that is drastically different from the comfort and security of the prenatal environment and, essentially, from
the pleasurable environment still being provided (Kernberg, 1980). In
a real sense, the pleasures associated with the earlier process of involvement provides the infant ego with a cushion to tolerate and eventually to integrate the increased frustrations of later phases. The evolving capacity to adapt to a world which exposes the child to a range of
threats, opportunities and losses has its foundation during these early
periods of development when ego functions are activated at a rudimentary level from the undifferentiated matrix. The smile response is one
of the first indications of cognition (at least in a perceptive sense)

which serves the process of involvement within which the functions of defense, memory, emotional sensitivity, reality testing and object relations are initially activated.

The presence and influence of constitutional factors are critical variables to development in the symbiotic phase. The question of hereditary and/or neuro-physiological factors and their impact on early dyadic involvement is an important one and not readily resolved at this stage of our understanding about childhood development. As Mahler observes, many mothers of autistic children do not appear "to lack warmth, genuine love or acceptance of the individual child, nor do they appear to be exceptionally possessive, infantilizing and restrictive." She observes, further, that "maternal psychopathology has rendered the adult partner unable to respond..." and concludes that "...damage to the ego which results in infantile psychosis occurs in children who have a hereditary or constitutional anlange for it" (Mahler, 1979, 134-135). Hereditary and/or constitutional factors are important not only in understanding that subgroup but play an important part in the early involvements of all neonates and the various forms of mother-child relationships that evolve during these critical months. No doubt, constitution contributes to the nature of the fit between the child's ego and the mothering alter ego, but exactly how these factors affect that relationship is unknown.

In view of the evidence now being accumulated from current studies, we cannot dismiss the importance of biological factors nor can we confine our understanding solely to psychosocial factors; we must be open to the role that heredity and constitution may play in the structuralization of the ego and its functions. Biological, psychological and social factors transact to affect the involvement process as well as subsequent processes. Although we may not understand fully the effect of these transactions on development, it is apparent that ego development can be understood only within a holistic perspective which takes into account the influence of all three spheres.

As the process of involvement proceeds, the child becomes increasingly capable of actualizing specific ego functions. While retaining an attachment to the maternal figure and continuing to need involvement with her for biological, psychological and social supplies, the infant gradually becomes ready, maturationally and developmentally, to assert his acquired capacity for beginning autonomy. In addition to maturation of physiological and neurological systems which facilitate the "quickening" of ego functions, the change in the nature of the involvement process is made possible by the incorporation of psychosocial supplies available in the primary dyadic relationship with mother.

These supplies are of a cognitive and emotional nature and serve as the initial resources in the building of a sense of separateness and object constancy which is essential for subsequent processes of ego development. Whereas the infant needed the physical attachment and intimate involvement with the symbiotic mother in earlier periods, he begins to need the mothering figure in a different way around six months of age. The gains of the attachment experience and those of the early involvement process facilitate the natural thrust toward separateness and provide the resources, in the form of positive memory traces, for differentiation from mother and the initiation of expanded involvements with the human and physical environment.

Subsequent involvements with the mother, with other primary figures in the family and eventually with secondary figures outside the family will be characterized by a greater sense of differentiation as a result of the development of inner and outer ego boundaries. That process of structurization of the defensive and adaptive systems continues throughout life and provides the framework within which executive functions of cognition, emotional sensitivity, reality testing and object relations may develop. The ego is thus protected from the vicissitudes of inner needs which have been satisfied by age appropriate responsiveness from mother and other primary figures. As a consequence, the child is equipped to engage in widening horizons of social opportunities for biopsychosocial growth and development.

The notion of boundaries in subsequent processes of involvement with the human world may be contrasted with the earlier qualities of involvement characterized by fusion with and lack of differentiation from external figures. Boundaries involve a sense of control over one's inner needs as well as a sense of separateness from other human figures in the social environment. These inner and outer perimeters are formed as a result of physiological and social developments during the preschool years. Three dimensions in psychosocial development appear to be instrumental in forming ego boundaries: at a cognitive level, the child acquires the fundamental tools of adaptation as he moves from the earliest sensori-motor phase, through the transitional pre-conceptual phase, and into the intuitive phase of cognitive development. Although he continues to experience life from an egocentric perspective, the child becomes increasingly able to think in terms of cause and effect relationships, to communicate his understanding of the world through verbal symbols, to work out his struggles to comprehend reality by the use of play, and to identify through imitation with the values of significant adult figures in his life.

At an emotional level, the child is negotiating important stages of psychosocial development during the separation-individuation period; these enable him to acquire a seminal sense of autonomy and a corresponding capacity to initiate new opportunities for self-enhancement. He develops a beginning confidence in his ability to take care of himself, to control his bodily functions, to become independent of others in specific aspects of life and to risk involvements in new relationships. At a relational level, these gains in ego skills will be facilitated in a progressively integrated way if the empathic responsiveness of and relatedness to significant human figures continues to be available to the child. The availability of an empathic alter ego(s) provides emotional nourishment for the child who still needs to retreat to the security and comfort of relationships with people on whom he knows he can depend. Concurrently, the same human caretakers need to help structure expanding and safe encounters with the external world and to support new involvements with that world. The natural rapprochement needs of the child, along with the availability of an empathically responsive alter ego(s) are the most critical variables in building a sense of object constancy, which will facilitate involvement in upper level processes of ego development (Mahler, 1975, 76-108; Anthony and Benedek, 1970, 109-136 and 337-352).

As a result, the child begins the life-long process of psychosocial learning in which the qualities of significant figures are incorporated into his sense of self. These three aspects of life—cognitive, emotional and relational—help the individual to distinguish self from others, to evaluate the properties of reality, to risk himself in new opportunities for learning about the world and to develop reasonably consistent self and object representations based on the constancy of positive memories of significant others. Before entering the world of human relationships outside the safe boundaries of the primary family group, the child needs to have experienced himself as a separate and individual human being who has mastery of the forces originating in his internal world and who is capable of engaging in new challenges for learning in the external world without being overwhelmed with feelings of loss or threat.

MID-LEVEL PROCESSES:
IDENTIFICATION, INTROJECTION AND DIFFERENTIATION

Identification, as the third process involved in ego development, has its origins in the attachment process and its roots in the process of involvement. Referring to the emergence of this process, Maier quotes

Piaget, who suggests that the child initially selects models of identification from within the primary group of the nuclear family since the child:

> feels close to those who satisfy his immediate needs and interests.... Under ordinary conditions the young child maintains a sense of respect and care for the superior powers of his caretaker(s). He places them in an omnipotent position. The child's sense of obedience and care...is derived out of a combination of love and fear and provides the foundation for his conscience (Maier, 1965, 134-135).

Beginning at this early level and extending throughout subsequent processes, the development of the ego is now interrelated with the development of its monitoring dimensions, the superego and the conscience. Experiences with the external world become more cognitively and emotionally associated with value, and internal representations are (ever more) linked endopsychically with goodness and/or badness. As Piaget observes, the process of identification with external figures involves elements of love and fear, which originate in earlier processes. While occurring along a continuum and rarely experienced endopsychically in their bipolar form except in early childhood, the "object" of love or hate perceived by a "subject" will profoundly affect the process of identification.

Optimally, identification builds upon the gains of early encounters with the human world, particularly in the sense of trust and satisfaction associated in being with others, even when one had no choice. The gains of these earliest experiences stimulates a desire for continued contact with other familiar figures and for expanded engagements with new figures. Unlike attachment, which was exclusively dyadic in nature and involvement, which was initially dyadic, the process of identification involves the individual in multiple encounters with other members of the primary family group, with one's peer group and with secondary figures in the human environment.

This process begins at the sensori-motor level as the child imitates the movements and mannerisms of the mother. Jacobson attributes these mirroring reactions to the primitive needs of the child for merger and "one-ness" with mother and suggests that these earliest experiences "are the foundation on which all future types of identification are built," and, "only when perceptive functions have sufficiently matured, can gratifications or frustrations become associated with the object" (Jacobson, 1964). The latter may become manifested behaviorally as "ambitendency," the behavioral precursor of emotional ambivalence. If ambitendency persists and opposite wishes are not synthesized by the developing ego, defensive splitting of the object world into separate internal images may become a permanent modus operandi for dealing with social reality (Mahler, 1975). These rudimentary imitative behaviors are the precursors of the identification process. Although imitation may remain as a critical factor throughout life, it eventually becomes less encompassing of the process of identification; this occurs as a result of both the structuralizing of more sophisticated functions of cognitive mastery as well as the resolution of higher level processes such as differentiation and separation. In fact, cognitive, emotional and behavioral alignments with figure(s) to whom the individual is attached and with whom he is involved become more parsimonious at two years of age, as the ego of the child struggles—on the one hand, to hold on to the symbiotic mother and, on the other hand, strives to become more self sufficient and independent through selective identifications (Jacobson, 1954). Thus begins the life-long process of alignment with others not only for narcisstic gratification of one's needs but, more importantly, for the purpose of one's growth toward progressive autonomous functioning of the ego.

Alignment with human models of identification, initially in primary and later in secondary groups, develops optimally within relationships that have a high positive valency for the individuals involved. Valency, the attractiveness of one person for another, is constrained initially by the availability of models. As ego functions become operationalized, the individual is able to be more selective about his identifications. That is, the child develops greater capacity for choice in aligning with specific characteristics of certain people. Valency is also affected by the "functional value of the behaviors displayed by different models," which is regulated by process of feedback and reinforcement (Bandura, 1977, 24). People tend to align with figures of identification to whom they cathect positively because of the attractiveness of qualities observed within the other(s). The desire to remain attached persists, however, only when there are rewards available within the encounter to sustain the relationship. These rewards are generally transmitted through the communication of positive regard and support which have significant value to the participants. The value of rewards will be shaped by the level of ego structuralization, which is contingent on the quality and resolution of earlier processes as well as on the capacity of the ego to anticipate future gain in these psychosocial supplies. For example, excessive deprivation or indulgence in the low level processes of attachment and involvement may tug at the individual to retain, to replicate, or to perpetuate the not-so-good-enough memories of earlier periods which may interfere with developmentally appropriate levels of subsequent identifications. In another respect, alignment may be facilitated by the anticipation of immediate or future rewards as in formal learning situations: for example, where the desire for a good grade or the approval of the teacher (i.e., positive feedback) may push the individual to succeed.

While the individual begins the process of identifying and of forming internal representations very early in life, the foundations of one's sense of self in all its dimensions is established during the second to sixth years. During that period, the evolving person is highly susceptible to the influence of significant adults in the immediate environment to whom are attributed unusual powers of omnipotence and omniscience. Several developmental events occur which have been identified by Piaget as "The Preconceptual Phase," by Freud as "The Oedipal Period," by Erikson as the "State of Initiative versus Guilt," and by Mahler as the "Separation-Individuation Phase" (Piaget, 1973, 49-62; Freud, 1949, 25-32; Mahler, 1975, 52-120; and Erikson, 1953, 247-274). A developmentally delicate time by any measure, it is a period when the child—relying on the gains of earlier experiences—becomes ready to engage the world in the process of broadening and deepening his biological, psychological and social sense of self. The impact and influence of significant others on the process of functional and moral identity cannot be underestimated. They are the resources which help to build ego functions and the vehicles through which self-esteem is shaped. The nature of feedback processes during this period determines how well the child will integrate a positive image of himself and, as a consequence, be freed, through the power of self-confidence, to engage the external world in ego adaptive rather than ego defensive modes of behavior.

Beginning in this period and extending throughout life, the individual is confronted with an array of human objects upon whom he may be dependent in many different social contexts and from whom he receives and must process innumerable expectations of preferred behaviors. A sociobehavioral outcome of those interpersonal experiences is the induction of the individual into important social roles. Ackerman has conceptualized social role as the "bridge" between intrapsychic life and the participation of the individual in social groups (Ackerman, 1958). He views social role as "an adaptional unit of the personality in action" which includes internal as well as external aspects. From an external or sociological perspective, the learning involved in the process of identification originates in the expectations which significant human objects or alter egos convey to the individual about appropriate or acceptable behaviors within the context of specific dimensions of life. These dimensions may include expectations related to gender, ethnicity, race, and one's position within the family and in other groups. From an internal or psychological perspective, a nuclear sense of identity will become organized if the constitutional endowments that push for expression, the developmental experiences already internalized as ego resources and the new encounters with the social world fit together in a complementary way. That nuclear sense of who one is (i.e., self-representation), which evolves toward a relatively steady psychological state of being (a separate and distinct person), originates within the primary family group; it is subsequently reinforced, modified and/or expanded upon as the individual encounters other models of identification outside the family. If one experiences his or her biological, ethnic and familiar identities (which are constitutionally determined and beyond personal choice) within primary and secondary contexts of support and positive reinforcement, the individual will associate—gradually yet progressively—favorable thoughts and feelings with these characteristics. It will feel good to be male or female, good to be black or white and good to be a member of this family rather than any other family.

As noted, the process of identification involves the individual with the primary group of the family and then with other groups such as peers and school. In trying to understand how these groups transmit expectations to the child, which eventually become internalized selectively as parts of the conscience (i.e., initial object representations) and as shapers of specific ego functions, the nature of external human communications is a most critical factor.

The importance of the quality of communications within relationships that form the matrix of earlier processes has been implicit in our discussion. Constitutional limitations, caretaking deficiencies, unexpected traumas such as an important loss, ordinal position in the family and the presence of siblings, sex and socio-economic status may singularly or in various combinations exert an impact on the processes of ego development. As mentioned, we know little about the interaction of hereditary and environment and the consequences of their interplay on human development. We may be reasonably certain, however, of the influence on the evolving ego of certain communication patterns within primary and secondary groups. For example, the personality configuration of the mother's ego may affect her responsiveness to phase specific needs of the child in early processes, while certain constitutional factors in the child may interfere with the normal reciprocal exchanges within the mother-child relationship, particularly during the symbiotic phase.

During the identification process, the nature of communication transactions become more complex and unpredictable not only because the ego has become more complex in its journey toward autonomy, but also because the child becomes increasingly involved in triadic and group encounters. The individual is exposed to multiple occasions of feedback and the corresponding challenge of establishing several forms of reciprocal contact and ongoing complementary roles with many different people. If the individual is exposed to competing or conflicting expectations from more than one significant figure in the human environment, he may be caught in an intrapersonal dilemma—just as he may have been caught in an interpersonal dilemma earlier if there were mixed messages from the dyadic mother. The ego that is caught in these dilemmas at both levels will inevitably have particular challenges in psychologically surviving and resolving mid and higher level processes in an adaptive way.

That dilemma and the challenge which it represents for the individual may be most keenly experienced by individuals who are the victims of sexual, ethnic or racial discrimination. Although the family may have offered the kind of inter-personal experiences and feedback that facilitate the internal development of positive representations related to gender, ethnicity and/or color, the nature of involvements in the wider social system may confront the individual with contradictory experiences. Continuity of supportive feedback facilitates the integration of positive self and object representations. Conflicting messages of a degrading and destructive nature undermine the integration of object representations with a positive self-representation. For those people who are confronted with the irrationalities of social discrimination, the process of internalization will present a unique struggle, which may not be empathically recognized or understood by the dominant culture. As a consequence, the supportive and ameliorative value of the family and other primary reference groups will be particularly critical to the process of identification.

Watzlawick and his associates have identified several "axioms of communication" which are useful in understanding mid-level processes, particularly that of identification (Watzlawick, 1967). They suggest that in any human encounter which involves two or more people "one cannot not communicate." This axiom is not contingent on intention or mutual understanding of the participants. It means simply that people communicate, in the sense of transmitting messages to each other, whether they use words or non-verbal behavior and whether they are consciously aware or unaware of their intentions. The second axiom suggests that "human communication is a multilevel phenomenon" which includes: a content dimension in which the sender (of a message) is defining the significance of the message, and a contextual dimension in which the parties are defining their relationship, one to another. This second axiom involves the concept of metacommunications which attaches (usually at an implicit level) meaning to the importance of the overt message while at the same time defining the nature of the role relationships between ego and alter(s). Watzlawick observes that meta-messages define relationships as: accepting of the receiver, rejecting of the receiver or as disconfirming the existence of the receiver. The latter two situations are the most undermining of ego development and self-esteem since they discredit the very being of the individual or relegate the importance of his being to insignificance. A third axiom hypothesizes that interactions within a social role relationship may be complementary or symmetrical; these are determined by the difference(s) or equality(ies) between ego and alter. Any constellation of factors—biological, psychological and/or social—may contribute to the symmetrical and complementary aspects of relations that are viewed as transactional encounters in which behaviors are evoked in a circular and interlocking way. Watzlawick identifies two additional axioms which focus on the punctuation of interactions as well as the digital and analogic aspects of communications. For our purposes, the three axioms related to the inevitability of communication, meta-communication and the nature of symmetry-complementariness seem most useful.

These ideas about communication transactions offer us an approach to understanding the interpersonal link in the identifying process between the internal dynamics of the individual and his involvement with the social environment. Identifications involve a dynamic interplay between the endowed potentials of the individual and the availability of social resources that are transmitted over time through human communication transactions within the context of social role relations. An important dimension of social transactions in the identifying process is that they involve mutual interacting effects of one person upon the other(s) so that each is affecting and being affected by the other at all times. Messages which contribute to one's sense of self are constantly being exchanged regardless of one's conscious wishes, a proposition which highlights the critical nature of preconscious and unconscious forces on ego development. The child has less choice in escaping complementary encounters; as a consequence, he must develop defensive as well as adaptive mechanisms to cope with the impact of interpersonal and social forces on his sense of self and on his esteem for self. The adolescent and adult may have more choice in contending with interpersonal encounters, but only if subsequent processes of ego development are worked out in growth enhancing ways.

Identification, which we have defined as a reciprocal process involving dynamic and interrelated transactions rather than linear and unidirectional interactions, occurs within relationships that are more complementary in childhood than in adolescence and adulthood, when they become more symmetrical. In complementary relationships one is more vulnerable since, by definition, these relationships are characterized by an unequal distribution of power. No human relationship, however, can ever be perfectly equal; as a consequence, complementary aspects never lose their significance. They continue to be important, at least at a residual level, in the most egalitarian of relationships because processes of internalization are never resolved completely even in the most optimal of circumstances.

The process of identification which leads to a nuclear sense of personal constancy and continuity is contingent upon complementary attachments that are primarily loving and interpersonal involvements that are optimally frustrating. Through these interrelated processes, a progressive sense of one's separateness is dependent on significant interactions becoming less complementary and more symmetrical. While the digital mode of communication, characterized by explicit and consciously intended messages, is essential in supporting ego development, the analagic mode, characterized by implicit and meta-messages, plays a critical role as in the insidious effects of sexual, ethnic and racial discrimination. The identification process evolves in an optimal direction when the two modes converge with the innate thrust of the ego toward autonomy and self-sufficiency.

An integral aspect of the identification process and a natural extension of interpersonal alignments in that process is that of *introjection*. Introjection involves the taking in and integrating as part of one's self those qualities and characteristics that were previously a part of another but which became available through the communication transactions in social role relationships. Cathecting to an external object or selective aspect(s) of an object within the context of a valued alignment is a precursor of introjection. In early childhood, the supplies available in the social environment are internalized through an assimilative mode since the individual has not yet acquired a capacity to distinguish among environmental inputs. As long as these biopsychosocial supplies meet the egocentric needs of the individual, they tend to be absorbed in an undifferentiated way. As structuralization progresses, however, the ego develops a capacity to accommodate to the human environment; the individual learns not only to adapt to realistic expectations but also to exert higher levels of choice through executive ego functions in his alignments and subsequent internalizations.

Historically, the concept of introjection was used to identify a form of defense. Freud viewed introjection as "a kind of regression to the mechanism of the oral phase" through which the lost object was incorporated "inside the ego" (Freud, 1960, 19). Although suggesting that the origins of introjection as a defense mechanism were obscure, Anna Freud observed that "introjection from the outside world into the ego could not be said to have the effect of enriching the latter unless there were already a clear differentiation between that which belonged to the one and that which belonged to the other" (Freud, 1946, 55-56). Hartman, in exploring the origins of defenses, suggested that introjection may originate "as a form of instinct gratification before it is used in the service of defense" (Hartmann, 1964, 124). Jacobson introduced the concept of representations in order to distinguish between human objects in reality and their endopsychic presence as images within the self. She emphasized the critical importance of forming representations through internalization or what we have referred to as introjections (Jacobson, 1964, 102-105).

Traditionally, the term has been used to describe a mechanism of defense in which the ego protects itself from anxiety associated with the loss of significant figures. The concept is used here in a more generic and positive sense to convey a process by which characteristics—ego skills as well as moral values—are incorporated into the three ego systems as a result of identification with another person(s) with whom one has experienced a positively cathected relationship. Second, the ideas cited above—especially those of Anna Freud— identify a critical ambiguity in our theory which involves the dynamic and quasi-sequential evolution of these processes of ego development. Elements of all processes from attachment to autonomy are present in some form within the individual at a very early age and become activated as development proceeds. Thus, the individual must have some rudimentary ability to differentiate self from others in order for a process such as introjection to take place. That distinction implies, as well, that some pieces of the adaptive system must already have been in place at a very early age so that the individual has a sense of psychosocial boundaries at the interface of his ego and the external world. Otherwise, introjections would not serve to fuel the development of object constancy which promotes the achievement of separation-individuation.

Third, there are qualitative changes in the process of introjection as the individual grows from infancy through childhood and adolescence into adulthood. Introjection may very well begin as a form of instinctual gratification and change to a mode of defense before it becomes a more adaptive vehicle of differential learning. Fourth, the process of introjection evolves primarily from relationships with external figures in which loving and affectional valencies outweigh aggressive and fearful countervalencies. Jacobson argues, for example, that the oedipal conflict is resolved via positive identifications and corresponding internalizations with the parent of the same sex, rather than by way of fear. The position here is that introjection, via a relationship that is positively cathected, is more instrumental in the building of internal structures than is a relationship that is characterized by intimidation. We are of course talking in terms of a continuum of reinforcers, since the reality of all relationships includes positive and negative aspects. Finally, introjections become available as internal resources to fuel the process of differentiation as the integration and consolidation of internalized representations is accomplished. As Bandura observes, "imitative responses are usually performed without the models present, long after the behavior has been observed" (Bandura, 1977, 27). The continuity of introjections over time is promoted by positive reinforcements available within relationships valued by the individual, which facilitates the conscious availability of positive memories of those experiences after valued figures have become history. That notion is another way of expressing the concept of object constancy.

The third mid-level process, *differentiation,* refers to two interrelated dimensions of human development: the internal or intrapersonal, and the external or interpersonal. At an intrapersonal level, the infant enters the world in an autistic state which serves his need to maintain a "homeostatic equilibrium...within the new extramural environment." That state is temporary and gives way to "increased sensory awareness of and contact with the environment..." as a result of involvement with the mothering figure and others (Mahler, 1975, 42-43). Over time, the ego of the child gradually emerges from the undifferentiated matrix. Concurrent with the activation of ego functions, the individual develops a capacity to monitor his behavior, an event which some would conceptualize as a higher manifestation of structuralization or formation of the superego. The natural movement of the human being toward greater independence and autonomy is facilitated by the internal organization of the psyche, which we refer to as intrapersonal differentiation.

The first manifestations of interpersonal differentiation (the sense of being separate from others rather than an extension of their being) occurs from five to nine months of age when the child "hatches" from the symbiotic involvement with mother. According to Mahler, hatching is a result of three aspects of early organization: the "gradual ontogenetic evolution of the sensorium," the maturation of a rudimentary capacity for locomotion, and the beginnings of object constancy (Mahler, 1975, 53-54). Physiological maturation makes possible the activation of the ego function of perception which contributes to the ability of the child to discriminate between self and non-self. These changes, when coupled with the internalization of positive identification (i.e., introjects) with mother (who was available fairly constantly within the symbiotic orbit) also contribute to the readiness of the child to experience himself as separate and distinct. Whereas he could rely on the physical ministrations and presence of mother earlier in their relationship, the child now may count on a reservoir of positive memories of her which promote the development of the adaptive boundary and the confidence to initiate expanded involvements with others in the primary family group and later in secondary groups.

As socialization experiences widen during the latter part of the first year, the child becomes involved in further explorations of the human environment that enable his ego to build upon the differentiation process. One of the manifestations of that capacity to discriminate among figures in his experiential field was identified by Spitz as "stranger anxiety" (Spitz, 1965, 108-114). Mahler adds to our understanding of this developmental event by connecting it with the quality of human experiences which have taken place up to that time. She observes that an "inverse relation [exists] between basic confidence and stranger anxiety" which she attributes to the mother-child relationship in earlier periods, particularly during the symbiotic phase. For optimal development of the child's ego and in order for the process of differentiation to occur, primary human relationships must have provided initially for fusion and then for gradual bodily separateness (Mahler, 1975, 46-63). In that process one sees, perhaps more clearly than in any other (process), the interrelationship and interdependence of biological, psychological and social dimensions of early ego formation.

At a higher level of development, Bowen makes a significant contribution to our understanding of the differentiation process in a way that more fully integrates the intrapersonal and interpersonal dimensions within the frame of reference of a social system. Bowen is concerned about *what* happens between people and bases his theory on observations of current relationships rather than on inferences that may explain the historical etiology of those relationships. Considering the concept a "cornerstone" of his theory, Bowen defines differentiation as the extent of union or separateness between emotional and intellectual functioning. He views the process of differentiation along a continuum, bounded at one end by people "whose emotions and intellect are so fused that their lives are dominated by the automatic emotional system" (Bowen, 1978, 337-387). Bowen appears to be talking here about people whose adaptive system is not well organized, whose defensive system is rigid and intrusive of the potential for adaptive behavior and whose executive ego continues to rely inappropriately and excessively on the social supplies of others for "refueling." These people may have experienced excessive degrees of either frustration or gratification prior to the differentiation process. As a consequence, their relations with others are governed by unresolved narcissistic needs and correlative emotions which tend to dominate efforts of the ego toward more adaptive functioning. At the other end of the continuum are people who are more autonomous in their behavior as a result of the capacity to distinguish between emotional feelings and intellectual thoughts. They "can participate freely in the emotional sphere without the fear of becoming too fused with others" (Bowen, 1978, 364).

Bowen introduces two additional notions as part of his theory about differentiation, the solid self and the pseudoself, which seem to be related to the level at which internalization has progressed. Bowen says that the solid self is "made up of clearly defined beliefs, opinions, convictions and life principles. . ." that have been "incorporated into self from one's own life experience." He attributes a rather high level of adult-like intellectual reasoning and cognitive reflection to that incorporation and seems to be describing a process of introjection leading to a consolidation of the self-representation. The level of the pseudoself is characterized by an assortment of roles which the individual plays out in his social relations with others, not from any conviction of their personal validity but out of a fear of not conforming to group expectations. As Bowen says, "the pseudoself is an actor and can be many different selves," which may be contingent upon the needs of the social situation and not on an internalized set of congruent ego and superego representations (Bowen, 1978, 365). His concept of the pseudoself is akin to object representations which remain fragmented yet significant to social role behavior under specific conditions.

The solid self reflects a higher level of differentiation than does the pseudoself, which tends to be fused with the emotional system in both intrapersonal and interpersonal aspects. There is a pseudo quality to human encounters which may generate considerable anxiety when these encounters have the potential for involving the person in a more intimate and durable relationship. Although people with low to moderate levels of differentiation may pursue close relations with others, the potential for emotional fusion–intrapersonally and interpersonally— is usually so threatening that their egos resort to defensive manipulation of others to keep the encounter on an emotionally superficial level.

As noted, one of the most important contributions of Bowen's theory about the differentiation process is the identification between the intrapersonal and interpersonal dimensions. Bowen observes that people tend to marry others whose level of differentiation is approximately equal to their own level. He observes, further, that "unresolved emotional attachment to the parents is equivalent to the degree of undifferentiation" in each spouse: 'The lower the level of differentiation, the more intense the unresolved attachment" (Bowen, 1978, 382). Finally, Bowen hypothesizes that the conflicts inherent in the undifferentiated marital pair will be manifested in marital conflict, dysfunction in one spouse or projection onto one child who will emerge "with a lower level of differentiation than the parents" (Bowen, 1978, 384). That child will eventually mate with a spouse with a comparable level of differentiation which, over several generations following a regressive pattern, will produce individuals who will have increasingly serious conflicts in distinguishing between thoughts and feelings. As a consequence, these people will experience great difficulty in maintaining an appropriate level of separateness in their interpersonal relations.

Differentiation involves not only a recognition of one's distinctiveness from others (an indicator of the internal structuralization of the adaptive boundary) but also an acquiescence in that recognition. The quiet acceptance of the ego in one's difference from others, which is an implicit acknowledgement of one's individuality, is a reflection of the adequate resolution of earlier processes and a signal of one's readiness to engage in the resolution of higher level processes. Although all of the processes which we have been discussing take place in one form or another throughout life, lower and mid-level processes are primarily characteristic of the developmental tasks of childhood and adolescence. Upper level processes of separation and autonomy take place generally during adolescence and adulthood.

Before the examination of upper level processes, it is important to review the inherent relationship between psychological and social dimensions of the internalization process. The developmental affairs which lead to organization of intrapsychic functions occur within a complex matrix of biological, psychological and social realities. Individuals resolve the needs of each level as completely as possible. No one ever emerges from these specific processes with a total integration of the biological, psychological and social dimensions of self. The work of human development remains unfinished and serves to fuel subsequent encounters with the world out of which growth may be more fully realized. The ego of the differentiated individual is not only in command of forces at play in his inner world but is also able to adapt to the realistic needs of the outer world through appropriate role relationships. He is able to confront new situations with a sense of challenge and opportunity without becoming overwhelmed by their dangers and threats to his well-being. He is able to maintain an inner sense of continuity over time even as he engages in social role relationships that may not be compatible with his innermost convictions and self-representation. He is able to see the gestalt while coping with the pieces. His sense of self, as a differentiated individual who is concurrently identified with and inherently in need of contact with others, is characterized by a progressive synthesis and acceptance of his assets and liabilities, his positive and negative qualities, without losing perspective of his realistic potentials and limitations as a fallible and evolving being. That state of integration of ego development is of course relative to and contingent upon the biological equipment with which he was born and the social supplies which the human environment has been able to offer him.

HIGHER LEVEL PROCESSES: SEPARATION AND AUTONOMY

The process of *separation* must also be understood within a biopsychosocial perspective in which every dimension is interrelated. The significance of a dimension for structuralizing the ego will vary according to the developmental stage and the corresponding needs of any individual. From a biological perspective, the physical aspect of separation begins at birth as the neonate emerges from the intrauterine environment which has been his home for months and enters a foreign external world. According to Rankian theory, this initial separation serves as a symbolic prototype of separation conflict inherent in all subsequent relationships (Ford and Urban, 1963, 366-385). From a psychological perspective separation—although rooted in earlier phases of development—becomes a nodal issue in ego organization as the child hatches from the symbiotic orbit with mother and becomes involved in the separation-individuation phase; this begins at about five months and extends through the two and one-half-year mark, with the attainment of beginning object constancy (Mahler, 1975).

Although birth and subsequent involvements with primary figures within the family of origin are also social affairs, the social dimension of separation has its most profound impact on the evolving ego toward the end of early childhood. The child is then faced with a more lengthy physical separation from the family as he enters school and must adopt a social identity as a student and as a participating member of peer groups. During late adolescence the individual is confronted with a dramatic series of biological and social realities which culminate in a permanent sense of physical separateness from childhood. Separation then takes on a more significant biopsychosocial meaning as the emerging adult faces the challenge of integrating several dimensions that shape his destiny, including the potential for becoming productive in a career along with the capacity for becoming a "sexual and loving being" (Erikson, 1968).

In a real sense, the process of separation starts as soon as there is rudimentary awareness, even at a visceral level, of the loss of one biopsychosocial state of existence and the need to adapt to a new and more differentiated state. The first such transitional state occurs as the infant emerges from the intrauterine environment, which is compensated by the psychological fusion of the symbiotic relationship with mother. Psychosocial development, propelled by biological maturation, is then contingent upon the gradual loosing of fused attachments and involvements which are gradually replaced with interpersonal identifications and, later, with introjects. As the latter become intrapsychically available in relatively constant form, they provide the individual with internal resources to give up the familiar and to encounter the new. Readiness to separate at all levels of ego growth is determined by the developmentally appropriate quality of preceding relationships and the anticipated gain from involvement in new relationships, even with the same person. The ego is able to confront the risks inherent in these transitions when the social supplies (i.e., nurturing) available in earlier processes have been integrated into the psyche of the individual and when significant figures in the human system in which he is then involved are willing to support change.

Figure 5 depicts the relationship between internal development of self/object relations and experiences with "significant others" which lead to a sense of separateness and individuality. In order for separation of a biopsychosocial nature to occur *within* the earliest and most influential encounters with the human world, two sets of interrelated events must have occurred. First, significant figures must connect and respond empathically to the natural, developmental needs of the child, initially for union with the significant other(s) and gradually for biological distance and psychosocial separateness. Second, libidinal sup-

A. <u>Birth</u>

U.M.- undifferentiated matrix
S.O.- significant other
S- self representation
O- object representation

B. <u>Self-other involvement</u>:
symbiotic unity to 6 months

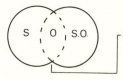 ⌐libidinal bond and empathic merger

C. <u>Self-other involvement</u>:
differentiation thru practicing and beginning identification: 6-18 months

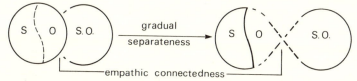

D. <u>Rapproachment</u>:
18-36 months

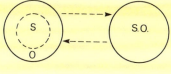

E. <u>Object constancy</u>:
integration to consolidation: 36 months and beyond

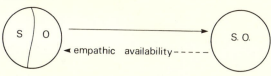

-identifications and introjects
 associated with value
-differentiation of emotional
 and cognitive functioning
-consolidation of solid self

**Figure 5   Development of Internalized
Self/Object Relations**

plies, available through empathic contact with the human world, must be incorporated intrapsychically as object representations and then transmuted into the self-representation which ultimately forms the nucleus of the "solid self." Although object representations persist as endopsychic incorporations of parental and sociocultural values, they must be integrated in a congruent way with the endopsychic representation of self in order for a sense of wholeness and "selfsameness" to become a "reality" for the individual. Once the self-representation becomes dominant and possesses continuity, the individual is somewhat freed, internally, to move on to the next higher plateau of human development. These early experiences with separation/individuation form the prototype for similar developmental plateaus in adolescence and adulthood.

As integration of object representations into the self-representation occurs within an ego whose structures are coalescing at maturationally appropriate periods, the individual is freed to seek out new attachments at higher levels of development. If primary attachments characterized by maturationally inappropriate dependency(ies) persist, the process of internalization will be retarded, and the individual will be handicapped in becoming involved and identified with new figures at more enduring, egalitarian and mutually satisfying levels of human relationships.

Loewald observes that "separation may be experienced as deprivation"..."if it is not facilitated or if it is prevented by others." He observes further

> that emancipation as a process of separation from external objects—to be distinguished from rebellion which maintains the external relationship—goes hand-in-hand with the work of internalization which reduces or abolishes the sense of external deprivation and loss. Whether separation from a love object is experienced as deprivation and loss, or as emancipation and mastery will depend, in part, on the achievement of the work of internalization (Loewald, 1962, 483-504).

The *loss* aspect of separation refers to the readiness of the individual to "let go" of familiar experiences, which become part of his object representations as they are placed in appropriate perspective, while the *gain* refers to the anticipation of one's capacity to take care of one's self and to reinvest one's energy into new experiences—even within existing relationships (i.e., the dominance of the self-representation). During these periods of change, equilibrium in the biopsychosocial dimensions is maintained when the loss is compensated by inner readiness to accommodate to the gain, and when external resources are available to support change. Through early adolescence, the separation process involves a gradual and progressive modification of introjects as a result of the expanding and deepening capacity of the ego to understand social realities in increasingly conceptual and analytic modes of problem solving. In other words, the cognitive and affective meanings associated with life experiences temper the process of internalization, such that inner representations lose their bi-polar quality and become integrated under the dominance of the self-representation. During the later phases of adolescence and throughout adulthood, the incremental character of change, as a product of gradual separations, continues; the individual is then capable of contending with more sweeping alternations in social realities, such as leaving home and accepting responsibility for managing one's life without reliance on familiar external resources. The latter becomes possible, however, only as the ego consolidates its inner resources through social experiences that were internalized as opportunities, albeit frustrating ones, rather than as persistently painful deprivations.

At its higher levels, the process of internalization is characterized by a consolidation of psychic structures and a continuity of one's inner sense of self as a consequence of the separateness experienced in one's biological, psychological and social relations with others. That state of ego development leads to a (conscious) awareness of alternatives in managing one's life, a capacity to exercise choice in conducting one's affairs and a willingness to accept responsibility for one's actions. To the degree that these aspects of *autonomy* exist within consciousness, they contribute to personal freedom.

The organizational state of the executive ego, coupled with the positive meanings associated with (internal) representations of one's identity, enable the individual to act on inner motives that fit with the reasonable expectations of his social situation at particular points in time. In other words, the individual is adaptively interdependent with his environment; he is not inappropriately dependent upon the environment for developmental supplies nor is he controlled primarily by external forces. His inner sense of separateness and the continuity of his inner self-representation (despite changes in social realities that may require adaptations to different social roles) sustain autonomy and promote independence of functioning in some areas without jeopardizing realistic dependency in other areas. The boundaries of the autonomous ego are organized to the point at which the defensive system (operating on signal anxiety) is capable of binding irrational intrusions of undifferentiated material into the executive ego; in addition, the adaptive system is capable of rational and empathic action to deal constructively with problems of a biopsychosocial nature.

The first manifestation of autonomy is evident at birth when the neonate is able to act biologically in the interest of his own survival without external supplies. Sustenance of initial neurophysiological functioning constitutes only partial autonomy in that sphere since the infant cannot survive indefinitely independent of a nurturing, human environment. Within the psychosocial dimensions of ego development, Erikson hyphthesizes that autonomy becomes a nodal issue during the second and third years of life as the child acquires the biological ability to control his bowels. During that muscular-anal stage, the child is held increasingly accountable by his caretakers for controlling a critical sector of his life which is represented psychosocially by the struggle to hold on or to let go (Evans, 1969, 18-23). How the human environment responds to that struggle, the crisis of developing a "sense of autonomy vs. a sense of shame and doubt," will influence the initial shape of a rudimentary sense of right and wrong. Whether the task of this life-stage will become a battleground for compulsive control or an opportunity to develop a beginning sense of inner directedness associated with pride and achievement will depend on the responsiveness of significant others to these developmental tasks.

As the child grows and acquires more sophisticated skills in caring for and caring about himself (i.e., ego functions and self-esteem), his sense of autonomy develops proportionally. The inner representation of freedom to care for and to control himself and his destiny will be determined principally by two interrelated factors:

—the availability of social supplies in the environment, familially and culturally, to support processes of internalization; and
—the gradual shift on the part of his caretakers to hold the child increasingly responsible for his behavior.

Autonomy will be affected adversely if either factor is unavailable or offered to the emerging ego by way of conflictual modes of human communication. For example, becoming productive as a worker will be contingent on the consistency of meaning associated with work roles within the family, the internalization of a set of beliefs about the value of work and, of equal importance, the availability of socioeconomic supports in the wider milieu which provides opportunities for the actualization of those values. In view of the importance of work to ego autonomy, social deprivation in the form of discrimination has to be one of the most significant sources of diminished esteem for self and of distorted representations of personal worth even when socioemotional supplies continue to be available within the primary group. While the family may serve as an island of acceptance and as a neutralizer of abrasive attacks on autonomy from the wider social system, its buffering functions may compensate only partially for extreme assault as the child, the adolescent and the adult encounters the external world: the school, the workplace, the community and society.

As with all processes of internalization, the nature of the autonomous process has an intergenerational character which Wheelis defines as "action which has been repeated over and over, and so has come to be a coherent and relatively independent mode of behavior" (Wheelis, 1969, 57). How inner directedly one comes to think and feel about one's self will be a reflection, in part, of how autonomous one's primary caretakers experienced themselves and how they represented their sense of autonomy to the developing individual. However, intergenerational, deterministic dynamics play a more influential role in earlier processes of internalization than they do in this higher level process when the ego is essentially self-determining and is constrained only by endowment and environment. The capacity to weigh options and to make choices now confronts the individual with a new human agenda to which he must respond, actively or passively.

One of the most dynamic examples of that capacity for active responsiveness, which reflects the resiliency of people to transcend sociocultural traditions, has occurred over the last several years among the ethnic/racial groups and women. Although born into a social system with powerful cultural traditions which overtly prevented or covertly undermined opportunities for the realization of autonomy, these groups have been able to effect change in significant aspects of the social environment. In spite of ingrained mores and conditions designed to maintain traditional relations between the relatively powerful and the relatively powerless, the potential for change toward a more egalitarian system has begun and some progress has been realized. Freedom of access to social resources is instrumental to the process of autonomy. Demise of access can have only a debilitating effect on that process.

In the day-to-day reality of living and in striving for a more autonomous existence, Frankl suggests that the "search for meaning" becomes a primary force in life. The person who is struggling, and indeed suffering, with matters of autonomy is concerned

in actualizing values, rather than in the mere gratification and satisfaction of drives and instincts, the mere reconciliation of the conflicting claims of Id, Ego and Superego, or more adaptation and adjustment to the society and the environment (Frankl, 1963, 164).

As this process evolves toward a higher level of existence for the individual, he is capable of transcending his immediate concerns in order to reach out to others, to make new commitments and to accept responsibility for contributing to the welfare of his fellow human beings. A sense of wholeness, integration and inner freedom tend to pervade human functioning, along with a willingness to hold one's self accountable for one's behavior. Rational choice, empathically informed, becomes a primary attribute of the autonomous person.

As with all processes which we have been discussing, autonomy is a relative matter, and one that must be understood within a sociocultural context. Although this paradigm of development has focused on generic processes (in the sense that the processes are instrumental to ego development across ethnic, social class and sexual "lines"), the ways in which each (process) is manifested and the value or meaning(s) associated with each (process) will be tempered and shaped by the value orientations of reference groups with which the individual is involved and with which he identifies. Once internalized at the level of mid-level processes, values influence significantly the nature of one's self and object representations. For that reason, values have a profound impact on how one views the world and how one relates to other people. Introjected values have a normative influence in the ego and its specific functions, as well as a more gestalt-like effect on one's generalized regard for self and for others, particularly between males and females, as Gilligan has so vividly brought to our attention (Gilligan, 1982). The tempering and shaping role of sociocultural values has been most explicit in our discussion of mid-level processes, but they are equally if perhaps more subtly influential in lower and upper level processes including that of autonomy. The autonomous process, in fact, helps to consolidate the adaptive system of the ego with truly humanistic values, so that the individual person is "the center of his own life,"

> capable of acting upon others as well as being acted upon, creator of himself as well as creature, able to use circumstances and human relationships to achieve his own purposes, including the purpose of continuous creation of himself (Smalley, 1970, 90).

SUMMARY

The three structural subsystems of the ego become organized through the process of internalization, composed of seven aspects:

—attachment
—involvement

—identification
—introjection
—differentiation
—separation
—autonomy

Although these processes may occur in more linear fashion during the early years of socialization, there is an increasingly critical transactional quality about them throughout the life cycle. Similar to Erikson's concept of the epigenetic principal, which he applies to the hierarchy of developmental stages, elements of the seven processes of ego development are present in the biopsychosocial realities of life at an early age and ascend to importance in relation to the evolving needs of the individual. Once actualized, these processes continue to play a critical role in development, although their character and mode of expression will change considerably from childhood, through adolescence and old age. While they are the vehicles by which potential ego structures become actualized, these processes tend to have a developmental line of their own which is shaped by endowment transacting through the ego with the environment. The cognitive and affective meanings associated with these processes become part of the individual's internal world in the form of endopsychic representations and serve a prototypical function for the ego in subsequent human relationships.

REFERENCES

Ackerman, N. *The Psychodynamics of Family Life.* New York: Basic Books, Inc. 1958.

Ainsworth, M. "Object Relations, Dependency, and Attachment: A Theoretical Review of the Infant-Mother Relationship," *Child Development.* #40 (1969) 969-1025.

Alexander, F. *Fundamentals of Psychoanalysis.* New York: W. W. Norton & Company, Inc., 1963.

Anthony, E. J., and Benedek, T. (eds.) *Parenthood: Its Psychology and Psychopathology.* Boston: Little, Brown and Co., 1970.

Bandura, A. *Social Learning Theory.* Englewood Cliffs: Prentice Hall, 1977.

Bion, W. *Experiences in Groups.* New York: Basic Books, Inc., 1961.

Bowen, M. *Family Therapy in Clinical Practice.* New York: Jason Aronson, 1978.

Brazelton, G. "The Infant as Focus for Family Reciprocity," *The American Family* Harvard Seminar Series, (cassettes), 1980.

Erikson, E. *Childhood and Society.* New York: W. W. Norton & Company, Inc., 1953.

———. *Identity, Youth and Crises.* New York: W. W. Norton & Company, Inc., 1968.

Evans, R. *Dialogue with Erik Erikson.* New York: Harper and Row, 1969.

Ford, D., and Urban, H. *Systems of Psychotherapy: A Comparative Study.* New York: John Wiley and Sons, Inc., 1963.

Frailberg, S. *Every Child's Birthright: In Defense of Mothering.* New York: Basic Books, 1977.

Frankl, V. *Man's Search for Meaning.* New York: Washington Square Press, 1963.

Freud, A. *The Ego and The Mechanisms of Defense.* New York: International Universities Press, Inc., 1946.

Freud, S. *An Outline of Psychoanalysis.* New York: W. W. Norton & Company, 1949.

———. *The Ego and the Id.* New York: W. W. Norton & Company, 1960.

Gilligan, C. *In A Different Voice: Psychological Theory and Women's Development.* Cambridge: Harvard University Press, 1982.

Hartmann, H. *Essays on Ego Psychotherapy.* New York: International Universities Press, Inc., 1964.

Jacobson, E. "The Self and the Object World: Vicissitudes of Their Infantile Cathexes and Their Influence on Ideational and Affective Development," *The Psychoanalytic Study of the Child,* Vol. IX. New York: International Universities Press, 1954, 75-127.

Kernberg, O. *Internal World and External Reality: Object Relations Theory Applied.* New York: Jason Aronson, 1980.

Kluckhohn, F. "Variations in the Basic Values of Family Systems," *The Family* (Revised Edition). Edited by N. Bell and E. Vogel. New York: The Free Press, 1968, 319-330.

Loewald, H. "Internalization, Separation, Mourning, and the Super-ego," *Psychoanalytic Quarterly,* 31 (1962) 483-504.

Lynd, H. *On Shame and the Search for Identity.* New York: Harcourt, Brace and World, 1961.

Mahler, M. *The Selected Papers of Margaret S. Mahler, M.D., Volume 1: Infantile Psychosis and Early Contributions.* New York: Jason Aronson, 1979.

———. et al. *The Psychological Birth of the Human Infant.* New York: Basic Books, Inc., 1975.

Maier, H. *Three Theories of Child Development.* New York: Harper and Row, 1965.

Papajohn, J., and Spiegel, J. *Transactions in Families.* San Francisco: Jossey-Bass, 1975.

Piaget, J. *The Child and Reality: Problems of Genetic Psychology.* New York: Grossman Publishers, 1973.

Pinderhughes, E., et al. "The Effect of Ethnicity Upon the Psychological Task of Separation-Individuation: A Comparison of Four Ethnic Groups." Paper presented at 56th Annual Meeting of American Orthopsychiatric Association. Boston, 1979.

Smalley, R. Boston, "The Functional Approach to Casework Practice," *Theories of Social Casework.* Edited by R. Roberts and R. Nee. Chicago: University of Chicago Press, 1970, 77-128.

Spitz, R. *The First Year of Life.* New York: International Universities Press, 1965.

Vincent, C. "Family Spongea: The Adaptive Function," *Journal of Marriage and the Family,* 28: 1 (Feb. 1966) 29-36.

Watzlawick, P., et al. *Pragmatics of Human Communication: A Study of Interactional Patterns, Pathologies and Paradoxes.* New York: W. W. Norton & Company, 1967.

Wheelis, A. "How People Change," *Commentary.* 47: 5, (May 1969) 56-66.

4

PSYCHOSOCIAL STAGES OF DEVELOPMENT:

THE EVOLVING NATURE OF THE SELF

Throughout the life cycle, there is an innate quest toward differentiation, integration and consolidation to achieve a sense of wholeness within the person. Once the ego reaches a state of organization characterized by the relative stability of its defensive, executive and adaptive subsystems, the individual is equipped to accept increasing responsibility for the quest. Even in optimal circumstances, however, processes of internalization remain unfinished as does the structurizing of ego systems that emerge out of those interpersonal relationships. Psychosocial maturity, an elusive and culturally relative concept, is contingent upon the state of internalization and the corresponding intactness of ego functions. Fortunately, no one reaches an optimal state of completeness or intactness in this development, a notion captured in such common expressions as "Nobody is perfect;" "I'm only human." To be human is to be unfinished and sufficiently restless to pursue one's inner fulfillment through involvement with the external world, an idea which sets the stage for further consideration in this chapter of the hypotheses about structure and internalization discussed in chapters two and three.

Initially, however, it is necessary to clarify two concepts which have been used extensively in our discussion: the ego and the self. The term "ego" is simply a conceptual tool for understanding a critical dimension of the human condition. It is a means of accounting for the behavior of the person as he struggles to cope with the complexities of life. The notion of an ego is a convenient mode for describing how the individual synthesizes the transactional effects on his well-being of internal biopsychological and external sociocultural forces. The task of synthesis is facilitated when the subsystems of the ego are relatively intact and is impeded when these systems, or parts of them, are impaired. To understand the synthesizing task of the ego is to assess the impairment to intactness of its functions along a dynamic continuum. That assessment needs to be made within a wider context which includes the biological and the sociocultural aspects of an individual's life. Taken as a whole, the biopsychosocial dimensions of existence define the concept of "self."

Consider for a moment how one might respond to a request to "describe yourself" as compared with "describe your ego." The latter, in fact, sounds preposterous. We generally do not pose questions to others which are as abstract as the latter. If we did, the response would probably issue more from the id or superego and tell us something about the narcissistic state (i.e., egotistical reply) or self-esteem (i.e., feeling good or bad). In contrast, inquiries about the self are common and fit with sensible modes of human communication. "Tell me about yourself" may elicit a range of responses such as: "I am a twenty-six-year-old woman; I'm intelligent; I'm Italian. The point here is that the notion of the self is not only more operationally understood but also is expressed cognitively in a holistic way: twenty-six-year-old woman (biological), smart (psychological), Italian (cutural). This notion (of self) approaches what Kohut meant when he referred to the self as a low-level abstraction, a "content" or "experience-near" phenomenon (Kohut, 1971, XIV-XV).

The ego, on the other hand, is an abstract idea which is useful for conceptualizing defensive, executive and adaptive functions. While closer to a general understanding of everyday reality, the explanation of the notion of self is also more inclusive and transcends the biopsychosocial dimensions of life. As a conceptual tool, the term "self" captures the synthetic and integrative aspirations of our being at any point in time. That is, we strive adaptively to experience ourselves and to behave as a whole human being rather than as a fragmented one. In fact, an indication of the intactness of the ego is the capacity of the individual to sustain a firm sense of the nuclear self, a constancy of the self representation, while responding to environmental stimuli in flexible and creative ways which are adaptive and autonomous manifestations of ego functions.

In contrast to the conceptualization of the self in "self psychology," one may say that the sense of self becomes integrated into the internal representations of self and other as the ego function of object relations becomes organized. The sense of self expands as the person identifies with selective attributes of figures in the human environment. These attributes initially form object representations which are transmuted into the self-representation as processes of differentiation, separation and autonomy are resolved. When fragmented introjects remain as object representations that have not been integrated into the self-representation, the individual is left to act out of fear of object anxiety rather than from his own inner convictions.

We have also suggested that the superego is not a separate and discrete structure but an infrastructure which interfaces with ego functions. The notion of self, which becomes operationally defined as the self-representation during mid-level processes of identification, introjection and differentiation, demonstrates the nature of that interface. Mid-level processes are, by their nature, always concerned with matters of value. That is, self and object representations are inevitably tempered and shaped by the values of reference groups with which the individual is involved and with whom he has identified. As object representations become less prominent and give way to the self representation, the value orientation of the individual may be affected by several variables which include innate constitutional predispositions (such as gifted intelligence) and the impact of secondary reference groups (outside of the family) whose values may be variant from those of the primary reference group. Adolescence is a period when the latter becomes a nodal issue in development, a time of achieving separateness but not rupture between self and significant others which facilitates the ascendancy of the self representation over object representations. If object representations do not become integrated into and congruent with the self representation, they remain as fragmented yet powerful influences on behavior. Social roles and relationships then continue to be structured out of object anxiety as the individual attempts to conform to his perceptions of the expectation of others. Of course, the state of ego autonomy is a relative matter and a "more or less" issue for all people as they struggle to act out of inner convictions while, at the same time, preserving their need for social approval and acceptance. The more complete the integration and consolidation of object representations into the self representation, the better equipped is the individual to become involved in new roles and relationships appropriate to his biopsychosocial stage of development.

We will now examine the relationship of the structural and developmental paradigm discussed in chapters two and three to stages of human development. Erikson's eight-stage model will be utilized in this discussion because of its biopsychosocial framework for understanding ego development. More than anyone, it seems, Erikson attended to inner and outer realities in constructing his paradigm and attempted to account for the complex transactions between the internal and external worlds of the individual and their influence on ego development.

The format for this analysis is shown in the following outline:

EGO STRUCTURE
  defensive system
  executive system
  adaptive system
INTERNALIZATION PROCESS
  lower level processes
  attachment and involvement
  mid level processes
  identification, introjection,
  differentiation
  upper level processes
  separation and autonomy

A. Infancy and Early Childhood
  Trust vs. mistrust
  Autonomy vs. shame and doubt
  Initiative vs. guilt
B. Childhood
  Industry vs. inferiority
C. Adolescence
  Identity vs. role confusion
D. Adulthood
  Intimacy vs. isolation
  Generativity vs. stagnation
  Ego integrity vs. despair

INFANCY AND EARLY CHILDHOOD: THE FIRST SIX YEARS

Basic ego systems become operational within an organized framework during infancy and early childhood which corresponds roughly with the first six years of life. Internalization processes evolve in a more linear direction during this period in contrast to subsequent periods when they occur primarily in transactional form.

Although the child experiences a beginning sense of separateness and autonomy in all three dimensions of his life, his sense of self continues to be influenced primarily by object representations. Some integration of object with the self-representation occurs but the level of sophistication of the cognitive function (the preconceptual ego) perpetuates dependence on external figures for biological and social supplies. That is, he can take care of his bodily needs and exercise a degree of autonomy over feeding, elimination, mobility and motility yet he remains highly dependent on external resources for the opportunities to exercise those functions.

Empathic attachments to loving figures promote a basic trust or faith in the "goodness" of others (as providers) and facilitates the internalization of positive object representations which Erikson views as the "cornerstone of a healthy personality" (Erikson, 1980, 58). The quality of early relationships with significant others, experienced progressively as a confirmation and reassurance of his worth and value (as a human being), supports involvement and identification processes. Deprivation of libidinal supplies undermines trust in others and reinforces the persistence of abandonment and annihilation anxieties which, if uncorrected, may lead to dependence on primitive defenses as a modus operandi for dealing with perceived dangers ascribed indiscriminately by the individual to the external world. Tolerance and firmness of significant figures, who are also able to connect empathically with the developmental needs of the child, support his natural thrust to risk involvement in relationships in which reciprocity is mutually gratifying and regulated through empathic connectedness with significant others. Boundaries between self and other (s) (the beginning of the adaptive system) are experienced as a rudimentary sense of separateness; together with the faith in providers, these contribute to subsequent identifications with the attributes of significant figures. The process of identification, within which the executive system of the ego becomes organized, requires initiative which Erikson suggests is necessary for all learning (Erikson, 1963, 247-274). Initiative is sustained, however, only as the individual experiences a mutual attractiveness or valency for maintaining the relationship, which is "fed" by verbal and nonverbal feedback of a prevailingly positive nature. During that process early shame—the basis of object anxiety that develops during the need-satisfying period—gives way to an inner sense of moral responsibility. As the child is progressively yet gradually held accountable for his actions and their social consequences, he begins to experience himself as a differentiated, separate and partially autonomous person. Within mid-level processes he becomes aware of constitutional "givens" over which he had no control–gender, race and ethnicity. Depending on the quality of feedback and reinforcement from the social environment, the child begins to value these important characteristics of his identity with a sense of goodness and badness.

We have suggested that lower level processes are antecedent to internalization proper, which has been associated traditionally with mid-level processes. However, development which is contingent on internalization is continuous. Recent research by Brazelton and others indicates that the infant, shortly after birth, may be more capable of reciprocal and differentiated relations with the external world than has historically been considered to be true. As knowledge becomes available on these important matters, we may find that lower level processes and the rudimentary ego structures which result from them have an even greater significance on subsequent processes at mid and upper levels of internalization.

By the time the child becomes involved more extensively in the world outside of the primary group, his basic ego functions have become activated and organized within the structure of subsystems:

A) He has experienced relationships of a qualitatively different nature within lower to higher levels of the internalization process.

B) His introjections of external figures become prototypical for future object relationships while the integration of object representations into the self-representation forms the basis of his self-esteem. These two aspects influence the quality of future role relations, particularly those in marriage and parenting.

Jennifer, a six-year-old black child, was initially referred to the clinic for an evaluation because of constant changes in her life starting at seven months of age. Although slim in build, her physical maturation was appropriate to her age. She was a bright and active child who did well in school and was highly responsive to her weekly therapy sessions, which she viewed as a time to play and to talk about her situation.

Jennifer is the oldest of four children born to an alcoholic mother, a single parent. At age seven months, the Department of Public Welfare obtained custody of Jennifer on grounds of parental neglect. She was placed in foster care and experienced several changes in her living situation over the next few years. For the past few months she has been residing (along with her younger siblings) with the maternal grandmother, who also has a 14-year-old daughter and a 19-year-old son.

Her play therapy reflects a pervasive sense of insecurity and fear of abandonment manifested in constant rearrangement of doll house furniture, people traveling from place to place, lack of food and children being removed from their parents. To defend against vulnerable feelings associated with these conflicts, Jennifer adopts a big sister role with her siblings, for whom she cares in a nurturing and protective way. Identification conflicts are manifested in confusion about her ethnicity and race as she insists that she was born white and became black as she grew. Her complexion is lighter than that of her siblings. Jennifer also appears to have a sexual curiosity which is unusual for her age. That (curiosity) may be the result of the living arrangement where there is some indication that she has witnessed sexual activity between grandmother and a male friend. Despite the trauma of her background, Jennifer appears to be adapting quite well to many aspects of her life. She enjoys and does well at school, and she has developed an active and ongoing relationship with the therapist.

In therapy, she is expressive and involved in play. During the second session, for example, she ran to the corner (of the play therapy room) to pick up toy furniture, which she placed in the doll house in a very orderly manner. She designated separate rooms for the male and female children as well as a room in which the parents were to sleep. A big sister was cleaning the grounds around the house. After she finished cleaning, the big sister jumped into the parents' bed and knocked the father out of the house. In the following session, a bear sneaked into the house and stole the children. When the mother awoke, she wept because of what had occurred and then began to search for the bear. When mother found the bear, she killed it and rescued the children.

In another session, Jennifer and the therapist were playing a board game which the therapist won. Jennifer became enraged and accused the therapist of cheating. When the therapist asked about her upsetting feelings related to losing the game, Jennifer said in an angry tone that she wanted to win and then withdrew in silence. The therapist commented that winning gave Jennifer the feeling of being in control and that she may have been upset about not being in control. After pouting, Jennifer insisted on another game and said confidently that she would win that one!

At the end of the sixth session, Jennifer asked to take some play dough home. Her initial response to the therapist's questions about her reasons for the request was to say that she liked it and then acknowledged that it would make her feel better. When Jennifer was not able to respond to a comment on how the play dough might help her feel better, the therapist asked if it would remind her of being here (with the therapist), to which Jennifer nodded her head in agreement and said "yeah."

Jennifer has experienced considerable difficulty in leaving the therapist at the end of each session, particularly in the first two months of their relationship. When she was reminded of the need to end each session, she would express anger by banging the toys and throwing them into a storage container. As the therapist acknowledged her feelings of anger at the separations and reassured her of their next appointment, Jennifer was gradually able to wind down the sessions with the therapist and not react with as much hostility.

Another theme in therapy was related to her confusion about racial identity, and her feelings toward the therapist, who was Chinese. In the initial session, Jennifer had insisted that she was half Italian and half American. As therapy progressed, she would make remarks about Chinese children with whom she would not play. When the therapist commented on her own Chinese identity, Jennifer responded that she liked the therapist and that Chinese women were O.K.

This six-year-old child, in spite of the discontinuities in primary relationships during her first six years, was able to adapt rather resourcefully to her present life situation. No doubt, her natural cognitive endowment was a significant resource in her efforts to adapt to the new living arrangement, school and therapy. That adaptation, however, appears to be based on tenuous internal structures.

The therapeutic relationship seems to be an opportunity to build object constancy, which was impaired as a consequence of mother's psychological unavailability and a lack of continuity with subsequent libidinal figures in her life. Her defense against vulnerability to annihilation and abandonment was to minimize the significance of mother and to adopt a pseudo identity as a mothering figure to her siblings. That pseudo identity was reinforced by her grandmother, who expects Jennifer to assume a caretaker role with them, thus providing fuel for premature autonomous development of her ego. Within therapy, Jennifer is able to relax defenses built up as a result of these developmental conflicts by experiencing the safety and constancy of a libidinally-oriented relationship with an adult. Although the relationship with the therapist can never substitute for the loss of similar qualities in a primary relationship, it can partially neutralize the narcissistic sting of these losses and permit the child to experience other dimensions of her self which have been denied via pseudo-independent behavior. Her anger at abandonment and the sadness felt in not having mother as well as the wish for her to be available in a protective and loving way are portrayed vividly in her dollhouse play. Within the safety of the therapeutic situation she can reveal these vulnerabilities, which are obscured in her seemingly adaptive behavior as a caretaker of her sisters.

The cheating accusation directed toward the therapist is a projection of her own behavior in playing games. Although cheating may reflect anxiety about one's competence and sense of self-esteem, it also is a way through which Jennifer may preserve her fragile control of relationships. Attachment to the therapist and personal investment in the therapeutic relationship helped to neutralize some of the anger and hurt associated with losing. The value associated with the relationship supported subsequent steps at reflecting upon and becoming aware of the meaning of cheating to her fragile identity, a gradual interpretative process framed within a therapeutic atmosphere that was protective of her self-esteem, limitations and capacities. These supportive and interpretative techniques may contribute to the strengthening and freeing of ego functions.

The ego building thrust of the therapy was evident in the way the therapist handled termination of early interviews. The play dough was a symbol of developmental struggles to establish libidinal object constancy which had been undermined as a consequence of the emotional unavailability of mother and the lack of continuity in primary relationships. By recognizing her feelings and gradually moving to interpret the meaning of Jennifer's behavior in tentative and questioning (rather than declarative) form, the therapist connected empathically with a nodal developmental issue and engaged the child in exploring the meaning of her behavior, both of which were potentially corrective of earlier experiences. It was necessary to maintain a delicate balance in the supportive-interpretative aspects of therapy within firm boundaries so that the relationship might become corrective but not a substitute for the unavailable object. Because of the deficiencies in the availability of constant significant others, object representations were distorted and their transmutation into the self-representation was manifest in precocious independence. The therapeutic risk in these situations is to generate excessive dependency rather than to respect and struggle to work with the child's potential for more autonomous ego functioning.

A critical dimension of identity during early childhood is race and ethnicity. For Jennifer, there was considerable conflict at this level of internalization processes. We do not know why she needed to deny her racial heritage and to see herself as a white Italian-American who had become black. The degradation to her self-representation as a worthwhile person appeared to be tied up with her denial of her identity as a person of color perhaps out of rage at mother who had abandoned her. Her rejection of self was projected onto others who may also have been identified as powerless. Her lack of confidence in the power of her self was projected on to Chinese children over whom she felt superiority. No doubt the behavior was also a displacement of her anger toward the therapist who was Chinese. As a potentially corrective experience and as an opportunity for building ego functions, the recognition of Jennifer's feelings and the acknowledgment of the therapist's ethnicity in an accepting manner (by the therapist) was a critical part of the process of strengthening this dimension of Jennifer's representation of self.

CHILDHOOD: SIX TO TWELVE YEARS

Childhood, which is synonymous with latency, is a time when an individual enters the wider world whether the world be "a field, a jungle or a formal school" (Erikson, 1963, 246). Erikson observed that all children—regardless of the sociocultural milieu in which they are raised—receive "some systematic instruction" which is designed to prepare them for meaningful roles in the future. During this time, which coincides with the stage of concrete operations, the ego function of cognitive mastery becomes an indispensable resource and focal point in the journey toward autonomy. Learning is enhanced as the child acquires the cognitive skill of deductive reasoning in contrast to earlier periods when his secondary processes were oriented to inductive thought. He is now capable of seeing logically the relationship between ends and their means, a skill that is essential to the ego function of cognitive mastery.

The term "latency" is significant to understanding the nature of internalization and structuralization during this period. Biologically, latency comes between two very rapid and dramatic stages of physiological change: early childhood (including infancy) and adolescence. In contrast to these periods, latency is a time of relative maturational stability instrumental to the consolidation of ego structures, which develop rapidly during the first six years and which will undergo dramatic reorganization during the adolescent years. The biological stability of childhood frees the ego to pursue tasks which will consolidate the psychological gains of earlier development and which will prepare the child for the developmental challenges of adolescence. Under optimal circumstances, consolidation of ego systems will be a stabilizing resource once pubescence is reached.

Lower level processes have a significance in childhood quite different from their significance in the earliest years. At that time, the process of attachment, manifested in the maternal-infant bond, was a sine qua non for psychological survival and biological well-being (Spitz, 1965). The self-confidence resulting from those primary experiences now becomes a vehicle for involvement with peers and for identification with tasks of learning. Comfort in one's separateness and confidence in one's success at autonomous strivings temper earlier needs to attach and to retain dependent involvements with primary figures. As a consequence, the child is freed to pursue productive work by identification with secondary resources of learning such as teachers and peers. Lower level processes are valued as a means to involvement in industrious activities, rather than as ends in themselves, which was true during infancy. Productivity as a learner helps to deepen the child's positive sense of himself, and positive reinforcement from significant figures for achievements strengthen his self-representation. Play and sharing in peer group activities also facilitate the sense of mastery as the child feels pleasure and reward in the exercise of executive ego functions in collaboration with equals.

Identification with peers of the same sex helps to strengthen gender identity, which became a nodal focus of the identification process during the preconceptual period when the child developed the capacity to differentiate by gender and to associate value with sexual identity. Collective associations with peers of the same sex was not as value laden an issue in that period as it appears to be during latency and early adolescence. Although changing social attitudes about acceptable behavior by gender is having an effect on traditional discriminatory practices and sexual stereotypes, the need of the latency age child for confirmation and reassurance of gender identity seems to be facilitated through group affiliations of a same sex nature which are characteristic of latency. On the other hand, contact with and involvement in activities—social, athletic and educational—with persons of the opposite sex is a means of promoting realistic and empathic attitudes toward those who are "different." Those experiences—when structured by adults whose values about gender are realistic and respectful of gender commonalities as well as individual variations regardless of gender—will serve to strengthen self and object representations related to sexuality and gender identification. Similar gains will be possible when the latency age child is involved with other children of different ethnic, racial and social statuses. The danger of this period, "a sense of inadequacy and inferiority" (Erikson, 1963, 248), may affect the shape of internal representations of self and others and as a consequence have an undermining effect on the adaptive capacity for productive work.

Latency is also characterized by significant gains in adaptation, which are derived from the strengthening of executive ego functions. As a result of these gains, self-confidence is enhanced. The dormancy of instinctual forces from the internal world focuses ego development at its outer boundary or interface with the external world. Inner needs are now oriented to the enhancement of adaptive skills of rational problem solving, intellectual curiosity and pairing with others to achieve collective goals. While the defensive system continues to serve as a buffering resource, it tends to be relatively quiet except in those situations in which the child ascribes to new relationships those affects and defenses which originated in early childhood. These self-protective modes may be most apparent in peer groups and in relation to new authority figures such as teachers. Otherwise, latency is characterized by an ascending of the adaptive system of the ego over the defensive system.

Paul, a nine-year-old white child, was referred to the clinic by his mother, who was concerned about his verbal and abusive behavior toward his two younger sisters, his association with older boys who were streetwise and tough, and his refusal to obey his mother. Her marriage of nine years to Paul's father has been punctuated by numerous separations as a result of his physical and verbal abuse of her. Both parents are currently separated and in individual therapy.

Paul always was an active yet manageable child and depicted by mother in macho-like terms; his aggressive behavior toward her and his sisters has exacerbated over the past year, which coincided with the most recent marital separation. Although prenatal history was normal, Paul's first two years of life were plagued with severe bronchitis for which he was hospitalized three times during the first year. With medical treatment these symptoms abated by three years of age. Mother recalls that Paul was a happy and outgoing child despite these illnesses, but she also reports that he has always been afraid of hypodermic needles, of the dark, of being alone, and of sleeping by himself. No other developmental irregularities were noted in his history.

In spite of abusive behavior toward his wife, father was described as a loving person with the children and, in fact, seldom punished them. Much of the abuse took place while the children were present. At these times Paul would run to his mother in a panic, screaming and crying, and the father would chastise him for being a baby, and then walk away. Paul appeared to be caught between the need to protect his mother and retain her love while risking annihilation by father whom he admired. To this day Paul has never been able to express anger directly and openly at this father. Despite these intrafamilial conflicts, Paul does well at school in his academic work and is not a behavioral problem in that setting.

His initial contact at the clinic was highly conflictual. Notwithstanding a tough-guy demeanor characterized by crude language and a swagger to his gait, Paul refused to separate from his mother until the second session, when the therapist was able to get him into the playroom through a gentle but firm stance. Once alone with the therapist, he began to play spontaneously and related in an appropriate and warm manner which, according to the mother, corresponded to his behavior when he was alone with her. Although his play was characterized by an aggressive quality, Paul was not destructive and showed no signs of being overwhelmed by his anger. Themes in his verbalizations tended to revolve around associations of strength with masculinity, weakness with feminity, fears of bodily injury, fears of abandonment and covert guilt about his badness.

In her therapy, the mother has expressed much anxiety about Paul's emulation of his father, particularly in his abuse of her and his sisters, and fears that he may grow up to be a carbon copy of father. Although she has some awareness of the significance of the most recent separation in increasing Paul's aggressive behavior, she does not appear to be empathically in touch with the counterphobic elements of his macho-like behavior. In brief, mother seems to view Paul as a scaled-down replica of his father rather than as a differentiated individual, a little boy who needs firm and consistent limits. Father appears overwhelmed with shame for abusing his wife and worries that Paul is trying to emulate him. His preoccupation with feelings of guilt also seems to get in the way of recognizing the fearful parts in his son.

This nine-year-old boy suffers from no physical or intellectual impairment at the present time and appears to be dealing with the task of learning in an adaptive manner. In spite of behavioral conflicts within the family, no complaints have been made by the school about his behavior. Paul is an average student who is apparently getting along well with peers and teachers.

Early physical illness which required numerous separations from the family and a history of fears which originated during that period are the precursors to current conflicts manifested in counter-phobic symptoms and separation anxieties. At the age of 22 months, for example, Paul experienced regressive enuresis when mother went to the hospital for the birth of the second child, but he regained bladder control when mother returned home with the new baby. In view of that regression occurring before, rather than after the baby and mother came home, his fear of abandonment may have prevented Paul from displaying any oppositional behavior that would have enhanced differentiation and separateness from mother.

We do not know how the father was available to him in these early years but we do know that Paul would cling protectively to mother when the father was abusive toward her, also risking the verbal wrath of father if he retained the "safe haven" with mother. Rather than experiencing a gradual separation/individuation, Paul was confronted with a dilemma which resulted in identification with the aggressor to the exclusion of libidinal ties with the nurturing mother. This interpersonal splitting along gender lines resulted in counterphobic behavior to keep his fears of abandonment from consciousness and in introjections of maleness inextricably associated with defeat of the weak female. His identification with the aggressive father was no doubt reinforced by the fact that he was the only male child and by the neighborhood, which was a tough place where little boys had to learn to take care of themselves. His identification with older, streetwise boys, a pattern for the past several years, served to feed his tenuous self-representation as a tough kid who could take care of himself and to seal off his sense of vulnerability and weakness, which was projected on to females. A hopeful prognosis that the splitting of self and object representations along gender lines can be modified is derived from the fact that Paul is able to relax this defense when he is alone with mother and with the therapist, who is also a woman. Another positive sign is that aggressive acting out associated with the splitting defense is confined to primary figures (mother and sisters) and has not contaminated his relationships with peers and other significant adults (such as teachers). Conflict-free ego functions, such as cognitive mastery, remain intact and facilitate adaptive involvement as a productive student.

Paul's sense of industry and self-confidence is tenuously grounded in his need to preserve differentiation of self and object representations, which are now rigidly compartmentalized by gender. For Paul, therapy may be an opportunity for relaxing his defensive need to preserve that split and of learning that the world is a safe enough place to be both strong and weak. These integrative gains will be contingent upon changes in mother's capacity to differentiate Paul from his father and as a consequence to relate to him as a separate little boy who needs love and firm control. Gain will be contingent, as well, on the capacity of father to make use of therapy to sustain recent changes in his relationship with mother and to help Paul modify his self-representation of maleness with aggression toward females.

ADOLESCENCE

With the beginnings of puberty, childhood ends and adolescence begins. This period is characterized by volcanic changes in the body and its physiological functions which reverberate on psychological and social dimensions of life. With the advent of significant biological maturation, the ego and one's sense of self are confronted with tasks that are qualitatively different from earlier periods. The discontinuities inherent in these changes are at least partially neutralized by psychosocial gains of the latency period. That is, the internalized resources related to enhanced ego functions and a strengthened self-representation enable the individual to cope with bodily changes and later with changes in social role expectations of early adulthood. In contrast to the needs of latency, which were for strengthening of ego systems, the needs of adolescence are for reorientation of those systems to meet the demands of more autonomous functioning in adulthood. The loss of the privileges of childhood, along with the challenges and responsibilities of adulthood, exert enormous pressure on the adolescent. His struggle to integrate these dialectic forces is manifested, not uncommonly, in rapid shifts in mood and in ambivalent behavior which may puzzle adults who have lost touch with the struggles of this period. Complicating this internal shift from representations of one's self as a child to one's self as an adult are external forces which define the individual as a child, at least in a legal sense, yet often treat him as if he were an adult.

The principal developmental task of the period is to accrue a sense of identity which Erikson defines as the ego's ability to integrate all identifications with the vicissitudes of the libido, with the aptitudes developed out of endowment, and with the opportunities offered in social roles. (Erikson, 1963, 250)

Integration within a new configuration of ego systems and self-object representations thus becomes a central task of adolescence. In contrast to the earlier gains in achieving identity, associated with a sense of separateness from significant others, the identification process in adolescence is concerned with an inner sense of self-continuity which was built up and consolidated from latency but which now must be modified in relation to vastly different social expectations of adult-like behavior. The means through which that shift is achieved has been referred to as the second separation individuation process which "connotes those ego changes that are the accompaniment and the consequence of the adolescent disengagement from infantile objects" (Blos, 1967, 167-168).

Our reference to the loss of childhood refers to the notion of interpersonal disengagement from significant others and the intrapersonal loosening of object representations accompanied by the ascendancy of the self-representation. Those significant shifts which occur concurrently in social relationships and psychological configurations involve the individual in parallel yet different tasks of earlier sub-phases of separation-individuation. Differentiation, practicing and rapprochement may again characterize behavior as the adolescent struggles to let go of the known past and to engage an unknown future. Within that process, the need to depend on familiar figures may be misinterpreted by the latter as regression to a more fixed state, which the adolescent actually fears, rather than as an adaptive attempt to cope with the challenge of becoming an adult. Patience, firmness and constancy are probably the most essential qualities that significant caretakers can offer the adolescent during this time (i.e., a "holding environment"). In a sense, the vicissitudes of this transitional period must be survived— even more than understood—empathically by parents and other significant figures if the adolescent is to become emancipated from the object ties of his childhood. Because of the powerful and unique transactional effects of biopsychosocial changes on inner states, empathic understanding will never be "good enough" to neutralize the inner struggles of the adolescent, nor need it be; the task of the adult world is to create and maintain parameters within which the adolescent may work out his own solutions that gradually strengthen reliance on his self-representation, and loosen continued dependence on object representations. Under optimal circumstances, that process leads to what Erikson has termed the integration of identifications.

The road to adult autonomy is paved with significant developments in the executive ego, particularly in the function of cognitive mastery. Formal operations, characterized by new skills of abstract reasoning, analysis and vertical thinking enhance the shift to reliance on self but they also lead to conflict. As a result of these gains, the adolescent is capable of understanding the imperfections of the adult world, of which he is to become a part, through a cognitive lens which was not available to him during earlier periods. He may see the inconsistencies and hypocrisies of that world more clearly; as a consequence, he is confronted with the need to assess the nature of his value system vis-à-vis the outside world. The peer group, as well as idealization of folk heroes which are instrumental to the loosening of object ties, are also instrumental to the resolution of this dilemma. Identifications with those who share similar conflicts help to reinforce the emergence of the self-representation which may be at variance with conventional mores and internal representations of the object world. In contrast to latency, the adolescent struggles to consolidate his self-representation, to rely more fully on himself in dealing with the world and to integrate into his representation of self those attributes of the object world which are congruent with his personal value system. These struggles also exercise other aspects of the ego such as the acuity of the reality testing function. The dangers of the period are in premature closure of the struggle through excessive independence leading to a pseudo state of autonomy or through surrender of individuation by excessive conformity to the expectations of the adult world. In relation to the monitoring function, the latter may arrest the individual at the "good boy -nice girl" stage of moral development (Kohlberg, 1964).

The distinction between the defensive and adaptive systems is perhaps more obscured during adolescence than in any other period. Although the peer group continues to fulfill adaptive needs as it did in latency, its value now is related to emancipation from object control and the reinforcement of a shifting and precarious self-representation by mutual identification with those with whom he has "something" in common. While peers may offer mutual support, pervasive involvement and exclusive identification with the peer group may be a perverse form of flight from an internal sense of emptiness, insecurity, fear of genital potency and the developmental needs which push him to become an individuated young adult. Idealizing phenomena may also serve this dual function of defense and adaptation as may involvement in heterosexual relations.

Intimate relationships are crucial to mid and late adolescence as well as to early adulthood; they offer the individual opportunities to explore and test the finished and unfinished aspects of the internalization process. "Playing the field" offers individuals the chance to assess the symmetrical and complementary aspects of relationships; that is, how their individual needs will or will not be satisfied through new relationships. Since that task is complex and includes highly significant preconscious and unconscious aspects, individuals need time and space to explore and test out relationships. Marriage may or may not be an adaptive resolution of this need. The important point is that development is continuous throughout adulthood and is contingent upon the playing out of lower, mid and upper level processes of internalization in relationships that are more adaptive than defensive for the adolescent and young adult.

Dan, a 17-year-old white adolescent, applied for therapy because of feeling depressed, isolated from peers, and troubled by his mother's alcoholism. During initial interviews, he presented as a bright and introspective person who said that he was troubled primarily about an inner sense of helplessness, powerlessness and lack of self-confidence. At the time of his application for therapy, Dan lived at home with his mother. An 18-year-old sister, who one month before (his application) had enrolled at an out-of-state university with a full scholarship, had been a patient at the clinic and had encouraged Dan to apply for help.

Although the developmental history is sketchy, Dan reported that he, an older brother and his sister lived at home with mother and father until nine years ago when the father died of a sudden heart attack. His early memories of the family unit were somewhat vague. He described the father as a hardworking man who spent much time at his job and was not available that regularly to the children. Mother was the primary caretaker, did not work, and stayed at home until after his death, when she sought employment in the business field. Apparently, she was quite dependent on her husband, not only to support her and the children, but to make important decisions. She was devoted to her role as mother to the exclusion of extra-familial activities, and from Dan's sketchy accounts, was an emphatically attuned and libidinally available figure in his early years.

After the death, mother and Dan's older brother became entangled in conflict, which led to the brother's therapy at the clinic. Mother refused to be involved in therapy and attempted to sabotage the oldest son's involvement (in therapy). She began to drink regularly and excessively to the point where she was fired from several different jobs. She became progressively less available to the children, who banded together for mutual support and to care for her. Although her behavior was very troublesome and characterized by unfounded suspicions about coworkers, mother refused to seek professional help. She appeared to become a figure with whom the children had to contend, protect and care for. Each of them turned to the clinic as a resource for maintaining their own sense of stability, almost like an extended family. Efforts by the clinic to reach out to mother were rebuffed, and no grounds could be established by the Department of Public Welfare for protective custody of the children.

Dan's request for therapy was doubtless precipitated by the realization that he would be the last sibling at home to care for his mother. He was concerned about her future since his older sister and brother were away at school. Given Dan's scholastic record as a straight "A" student, it appeared likely that he too would be able to leave home in a year to attend college. Yet his presenting concerns were more related to his withdrawal from peers, to whom he felt inferior despite his outstanding abilities. His sense of inferiority was reinforced a few weeks before the initial interview when he was unable to become sexually potent with an adolescent girl with whom he was involved.

Dan had compartmentalized his life by filling his leisure time with study and avoiding social relationships outside of school which might jeopardize the secret of mother's alcoholism. Despite the pain which he was experiencing, Dan did not seek refuge in drugs or alcohol.

Dan presents a rather clear picture of the difficulty in distinguishing between ego defensive and adaptive behaviors during adolescence. At one level, his achievement or over-achievement in school appears to be highly adaptive as it apparently was for his sister who, through her success as a student, was able to earn a scholarship to college. Her success and, potentially, that of Dan's, was also a means of breaking away from a pathological family situation without becoming ovewhelmed with guilt. For Dan, the status of being the youngest and last child at home and the only one left to care for mother was creating a superego dilemma which, no matter how it was resolved, would demand an enormous price from him. The involvement with school work and his outstanding achievement helped to bind underlying depression and a fragile sense of self-esteem. Adding fuel to this adaptive/defensive dilemma was a mother who was never satisfied with her son's achievements even when his academic record was near perfect.

Despite the tragedy of the present situation, we may hypothesize that libidinal supplies were adequate, if not plentiful, in the early years of the mother-child relationship. It appears that the sibling subsystem took over when the parental subsystem became so impaired that maternal supplies were no longer available. All three children banded together for mutual support and nurturance and turned to the clinic to meet their individual needs for adult stability. Their psychological hunger for object availability was not so all-encompassing that it resulted in severe impairment in ego functioning; this lends support to the hypothesis that maternal supplies were once available and adequate to early internalization processes.

Role reversal of this nature, however, may deprive the ego of a gradual and balanced means of integrating object representations into the self-representation. Dan and his sister had precipitously become adult-like adolescents in a reciprocal relationship with a child-like adult. Premature closure of the adolescent struggle and the premature consolidation of the self-representation may lead to depression as a defense against underlying rage toward the depriving object. When the superego is unusually severe, as it appeared to be with Dan, the esteem for self may be undermined by the impossibility of never measuring up as a parental object and never being good enough for one's peers because of shame associated with the object representation of one's parent. In a sense, there is a short circuit in the shift from representations of one's self as child to one's representation of the self as an adult.

The second separation/individuation process of Dan's adolescence is impaired because disengagement from infantile object representations has not been reinforced by reality. The ego of the parental self had become impaired and was compensated by the child who became a parental object. In that configuration, rapprochement became impossible with the actual parent. The seeking of therapy at that time by all three children may be indicative of their need to find an adult object to whom they may relate in order to work through final stages of adolescent separation/individuation including remnants of superego anxiety. Loyalty to the parent and the privacy of the struggle was fueled by guilt and shame, which undermined involvement in intimate relationships. The impotence of which Dan complained in his initial interview may have been a consequence of that internal conflict, which may also interfere with involvement in future relationships unless the developmental lesions can be healed.

ADULTHOOD: MARRIAGE

Today, adolescence seems to merge with young adulthood with no particular chronological age or rites of passage distinguishing clearly between the two periods. That ambiguity is characteristic of modern Western cultures and is not universal either in an historical or contemporary sense. Certain events may gradually accrue adult status such as a driver's license, the right to vote, the right to purchase and drink hard liquor and graduation from high school or college. In our culture, the ambiguity of visible symbols related to that transition parallels the process of psychosocial development, which is highly relative and influenced by a complex of variables.

Recent research suggests that sexual preference is already established by late adolescence and is likely to have been influenced, if not determined, by a biological precursor(s) (Bell, 1981). In relationship to the nodal issue of intimacy, we will focus on heterosexual relationships although the theory may also be relevant to understanding ego development in homosexual relationships. As future research uncovers the motivations not only for sexual preference but for involvement in homosexual relationships of an enduring nature, the mystery of sexual preference may become secondary to the generic question of why people choose to commit themselves to specific partners within intimate relationships. We also table the question of intimate and enduring relationships of a heterosexual nature, which do not constitute marriage in a legal sense. Although our discussion of the nature of ego involvement in the intimate relationship of marriage may have relevance to intimate relationships in general, the focus here is on marriage. The second aspect of our discussion will focus on the parenting role which is one expression of the adult need for generativity.

In his research on identity formation in adolescents and among young adult college students, Marcia found that the achievement of an integrated sense of identity is most likely if the individual has been involved in several situations which confront him with choices related to his moral values, life goals and personal relationships. Mature identity is characterized, according to Marcia, by an investment of the individual and a subsequent commitment to the choices that have been made from the alternatives available to him. Until the individual is ready to commit himself to these choices, a moratorium on the achievement of identity results. In situations where the person has been protected or deprived of normal adolescent crises and has persistently avoided personal investment in choices, role confusion may become a chronic problem, and relationships will tend to be characterized by a superficial quality. Where the person remains attached uncritically to parental values and clings to his perception of their aspirations for him, the individual may foreclose on his identity and look to others to make decisions for him (Marcia, source unknown).

Erikson suggested that each of his eight stages must be transcended "in such a way that the individual can take chances in the next stage with what was most vulnerably precious in the previous one" (Erikson, 1963, 250-251). With the achievement of identity emerging out of adolescence and young adulthood, the adult is ready to form new attachments and to become involved in relationships of a more intimate nature. Of course, this notion connotes an ideal state of ego integration which is impossible to achieve even under optimal circumstances. People consolidate their representation of self and achieve identity in more or less a holistic way and carry moratoriums, confusions, foreclosures with them into intimate relationships.

When a sense of identity has been achieved at an adaptive rather than a defensive level, the self-representation becomes dominant over object representations. However, even where ego systems become integrated into a sense of wholeness within the individual, the self-representation continues to be affected by the remnants of internalized objects, especially when there is lack of congruence between the two sets of representations. Absolute congruence is neither possible nor desirable, for it is the "unfinished business" in internalized human relations which provides the fuel for new attachments and involvements in the adult. Because of that "unfinished business," people continue to need people throughout life.

In Bowen's conceptualization of differentiation, the "solid self" appears to be synonymous with the self-representation and "pseudo self" with object representations in the adult (Bowen, 1978). The self-representation contributes to autonomy while object representations, if they persist as dominant forces in adulthood, will fuse with and absorb a tenuous self-representation and interfere with the separation process. The more unfinished the process of establishing a firm sense of the nuclear self (i.e., consolidated self-representation), the more likely is the individual to form new attachments that resemble the unresolved attachments with primary figures in the past. The more complete the process of differentiation, the less fused is the self-representation with object representations. As a consequence, the person with a relatively solid representation of and esteem for self is equipped to become involved in relationships with a confident sense of his individuality, separateness and autonomy. The person with a tenuous sense of the self-representation and corresponding tendency to devalue himself will become involved in a relationship in a more fused and symbiotic way and look to the other for supplies to make up his deficiencies. Although these distinctions may make sense conceptually, pure types or extremes when viewed along a continuum are simply theoretical possibilities. As Karpel suggests, most, if not all, intimate relationships will be characterized by ambivalence (to a greater or lesser degree) in relation to the levels of differentiation within each person (Karpel, 1976).

The Blancks identify five aspects of marriage that have the potential for ego development. They are:

—establishment of sexual relations, which offers the opportunity to resolve genital prohibitions of childhood;
—establishment of a new level of object relations, the continuity of which offers new opportunities for development;

—an opportunity to strengthen psychological separateness from
parents;
—an opportunity to exercise autonomy; and
—an opportunity to internalize new identifications (Blanck, 1968, 306).

Viewed along a continuum, the valency or attractiveness of one person for another is contingent upon conscious, preconscious and unconscious perceptions of the potential of the relationship to fulfill developmental needs. The degree of symmetry or complementariness—the
relative equality to inequality of ego to alter in role relations—will be
related to the level of intactness to impairment in ego systems within
each person and to the level of enmeshment to differentiation in self
and object representations. The more intact the ego of each person,
the more likely will the relationship be formed and sustained by an
integration of symmetrical and complementary transactions under the
dominance of symmetry. The more impaired the ego of each person,
the more likely will the relationship be formed and sustained by a rigid
compartmentalizing of transactions carried over from unfinished
aspects of earlier object relationships. These transactions will be of a
complementary nature. Such distinctions do not imply that one is
necessarily more functional than the other or that one will be more
gratifying or have a better chance of surviving without separation or
divorce. It simply is a method for understanding the relationship between internal and external phenomena as these interact within the
intimate relationship of marriage. In reality, marriages are characterized by degrees of symmetrical and complementary aspects at both
manifest (conscious) and latent (preconscious and unconscious) levels.
The motivation of people to enter into union with one another may
be attributed both to conscious attractions of similarities and differences as well as by attractions that lie outside awareness. Both symmetrical and complementary aspects may contribute to or detract from
the ongoing viability of the marital relationship.

    For example, some people may be attracted to each other because
of conscious similarities in values related to religious beliefs, age, ethnic and racial identifications, social and educational status. For others,
the symmetrical aspects of these attributes may be valued less significantly because of the conscious attractiveness of other attributes such
as kindness, sensitivity, closeness, respect for individuality and mutual
feelings of support. Valency, the attractiveness of people for one another in a reciprocal relationship, may also be affected by conscious
complementary attributes such as the manifestation of dependence/in-
dependence perceived within each person, objectivity/subjectivity in

solving problems, level of initiative/reticence in the relationship, and openness/closedness in sharing thoughts and feelings. At a level beyond awareness, people may be attracted to each other because of similarities in their levels of differentiation (as Bowen suggests), separateness and autonomy and their use of similar defenses in contending with the unfinished aspects of primary relationships in the present relationship. Both may look to the other in an unconscious way to take care of needs that remain unmet from previous relationships. A sense of emptiness may pervade the relationship and be defended against by mutual denial or externalization of affect. Complementary needs, defenses, object relations and levels of internalization may also influence valency in an unconscious way. One needs to be taken care of and the other needs to take care; the projector needs a "cooperative" target for his defensive behavior; the person who feels trapped within a separation struggle with his parents needs a rescuer who needs to rescue. Thus, the nature of marriage requires that we examine the reciprocal and interacting nature of the relationship both in terms of its defensive and adaptive aspects.

Ego development in marriage is interrelated with the state of ego development of the spouse. The meaning and value of a marriage will vary according to the developmental needs of each person and how these needs are met through the symmetrical and complementary valencies within their relationship. Although each marriage is unique, all marital relationships will be structured according to the nature of the intactness to impairment in ego systems of each person, and the level of arrest in internalization processes which each brings to the relationship. The more complete the internalization process and the higher the level of ego organization, the more equipped are individuals to psychologically form and maintain a mutually empathic and symmetrical relationship.

This point of view does not deny the capacity of people to transcend their history and to experience marriage as a corrective and growth-oriented relationship. Although the past is always a part of the present, the past, in and of itself, does not determine the outcome of new relationships. The resiliency, creativity and strength of the human being to overcome adversity is one of the remarkable and reassuring derivatives of a loving relationship. Marriage offers an opportunity for integration and consolidation of ego systems with the self-representation; its potential to fulfill that need is contingent upon the internal resources which each person brings to the relationship and by the catalytic effect of the relationship itself in freeing latent adaptive potentials. Development is continuous and marriage is one of several opportunities in adult life which may contribute to the quest for wholeness and fulfillment.

The Timms, a black couple in their late twenties, applied for therapy because of mutual concern that they were growing apart rather than closer together in their relationship. Both were well established in their careers and recognized professionally for their competence. They met in graduate school and had been married for three years. Each described their relationship as mutually gratifying and supportive during the first two years of their marriage. Mrs. Timms was employed full time in her profession for those two years, while Mr. Timms finished work on his degree. At that time, one year ago, they moved to this geographic area because of an exceptional professional opportunity for Mr. Timms. Since that time Mrs. Timms has felt increasingly estranged from her husband and views him as a good person who is like a friend but not someone with whom she wishes to spend her life. She is not happy living in this area, misses friends and family, is troubled that her husband seems settled for life, and feels trapped. Mrs. Timms had suggested a separation to have room to think through her situation, which precipitated his applying for therapy for both of them.

In individual interviews each appeared reasonably comfortable in talking about the situation. Mr. Timms was perplexed by his wife's behavior over the last several months. He expressed puzzlement about the change in her since the move. Neither felt at home in this area and both missed the comaraderie of the university neighborhood and closeness to her family. He came from a poor background and, like his older two brothers and a sister, had done well in school; as a consequence, he was able to obtain employment with a highly prestigious technological firm in this area. He describes his family as close and supportive; he is proud of their accomplishments. His father was a hardworking person who enjoyed his family. Mother was a loving and firm parent who had the primary role in disciplining and looking after the children. Mrs. Timms describes herself as an expressive individual, in contrast to her husband whom she views as a very logical and conservative person. To her, he is more interested in his job than in her and, although concerned, he does not seem to understand how unhappy she is with the way the marriage has turned out. She came from a middle-class family which was composed of her and an older brother. Her mother was a housewife and father a successful lawyer who, she feels, spoiled her by giving her anything she wished. Like her husband, Mrs. Timms remembered the family as close and cohesive; she thought that her father was the dominant figure and mother went along with what he wanted. She knew that they, particularly father, would be very upset if her marriage did not work out.

In conjoint interviews, this couple related initially in a reasonable and polite manner. There was a tightness and intellectual quality to their interaction that suggested a highly controlled and guarded relationship. Neither wished to hurt the other and, as a consequence, they avoided areas in their discussions that might provoke strong emotions, especially anger. Both reported that they had gotten along well before the move and attributed that happy period to the busyness of their lives as students as well as the supportiveness of friends and her family. Mr. Timms was initially attracted to his wife's carefree and independent life style and by her wit and intelligence. She was attractive to his evenness in temperament and his goal directedness. Each recalled their relationship together as close and exciting, qualities which had gradually disappeared over the past year along with a diminution in their sexual relations.

This couple is experiencing the expected developmental conflicts of early marriage which have been exacerbated by the loss of familiar, collateral relationships which both valued, Mrs. Timms more so than Mr. Timms. The conflict between them now (in contrast to the harmony which each says characterized their relationship prior to the move to an unfamiliar geographic area) is being defended against by a pulling-back from meaningful discussion of the issues that have created a change in their feelings for one another. Historical data suggests that each was able to form an individual identify characterized primarily by the dominance of self-representations over object representations. Their attractiveness to each other, in fact, seemed based on a mutual perception of the other's level of differentiation, manifested in their autonomous and goal-oriented behavior in adapting to life. The stress associated with the move, along with the sense of isolation (particularly within Mrs. Timms), have created an imbalance in their relationship. One wonders if they would be experiencing this disequilibrium if there had not been such a dramatic change in the social environment.

As therapy progressed, it became increasingly clear that Mrs. Timms resented the sacrifices that she thought she had made in helping her husband complete his professional education. She tended to dismiss these resentments as unimportant until they moved (in order for Mr. Timms to take advantage of an excellent employment opportunity in this area). During the past year, these resentments were increasingly on her mind as they could not be neutralized by the satisfactions of her work and the availability of supportive relationships with friends and family. The loneliness associated with a strange environment precluded avoidance of these feelings, which became manifested in sexual and interpersonal withdrawal from her husband. For his part, Mr. Timms was unaware of how his wife viewed the situation and he reacted with puzzlement and absorption in his work. The more she withdrew, the more he invested his energies into a highly interesting and rewarding career.

Mrs. Timms was reluctant to confront Mr. Timms with her feelings, which were not compatible with her expectations of herself as a wife. She was modeling her role after that of her mother, who was devoted to the career of her husband. Mother never complained nor had she put her own needs before those of her husband. In significant respects, Mr. Timms resembled her father, a competent, decent, logical and goal-oriented person. For his part, Mr. Timms saw in his wife much of the strength and warmth that he associated with his mother. Their symmetrical investments in the marriage were related to sociocultural aspects of their individual identities as well as to the level of differentiation that each had reached in their individual development. They appreciated their commonalities but tended to avoid dealing with complementary aspects, which derived from object representations that did not fit with their idealized images of themselves. Her guilt for feeling resentful prevented Mrs. Timms from sharing this part of her self with Mr. Timms. He resented the change in Mrs. Timms, to whom he had been attracted by her warmth and support.

The nature of the complement was not polarized, and this couple was able to reestablish contact with one another by using therapy as a vehicle for opening doors that had begun to shut between them. Each had brought into the marriage individual identities that were grounded on reasonably well consolidated self-representations. Their motivations to marry were based on complementary qualities that were not extreme nor rigidly ingrained into psychological structures. The precipitating event of geographic relocation had deprived Mrs. Timms of familiar resources upon which she depended and had heightened her awareness of resentments toward Mr. Timms that had been bound at a preconscious level. Their individual levels of ego autonomy and their commitments to the marriage were strong enough to absorb the threat to their relationship and available enough to free adaptive potentials for a more intimate relationship.

PARENTHOOD

Although the dyadic relationship of marriage may be an end in itself, a value which is reflected in contemporary marital trends, an important development which may evolve from that relationship is parenthood. Shifting mores about the notion of parenting have had a significant impact on traditional practices related to this aspect of generativity. For example, the role of the contemporary father in parenting has been a focus of recent inquiry as a result of changing values related to the egalitarian aspects of male and female roles. The traditional role of the father as provider, companion and disciplinarian is under review as is his involvement in birth and early care of the infant. His role as a more equal participant in the nurturing role, traditionally ascribed to the mother, is an important consideration in understanding ego and self-involvement in parenting and the effect on children of that shift. Another aspect of parenting on the contemporary scene is the single-parent family, which has usually consisted of the mother and her children; this is also undergoing change. Fathers are now more likely, although not commonly, to have custody of their children after a separation or divorce. Because of the recent shifts in beliefs and practices related to the role of parenting, there is, at present, only a modest amount of research on the subject. The role of father in early socialization, for example, is almost nonexistent. Although the sexual identity of the parent will no doubt have a significant impact on the socialization of children and on their self-object representations related to gender identity, our concern will skirt that issue and focus on the generic aspects of differential empathy and connectedness of the parent with the needs of the child at specific developmental levels. As with the intimacy of the marital relationship, parenting is also a reciprocal relationship in the sense that

> mature man needs to be needed, and maturity needs guidance as well as encouragement from what has been produced and must be taken care of (Erikson, 1963, 251).

Our culture provides little genuine support for the parenting role despite the plethora of popular literature on the subject and the proliferation of programs designed to teach parenting skills. The fragmentation and compartmentalization of contemporary life provides few opportunities for prospective parents to learn from the previous generation. Even when opportunities are available, the rate of change in notions about "correct" parenting raises questions about the adequacy or validity of one's models. Changing familial circumstances, such as both parents working, also contribute to ambiguities about parenting and may require adaptations that do not fit with practices of a generation removed. Shifting social values about discipline, adolescent sexuality and the role of the father require new adaptations which may be quite different from the experiences in one's family of origin. Turning to experts on parenting may only exacerbate anxieties and confusion about becoming a parent because of their varying and often conflicting advice. Finally, many responsibilities that were considered to be within the periphery of the mother's or father's role have been assumed by or delegated to other societal institutions.

Along with these trends has been the emergence in our culture of a consciousness about the importance of parenting to the well-being of children. Indeed, much of the popular literature on this topic may feed on the guilt and insecurities of parents while at the same time reminding them implicitly of their power over children and holding them accountable for the way their children turn out. Until quite recently, much of the professional literature also focused heavily on the parent-child relationship as the toxic element in understanding psychopathology while ignoring constitutional and environmental factors. We also fail, too often, to acknowledge the limitation of our methods for diagnosing pathology and the inferential nature of our understanding of etiology, which may or may not be linked primarily to parent-child relationships.

Within this atmosphere, parenting may truly be considered an adaptive function. Although it may often be a lonely, confusing and difficult role, it is also one of the most critical responsibilities in society. Along with marriage, it is probably one of the most intimate relationships with which one may be involved in a lifetime. Parenting consists of skills that can be learned but, more importantly, it is a relationship which one experiences in an inter-generational context. While parents may not always act toward their children as their parents acted toward them, mothers and fathers are influenced significantly in the parenting role by their object representations of experiences with their own parents. In addition, "parents meet in their children not only the projections of their own conflicts incorporated in the child, but also the promise of their hopes and ambitions" (Benedek, 1959, 405).

Parenting is an ego-adaptive response to the task of generativity when rational and empathic skills are employed to help the child negotiate developmental stages. Popular literature and programs to enhance parenting tend to focus on the skill aspects of parenthood. Parenting, however, consists of a relationship which, in optimal circumstances, is characterized primarily by empathy, differentiation and responsiveness to the needs of children; the parenting relationship may also include displacements from the parents' experiences as a child and projections of their unfinished agenda in structuralization and internalization. If the latter become available to parental consciousness and are transmuted from narcissistic sufferings into empathic sublimations, they may serve as powerful resources for attunement to the developmental needs, challenges and conflicts of the child. Emotional sensitivity, in other words, becomes empathically adaptive in the parental relationship when the responsiveness of the parent "is not in the service of narcissistic needs but in that of mature object relations" (Olden, 1958, 505).

Responsiveness of the child to his parents has a significant effect on the quality of empathy over time. Parents are only human and, therefore, take pleasure in the practice of adaptive skills as their efforts are rewarded in the developmental achievements of their child. As with any meaningful relationship, parenting must also be understood within a reciprocal and transacting process in which the subject is affecting and being affected by the object at all times. Individuality, as a manifestation of constitutional predispositions, is probably the least understood aspect playing upon the parent-child relationship, yet is a significant factor in influencing parental responsiveness to each child. While that variable may not be understood well in its effects on parenting, it does need to be acknowledged as an important factor in this critical process.

Parental empathy refers not only to the capacity of one to feel for or like another but also to the intuitive ability to connect with less visible development needs as the perception of those needs is informed by accurate understanding of human development. Empathy, unlike sympathy, involves both emotional and cognitive aspects of ego functioning and is characterized by attunement to, yet separateness between, self and other. Under optional circumstances, boundaries between the parental and child subsystems are maintained within the empathic encounter without recourse to enmeshment or disengagement between the two subsystems (Minuchin, 1974, 53-60).

One of the great challenges to effective parenting is in empathically understanding and responding appropriately to the needs of children at different stages of parental and child development. Processes of internalization, from attachment to autonomy, require different responses from parents. The needs for libidinal and unconditional attachments of infancy shift as the child becomes self-reliant and needs more room to exercise his beginning sense of autonomy. The child of rapprochement continues to need the parent but in a different way from earlier periods. The child of identification and separateness needs more space and opportunities to form new attachments and to become involved in new relationships. Adolescents, while demanding independence from parental controls, need the constancy of parental concern for their struggles while, at the same time, clarity and firmness of limits. The parenting relationship as a holding environment requires flexibility within structure, empathy within firmness and tolerance within constancy in varying combinations throughout infancy, childhood and adolescence; all of these parents struggle with as they themselves are experiencing developmental changes. The latter may be a particularly vexing issue to the parent(s) of adolescents when the parent(s) may be facing their own mid-life crises while contending with the crises of their son or daughter (Levinson, 1977, 89-112). The creativity in integrating these seemingly contradictory qualities is the essence of the adaptive task of parenthood.

For the parent, a consequence of effectiveness in the parenting role is enhanced self-esteem and further consolidation of ego systems. In addition, parents, as they reflect upon the meaning(s) of their experiences in raising their children, may modify their value orientations and realize significant internal shifts in self and object representations. As Benedict observes:

> The conflicts which were incorporated in the superego when the parent was a child was "worked over" through the experiences of parenthood... Through the successful relationships of the parent with his child or children, his superego loses some of its strictness; and as it allows for a broader, deeper capacity of experience, it indicates a new step toward the dissolution of its infantile origin (Benedek, 1959, 415).

Conversely, parents who do not measure up to their ego ideal of parenthood may experience a hardening of their values, a stagnation in their capacity to consolidate ego systems and a despair in their self-confidence, all of which may persist to affect the integrity of old age.

Mrs. Bennett, a 34-year-old mother of a 12-year-old son, Tom, applied for therapy because she and her husband were in constant disagreement about disciplining their son. She complained that Mr. Bennett picked on Tom and related to him in a deprecating manner. No matter what Tom did or how well he did it, father was critical and demeaning of the boy, according to mother. Recently, Tom had begun to fight back and Mrs. Bennett has found the situation intolerable. In a tearful manner she described how she had been screaming at the two of them. She feels at a loss in dealing with the conflict and worries that her son could suffer permanent psychological damage if Mr. Bennett continues his unjust attacks.

Mrs. Bennett was the second child and oldest daughter of five children. She recalled a chaotic childhood because of alcoholism of her father and mental illness of mother, who was hospitalized for prolonged periods of time through Mrs. Bennett's early adolescence. As a consequence of a suicide attempt by the mother when Mrs. Bennett was 12, father joined Alcoholics Anonymous and was able to master his drinking problem. During her adolescence, mother was able to remain at home but began to drink regularly and to excess. Mrs. Bennet was ascribed a caretaking role by the mother with the father's passive acquiescence. She was required to look after her younger brother and her sisters and to take care of the house. Because of her good academic record, Mrs. Bennett had an opportunity to be selected for a special college-bound preparatory program, but the mother would not permit her to enroll (in the program). She resented her mother's selfish and unreasonable behavior and looked forward to a time when she would be free of mother's domination.

Mr. Bennett was the youngest of three children and was always treated as the baby in his family. His mother was described as an overbearing and smothering person who tried to run Mr. Bennett's life even after their marriage. The father was a rather docile individual in relation to his wife and did not have much to do with Mr. Bennett except to criticize his marginal work as a student. He died when Mr. Bennett was 13.

Mr. and Mrs. Bennett married when they were both 18 after a brief premarital relationship. Mrs. Bennett had not dated during high school. She was pregnant at the time of the marriage. Shortly after the birth of their only child, Tom, Mr. Bennett lost his job as a mechanic and the young family moved in with his widowed mother who had lived alone since Mr. Bennett's marriage. According to Mrs. Bennett, the mother-in-law infantalized Mr. Bennett, discouraged him from taking a job below his abilities and paid little attention to Mrs. Bennett and Tom. After several months, Mr. Bennett obtained employment but refused to move out of his mother's house, a stand which the mother supported. Mrs. Bennett tolerated the living arrangements for two years and then separated from her husband. He had no contact with them for over a year and then began to ask Mrs. Bennett out on dates. He paid little attention to his son, and apparently used visitation privileges as a ploy to see her. For several years Mrs. Bennett and her son lived alone, surviving on welfare and her part-time earnings. They reunited with Mr. Bennett when Tom was 10 years old. For religious reasons, she did not seek a divorce nor did she become involved with other men during the separation.

Since the reconciliation (three years ago), the relationship between Mr. and Mrs. Bennett has been relatively peaceful, but the relationship between him and Tom has been progressively more conflictive. Mrs. Bennett becomes a mediator between the two and feels strained in her loyalties. The couple discuss their differences as parents but conflict persists. She sees her husband as rigid and critical and herself as flexible and supportive of Tom. At the present time, Mrs. Bennett is requesting help with conflict related to parenting and not with the marital relationship.

Mr. and Mrs. Bennett's marriage during adolescence occurred before either had been appropriately separated from ambivalent object representations of childhood. In that sense, their precarious level of differentiation was symmetrical as both struggled to sever conflictive ties to parental figures. Mrs. Bennett was seeking rescue from an unhappy family situation while Mr. Bennett may have been seeking a replication of his symbiotic-like attachment to mother. Rather than acting from a secure sense of self, both appeared to be object oriented in their complementary attraction for the other. The second separation/individuation process of adolescence appeared to be stuck at the practicing subphase for Mrs. Bennett as she sought in Mr. Bennett a safe haven of rapprochement which developmentally had been un-available to her in the family of origin. Mr. Bennett, on the other hand, appeared to be seeking a mother who would complement his symbiotic-like self-representation.

In their quest for a more complete sense of wholeness, each looked to the other for resources and supplies which neither felt could be found within the self. With the birth of their son, an overadequate complementarity developed between Mr. and Mrs. Bennett. As she devoted herself to the care of the infant and derived much gratification from that symbiotic involvement, Mr. Bennett was left out and retreated to his own symbiotic-like involvement with his mother.

The separation tended to reinforce and prolong the symbiotic ties between mother and son. Mrs. Bennett, a highly competent person, worked to financially sustain the living arrangement which doubtless helped to neutralize the strength of the symbiotic bond between them. Mr. Bennett remained outside the mother-son orbit and only gradu-ally made efforts to reenter the family, not because of concern for his son but because of a need to reestablish a relationship with his wife. Because of incomplete consolidation of the self-representation, an ob-scure boundary exists within Mrs. Bennett in her perception of Tom and his relations with Mr. Bennett. She cannot tolerate Mr. Bennett in the parental role because of enmeshment of her object representa-tion of Tom with her self-representation. Even as Mr. Bennett's be-havior becomes more empathically attuned to the son's age-appropriate needs, Mrs. Bennett continues to experience his discipline of Tom as a personal attack.

Although we know that religious convictions reinforced Mrs. Ben-nett's need to hold onto the marriage and not to seek a divorce, we may also assume that her need to hang on to the marriage had a de-velopmental significance. With the onset of the genital stage of early adolescence in Tom, Mrs. Bennett permitted her husband to return home. Her anxiety that Tom was moving from a pregenital to a geni-tal level of sexual development may have triggered preconscious fears for her relationship with him that had been played out up to that time at a need-satisfying plateau. The reentry of Mr. Bennett onto the scene created a triangular conflict in which both males were competing for the mother. The outsider was infringing on psychosocial territory that had been the exclusive province of mother and son for years. In con-trast to their earlier motivations to marry, both Mr. and Mrs. Bennett appear more developmentally ready now to fulfill their emotional and sexual needs through the marriage. The familial reconciliation proc-ess, however, took place in a highly delicate period. Its success now appears to exercise and perhaps to strain the ego capacities of each to adapt to a new level of development. Mrs. Bennett must relinquish her symbiotic object enmeshment with her son, while Mr. Bennett must accept more autonomous responsibility as an egalitarian partner in marriage. These tasks confront them at a time in their son's life which corresponds to significant nodal conflicts in their own development. The narcissistic wounds of their own struggles in separation/individuation (which will never heal) may nevertheless be transmuted into empathic sublimations for the well-being of their son. If not, the child will carry on to the next generation the conflicts which plagued them in their own adolescence and which confront them today in their relationship with their child. In transcending their sufferings, these parents, like so many, meet in their children what Benedek referred to as "the promise of their hopes and ambitions" (Benedek, 1959, 405).

SUMMARY

In this chapter, we have tried to relate the paradigm of structuralization/internalization to psychosocial stages of development. Two conclusions may be drawn from this discussion: One is that development is continuous from birth to death. Structures emerge from unions which provide the resources through which processes of internalization are played out and by which ego systems become differentiated, integrated and consolidated. Second, in any human relationship individual development is contingent upon a complex of variables, the most important of which is perhaps the interdependence of intrapersonal change with the capacity of important relationships to change as well. Rare is the individual who can adapt to developmental change independent of change in family, marital or parent-child relationships. Throughout life, people are concurrently the subjects as well as the objects of change. As a consequence, development is not only continuous but potentially contagious within the transactional relationships of the primary family group.

REFERENCES

Bell, A., et al. *Sexual Preference: Its Development in Men and Women.* Bloomington: Indiana University Press, 1981.

Benedek, T. "Parenthood As A Developmental Phase: A Contribution to the Libido Theory," *Journal of the American Psychoanalytic Association,* 7 (1959), 389-417.

Blanck, G., and Blanck, R. *Marriage and Personality Development.* New York: Columbia University Press, 1968.

Blos, P. "The Second Individuation Process of Adolescence," *Psychoanalytic Study of the Child,* Vol XXII (1967) 162-182.

Bowen, M. *Family Therapy in Clinical Practice.* New York: Jason Aronson, 1978.

Erikson, E. *Childhood and Society.* New York: W. W. Norton & Company, 1963.

——. *Identity and the Life Cycle.* New York: W. W. Norton and Company, 1980.

Karpel, M. "Individuation: From Fusion to Dialogue," *Family Process,* 15: 1 (March 1976) 65-82.

Kohlberg, L. "Development of Moral Character and Moral Idealogy," *Review of Child Development Research.* Edited by M. Hoffman and L. Hoffman, New York: Russell Sage Foundation, 1964.

Kohut, H. *The Analysis of Self.* New York: International University Press, 1971.

Levinson, D. "The Mid-Life Transition: A Period in Adult Psychosocial Development," *Psychiatry,* Vol. 40 (May 1977) 99-112.

Mahler, M. *The Psychological Birth of the Human Infant.* New York: Basic Books, 1975.

Marcia (source unknown)

Minuchin, S. *Families and Family Therapy.* Cambridge: Harvard University Press, 1974.

Olden, C. "Notes on the Development of Empathy," *Psychoanalytic Study of the Child,* Vol. XXIII, 1958, 505-518.

Spitz, R. *The First Year of Life.* New York: International Universities Press, 1965.

5

EGO STATES

Before proceeding to examine the relationship of this paradigm of ego psychology to clinical practice, I would like to discuss some ideas which have been touched upon in the last three chapters and that have been implicit in our discussion of theory. The ego is not a static psychological structure but a dynamic entity which is in a continuous state of change throughout one's life. While internalization tends to slow down with age as ego functions become organized within stable subsystems, the need to adapt one's life to changing biological and social conditions persists. The resiliency of the human being and the capacity of intact ego functions to compensate for impaired functions are indications of the potential within people to respond to change in adaptive rather than defensive modes of functioning.

Various aspects of the intrapersonal life of the individual respond to the ubiquity of change in differing ways. Once the defensive system is established, for example, it remains impervious to significant change although modifications in defensive styles are possible. The most generic and fundamental of all defenses, repression, is least likely to change because of its special purpose in the psychic economy of keeping from consciousness any instinctive threat to psychological survival. Lower level defenses are more resistive to modification than are higher level defenses because of the latter's more significant preconscious, cognitive and adaptive characteristics. After object relations development reaches a point at which the self-representation becomes dominant over object representations, there is a further resistance to change in the interest of one's need to maintain continuity of "self-sameness." That state is an indication that the level of consolidation in object relations has been reached. Emotional sensitivity or empathy seems to reach different plateaus in the course of human development and may be more amenable to modification but usually in the context of specific relationships such as marriage, parenting and psychotherapy. Unless ego and self systems are severely impaired in general (as in psychosis), the functions of cognitive mastery and reality testing are probably most responsive to change without heroic effort. Of all aspects, the adaptive system has the potential to respond progressively rather than regressively to biological or social alterations in the form of losses, threats and challenges. In fact, progressive change is always a reflection of the creativity and resiliency of the adaptive system of the ego to encounter and to deal with conflict.

Our use of the term *system*, in referring to the three aspects of psychological structure which make up the ego, is deliberate. The notion of system, in this context, refers to any set of interdependent elements which tend toward equilibrium in their interaction with one another. Taken together, the interdependent and interacting aspects of the elements in a human system are its transactions. Equilibrium, which characterizes human systems, is the tendency of elements to exist, more or less, in a state of balance, such that a change in the state of one element produces reactions in other elements to return the system, as a whole, to a steady state. The term *state* refers to the dynamic nature of the ego system and its subsystems as well as their inherent relationship with the biological, interpersonal and sociocultural worlds. The concept of systems, or more precisely subsystems (since no systems exist in isolation from reciprocal influences of other systems) is useful for understanding behavior in intrapersonal, familial and other group contexts and the transactional effects of one aspect on another.

The transactional nature of internal (ego) and external (environmental) aspects of these subsystems are shown in Figure 6. The diagram depicts the interlocking nature of ego subsystems, which become organized as a result of the spiraling effects of internalization processes, and the interrelationship of these subsystems with important environmental subsystems. The dotted extensions of the spiral at the outer boundary of the ego are intended to show the partially open nature of ego systems to the influence of the external world at the interface of the adaptive and environmental subsystems. Of course, the notion of interface also connotes a reciprocal relationship of the person with the environment (people may influence the environment). As we have suggested, any substantial (in contrast to superficial or incidental) change at any subsystem level or combination of levels will impact on other levels and result in alterations in their functional states.

The transactional nature of internal (ego) and external (environmental) aspects of these subsystems are shown on the following diagram: The diagram depicts the interlocking nature of ego subsystems, which

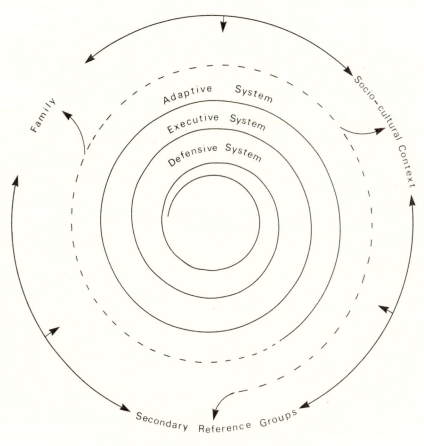

Figure 6   Intra and Interpersonal Subsystems

become organized as a result of the spiraling effects of internalization processes, and the interrelationship of these subsystems with important environmental subsystems. The dotted extensions of the spiral at the outer boundary of the ego are intended to show the partially open nature of ego systems to the influence of the external world at the interface of the adaptive and environmental subsystems. Of course, the notion of interface also connotes a reciprocal relationship of the person with the environment (people may influence the environment). As we have suggested, any substantial (in contrast to superficial or incidental) change at any subsystem level or combination of levels will impact on other levels and result in alterations in their functional states.

The utility of the systems metaphor adds a critical dimension to our paradigm for understanding the complexities of human behavior. It is a valuable tool in understanding the motivation of people to seek professional help, which is a significant focus in the beginning phase of clinical work. It is also a piece of theory that is useful to the practioner in structuring interventions. To amplify upon these three aspects, we turn now to a consideration of crisis theory.

People seek help for an infinite variety of reasons under circumstances that are unique to each person. Because of the variation and idiosyncratic nature of these motivations, it would be fruitless to attempt a listing of reasons. However, we may assume on the basis of commonsense, clinical research and experience that the applicant for clinical services has experienced some upset or sense of imbalance in the system of biological, psychological and/or social forces that affect his life. Sometimes the journey to the initial interview has been lengthy and the applicant may have been involved in rather complex intrapersonal and interpersonal experiences which have influenced him to seek help. At other times, the trip is a short one and has been precipitated by recent circumstances which have caused an upheaval or sense of imbalance in the life of the applicant. A significant part of exploration and evaluation in the early phase of the clinical process must include a consideration of the applicant's reasons for seeking help at that particular time as well as an understanding of his defensive, executive and adaptive attempts to cope with the focal conflict now and in the past. Is the conflict chronic in nature and a reflection of persistent difficulties in ego functioning—intrapersonally, interpersonally or both—or is it the result of more acute distress of recent origin? Not everyone who seeks help is in crisis but every seeker is experiencing some degree of anxiety about his state of well-being, which is generally experienced as an imbalance within or between intrapersonal and/or interpersonal aspects of his life.

Crisis refers to:

> ...the acute and often prolonged disturbance which may occur in an individual or social orbit as the result of an emotional hazard. It is the emotional reaction of an individual to an important and upsetting life situation in which he is not able to cope with the external events nor his internal impulses by use of his usual defenses. (Klein and Lindemann, 1961, 5).

Along with impairment in the defensive system, we would add to this definition that crisis also involves an impairment in the adaptive system which leaves the individual vulnerable to the consequences of upset at the interface of the ego and environmental systems. For our purposes, the idea of crisis has a qualitative meaning and refers to the degree of imbalance and upset rather than to any quantitative state. Whether or not people are in crisis is less crucial than recognizing that people experience intrapersonal and interpersonal upset as a result of their inability to defend against and adapt to change.

Another form of crisis may involve a disequilibrium in role relations between and among people in a group. Taking the family as an example, one can see how the upset of an individual may be a manifestation of a group upset, or conversely, the group upset may be a manifestation of an individual upset in a family member. For example, the entry into adolescence may produce disequilibrium for the teenager which may in turn affect the equilibrium of the entire family, particularly in the parents' roles. Going away to college and leaving the security of his home for the first time may be an emotional hazard for the older adolescent, create an upsetting situation for the entire family, and may develop into crisis around the separation. In another respect, the loss of employment by the principal wage earner inevitably leads to repercussions throughout the family constellation which may result in a crisis state if intra-and interpersonal resources within the group are not adequate to cope defensively and adaptively with the situation.

Spiegel hypothesizes that equilibrium in role relations among members of a primary group, such as the family, cannot be maintained for indefinite periods of time (Spiegel, 1968). Bowen suggests that this type of instability (disequilibrium) is characteristic of dyadic relationships and is the basis for triangulation (Bowen, 1978). In interpersonal relations, equilibrium is maintained only as long as individuals are able to meet each other's expectations. When the mutuality of that complementary association breaks down, people may attempt (defensively and/or adaptively) to resolve the imbalance by involvement of a third party.

Imbalances of an intrapersonal and interpersonal nature occur in response to events which have been referred to as "hazardous situations." These situations may involve:

> any alternation in the field of social forces within which the individual exists, such that the individual's expectations of himself and his relationships with others undergo change. (Klein and Lindemann, 1961).

Potential hazards may be classified as follows:

A. *Developmental*—Transitions in biopsychosocial states as a result of maturation and development; examples: Erikson's stages of psychosocial development, each of which confronts the individual with significant alterations;

B. *Role Transaction*—Achievement of a new social status as a result of horizontal or vertical social mobility; examples: entry into school, marriage, job-promotion, geographic relocation;

C. *Accidental*—Loss or threatened loss of significant relationship(s); examples: divorce, death.

Depending on the significance of life changes—always potentially hazardous—the individual (through his ego functions) and those significant others with whom he is involved (through their role relations) may respond in different ways. If change is perceived as a threat, an individual may become fearful, which may trigger defenses to avoid the anticipated consequences (of the threat). If change is experienced as a loss, depression may result. If it is seen as a challenge, an individual may respond adaptively with hope and purposeful problem-solving activities (Rapaport, 1970, 277). Most responses to change will include varying degrees of all three of these responses.

> Mrs. Allen, age 44, came to the agency after being referred by the local public school system; her 15-year-old son, Donald, was failing all courses in school despite above-average intelligence. She was 15 minutes early for her appointment, and when the clinical social worker greeted her in the waiting room, she appeared tired and forlorn. While continuing to hold in her hand a cigarette which she had been smoking, Mrs. Allen rather hesitatingly stood up and limply shook hands with the therapist. She continued to carry the cigarette as she preceded the social worker down the hall toward his office. She was tall and very thin and her cotton dress appeared loose fitting, as though she had recently lost much weight. Possi-

bly in an attempt to disguise her rather sickly appearance, Mrs. Allen wore a noticeably heavy amount of makeup.

Throughout the interview, Mrs. Allen chain-smoked, lighting each new cigarette from the burning butt of the previous one. She showed little emotion in revealing her problem with Donald although much of the content was of a sensitive and painful nature. She spoke in a somewhat high-pitched, piercing voice, giving the impression that she was trying hard to control her feelings. Talking in a well organized, chronological and sophisticated manner, Mrs. Allen maintained her intellectual, defensive style of relating throughout the hour. In retrospect, she was not to allow herself much affective involvement with the therapist for many additional interviews.

At the beginning of the interview, the therapist had only to indicate that he was interested in understanding her reason for coming to the agency for Mrs. Allen to begin talking. She went into much historical information about her difficulties with Donald as well as her marital problems and present physical condition.

Donald, an only child, was born while his father was away from home on an extended business trip. Because the father traveled extensively in his work, neither the child nor the mother saw much of him. Pregnancy and birth were without physical complications. In subsequent interviews, Mrs. Allen told that she had never wanted children because of the nature of her husband's work, and revealed reticently that they had not planned on the child's birth. She was disappointed and extremely unhappy about the pregnancy and often wished that something would happen to the fetus so that she would not have to bear a child. Despite her feelings, Mrs. Allen said that she was able to rally herself and care adequately for Donald throughout infancy. She described the beginning of fond and tender feelings for him as he filled an emptiness in her life due to the long periods of loneliness when Mr. Allen was away.

Donald's childhood was uneventful, according to the mother. He was a healthy child, experiencing only the usual childhood illnesses. Mother worked as a nursery school teacher to supplement the family income and Donald attended the same nursery school; later on, when he entered kindergarten, Mrs. Allen switched to elementary school teaching. She was able to verbalize her guilt toward the child after several interviews, saying that she made this transfer so that she could be close to Donald. When Donald was in latency, his father resigned from his job and went into business for himself. A few months later he was killed in an automobile accident. The death apparently had little effect on Donald and Mrs. Allen for there had never been much warmth or closeness between the father and his wife and child. The distance of their relationship to father was magnified by the fact that he had been away from the family most of the time.

After her husband's death, Mrs. Allen continued to teach at the same school Donald attended. However she was careful not to have him in her classes as he went through the elementary grades, accomplishing this feat by specializing in kindergarten teaching. Four years later, as Donald was beginning puberty and making the transition from elementary to junior high school (leaving his mother's school for the first time), Mrs. Allen remarried. In this new union, she was hoping to find a father for her child, especially since he was entering adolescence and would need "a man" with whom he could identify. In a few months she discovered that her husband was an alcoholic. He made promises to stop drinking but never kept them. Because of the severity of the alcoholism, he could not work and embarrassed his wife by begging money from her friends and professional colleagues to buy liquor. When confronted with empty bottles which were hidden under the couch and elsewhere around the home, her husband would deny drinking.

The marriage remained intact for about two years until Mrs. Allen with mixed feelings of pity and disgust, initiated proceedings for a divorce. At that time, four months before she was seen at intake, Mrs. Allen separated from her husband and had a restraining order sworn to keep him away from the home. Mrs. Allen said that she had tried to encourage her husband to get professional help with his problem and, although he would often tell her that he was getting medical and psychiatric help, she became convinced that he was lying and would not change.

Donald never got along with his stepfather. He had nothing but contempt for the man, and on a few occasions the two of them nearly came to blows. For the first time in his life, Donald had to share his mother with another man, a man for whom she had obvious affection. He had to contend with this threat while experiencing the intense, sexualized drives of early adolescence. Soon after his mother's marriage, Donald became rude and rebellious toward her for the first time in his life. His school work deteriorated from a satisfactory level to the point where he was required to repeat the eighth grade. At the same time, his mother began to have interpersonal difficulties with her immediate supervisor, and subsequently transferred to a different school.

In the midst of this complex dilemma, Mrs. Allen entered the period of menopause and underwent a hysterectomy only one month before the intake interview. When she came to the Center, Mrs. Allen was still in poor physical health, as her appearance testified.

Despite the enmeshed quality of their relationship, evidence from the family history supports the hypothesis that this mother and child functioned reasonably well for many years. The anxiety associated with giving birth to an unwanted child within a marital relationship that was tenuously grounded confronted Mrs. Allen with a hazardous dilemma. The harshness of her super-ego, which was explored later in psychotherapy, contributed to the prolonged symbiotic nature of the role relations between mother and child. Despite the overprotectiveness, Mrs. Allen was able to mobilize enough adaptive skills as a mother to help Donald through the first separation/individuation phase; this was successful despite the tenuous nature of object constancy which was tempered negatively by the persistence of physical closeness through elementary school. No doubt, the nature of equilibrium within each and between them was balanced precariously and was drastically upset when each was exposed to several hazardous events, which occurred in rapid succession, shortly before Mrs. Allen applied for clinical services.

An important internal resource which helped to neutralize the potentially damaging features of the maternal relationship was Mrs. Allen's background in early childhood education. As she said later in treatment, her knowledge of child development served as a check on her inclinations to use the mother-child relationship as a substitute for an ungratifying marriage. Her adaptive system, in other words, partially neutralized powerful inner needs to defensively maintain fusion with her son. The other adaptive strength in the situation was her genuine love for the child which developed as she became more involved and comfortable with the maternal role.

No data emerged to suggest that Donald was symptomatic until age twelve. At that time, several events occurred. Donald faced the threat of leaving the protective custody of an elementary school in which he had always been physically close to mother. He was about to enter a new and strange school where she would not be accessible to him. Around the same time, he was confronted with the necessity of sharing mother for the first time in years with another man with whom he was not prepared to compete. These events and transitions in role relations were taking place while he was experiencing the genital hazards of puberty. In attempting to reestablish a sense of equilibrium within self and his family, he began to fight his mother and stepfather. Simultaneously, his academic record deteriorated for he was too overwhelmed with trying to resolve the crises to concentrate on intellectual matters.

Donald was subsequently sent to a private school where he was given special help in catching up on missed work. Mrs. Allen consented to the plan and took major responsibility for the placement—not only for scholastic reasons, but also because she wanted to remove Donald from the unstable home situation. Later, he returned home to live with his mother while attending another private school in the area. Although he continued to have some difficulties, Donald seemed to enjoy school and participated in sports, for which he had considerable natural talent.

Mrs. Allen also had been greatly affected by her encounters with emotionally hazardous situations. Out of her compelling need to control interpersonal relationships, a theme which emerged later in her therapy, she married an alcoholic. When his behavior became intolerable to her, she instituted proceedings for a divorce and took legal steps to keep her husband away from the home. Her image of him was that of a hopelessly sick man, yet she longed to return to him. This feeling was amplified again and again when she returned home from work to an empty house. By sending her husband and her child away, she had started to resolve the crisis. Throughout the dilemma, Mrs. Allen was going through menopause and her feelings of loss were even more pronounced than they might have been at another time in her life. The hysterectomy had produced a physical crisis, and it was many months before she was able to regain her strength. The physical and social problems fed on each other, making both more acute and further preventing Mrs. Allen from resolving the psychological conflict with her adaptive resources.

To put this analysis into a broader perspective, data became available within the ongoing treatment relationship that illustrate salient concepts discussed in the last chapter. First, however, let me explain that the therapeutic relationship was of a supportive and clarifying nature during the early weeks of intervention. Mrs. Allen was a competent person who used therapy as a vehicle for expressing her pent-up feelings about the conflictual situation with which she was involved and as a means for reinforcing decisions which she had already made about placement of Donald and separation from her husband. Later, as the crises of placement and separation abated, she chose to move into more intensive therapy where she examined her feelings about herself and her relations with people in more depth.

One of the more interesting and, initially puzzling aspects of this case was the fact that this person sought professional help after having made two key decisions in her life: placement of her son and separation from her husband. As she revealed more of herself in therapy, the reasons for the peculiar sequence of events became clear. She had applied for clinical services out of a deep sense of loneliness and depression related to the losses not only of her husband and son but to the hysterectomy. The object loss which she felt that she could retrieve was her son but she was anxious about his coming home and feared that the two of them would not get along after the events of the preceding months. She also valued her independence and capacity to manage her life without relying on anyone else. She was accustomed to relying on her own judgment for important decisions and felt vulnerable if she had to depend on someone else. Her conscious self-representation was of a self-assured and competent woman who had always had to manage her life by herself, which she did with confidence.

Her developmental history revealed a child, born into marginal circumstances, who remembered never being able to please mother and never feeling that father cared about her because he was only sporadically at home. She excelled as a student and became the first member of her family to go to college; she graduated with honors and received a scholarship to graduate school where she was also highly successful. Behind the presentation of herself to the world as a competent person was a very frightened sense of self who felt highly vulnerable whenever she was not in control of relationships and situations. To neutralize the anxiety connected with her feelings of low self-esteem and vulnerability, she became a perfect student and later in her career was considered a "model" for others in her profession. Her ego had indeed compensated effectively for impairment in object relations by extraordinary achievements in cognitive functioning which contributed to adaptation in the academic and professional worlds.

Her self-representation, at a conscious level, was congruent with her successes (self-assured and competent) and was a reflection of how she had always viewed her mother. At a deeper level, she was a frightened, confused and lonely child who maintained distance in control of human relationships by being the competent "one." Her object representations in relation to men were fragmented and derived from her perception of her father as weak and unavailable, qualities that were found in both of her husbands.

Her ego systems were highly efficient in dealing with her inner world of low self-esteem and the external world of high occupational esteem. The painfulness of her self-image was balanced in a deceiving yet reassuring way by her professional successes. Only when her ego systems became overloaded as a result of multiple imbalances in the biological, psychological and social dimensions of her life did she seek professional help.

CONCLUSION

This essay was designed to explore an important aspect of the mediating role of the ego. Its subsystems of organization exist in a dynamic state of balance to each other as well as to the internal world of need and the external world of social expectations. Although the ego may function optimally when there is a fit between inner and outer worlds, a perfect fit is never possible. The task of the ego is to negotiate discrepancies between the two (worlds) which are ubiquitous throughout life. In situations of major biological or social change the ego through its subsystems may not be able to carry out its mediating role, a consequence of which may be experienced as a sense of imbalance within the self or between the self and others. Although social behaviors are indicators of the intactness to impairment in ego functions which support the mediating role, observation limited to manifest behavior may only obscure the more private and invisible sufferings of people as they struggle to restore a sense of wholeness within themselves. At those times, people are more likely to seek help from others. Although crisis theory is useful in understanding these phenomena, people are not necessarily "in crisis" when they apply for clinical services. Inevitably, they will be experiencing a state of disequilibrium in the capacity of their ego systems to negotiate, intrapersonally and/or interpersonally, the imbalance which will adversely affect their sense of confidence in self to manage their lives.

REFERENCES

Bowen, M. *Family Therapy in Clinical Practice.* New York: Jason Aronson, 1978.

Germain, C., and Gitterman, A. *The Life Model of Social Work Practice.* New York: Columbia University Press, 1980.

Klein D., and Lindemann, E. "Preventive Intervention in Individual and Family Crisis Situations," *Prevention and Mental Disorders in Children.* New York: Basic Books, Inc., (1961) 283-306.

Mackey, R. "Crisis Theory: Its Development and Relevance to Social Casework Practice," *Family Coordinator* 17: 5 (July 1968) 165-173.

Rapaport, L. "Crisis Intervention as A Mode of Brief Treatment," *Theories of Social Casework.* Edited by R. Roberts and R. Nee. Chicago: University of Chicago Press, 1970, 265-311.

Spiegel, J. "The Resolution of Role Conflict Within the Family," *A Modern Introduction to the Family* (Second Edition). Edited by N. Bell and E. Vogel, New York: The Free Press, 1968.

6

AN EGO-ORIENTED MODEL
OF CLINICAL SOCIAL WORK

OVERVIEW

As noted, no approach to clinical practice may be understood apart from its theoretical perspective. The parameters of a particular approach or combination of approaches are defined by the set of ideas which give substance and focus to clinical work. These ideas, when put together in a systematic way, constitute models of practice which may have the following characteristics: Models may be implicit or explicit, simple or complex, unidimensional or multidimensional. Contemporary trends in theory building have emphasized the explication of more intricate and multidimensional models of clinical practice which reflect the realities of practice today and the awareness of the impact on well-being of a complex of interacting forces in biological, psychological and social spheres of life. Theoretical models play a critical role in the development of one's approach to practice and influence significantly the individual style or artistic use of self in working with troubled people.

While we may strive for validity of a scientific nature in constructing models for practice, the realization of that aspiration is constrained by several factors, not the least of which are:

—the boundaries and limitations of knowledge at particular points in time;
—the mysteries of biological, psychological and social factors and their interrelationship, which are most difficult to measure and to control;
—one's own predispositions and assumptions, which may reinforce closedness to new ideas rather than openness;
—the unpredictability of human nature; and
—the capacity of individuals to transcend incredible obstacles in human development and, as a consequence, to become exceptions to normative expectations.

Although our best efforts will always fall short of creating an ideal model of clinical practice, we do have a responsibility to think about the relationship of theory to practice and to reach for a more integrated approach, in which clinical practice becomes more congruent with its theoretical base. That effort involves an honest search for valid knowledge, a respect for the unknown and a willingness to evaluate the impact of ideas on one's vested interests as a practitioner.

THE HUMAN CONTEXT OF CLINICAL PRACTICE

Within an ego psychological perspective, theory is useful for understanding structural assets and liabilities of a client and for identifying areas of vulnerability in psychosocial development. The perspective also is helpful in understanding the nature of the clinical process itself, which may recapitulate or replicate—depending on the ontogenetic state of the client's ego—earlier processes of internalization. To meet the client "where he is" is to invite him to tell his own story in his own way and to connect empathically with his structural and developmental sufferings as they are shared with the worker within the perimeters of the interview. To "stay with the client" is to understand and to respect the need of the client to move at his own pace, which is a reflection of his level of internal organization and his capacity to become involved in a relationship that may represent an additional risk to his intrapersonal and interpersonal equilibrium. Although the worker is always the "guardian of autonomy" for the client's ego, the nature of autonomy will be related to the quality of earlier experiences with significant figures, memories of which will be present in the dynamic matrix of the therapeutic relationship at unconscious, preconscious and conscious levels.

The individual practitioner may give the client nothing but can offer him a great deal. The client has the power to decide, proximately or ultimately, to accept or reject what is offered. In fact, a significant dimension of therapeutic work throughout the helping process is for the therapist to engage the client in exploring and deciding about his interest in accepting the help which the therapist offers. The therapist needs to take special care in respecting the integrity of the client to make his own decisions and to accept his right to choose, as freely as possible, whether or not to make use of the service which is offered; this choice is crucial in building a therapeutic relationship as well as strengthening the defensive and adaptive boundaries within which executive functions can be exercised. The essential elements of the process are, thus, concerned with matters of exploration, involvement and commitment rather than with manipulation, exploitation and coercion. An atmosphere of progressive openness and directness rather than closedness and deception is essential to the promotion of structuralizing and the restoration or enhancement of the client's thrust toward ego autonomy and wholeness.

The most viable, but not necessarily reliable, resource in clinical work is the self of the therapist—the self, as represented in one's biopsychosocial history tempered by professional knowledge, values and skills. While the therapist serves the client most effectively when she is able to offer—and the client is capable of accepting—assistance to help himself, the reality that one human being has sought another for assistance suggests that the empathic presence of the latter has a special and potentially profound effect on the outcome of the work between them, an assumption which recognizes the critical value of respecting the separateness and autonomy of our own existence and that of the other person whom we call client. As a special type of human relationship, the therapeutic relationship is an opportunity for freeing the potential for psychosocial development which the client brings to that encounter. It is also an opportunity to contribute to the consolidation of the self-representation within the client and as a consequence to enhance his sense of self-esteem, an opportunity that may be circumscribed by the therapist's own impairment in ego functions.

At one level of self, primarily an ego-oriented level, therapist and client are different from each other. Endowment coupled with opportunity play an important role in the development of our ego assets and liabilities. The family into which one is born and the social environment in which one is reared play the most fundamental roles in structuralizing defensive, executive and adaptive subsystems of the ego. However, there is a deeper level of life in which all persons share and which is not affected substantially by endowment or opportunity. It is the world of basic human needs and the feelings associated with the fulfillment or frustration of those needs. At this level, all people share a common heritage which is undifferentiated in its primary core but which is manifested in various ways depending on the life experiences of each person as he connects with and is involved with the world of significant others, the family and the wider social milieu. Because this basic level of existence is relatively unaffected by the social environment, people are one: there are no teachers, no students; there are no caseworkers, no clients; there are no therapists, no patients. Differentiation occurs at one level and results in manifest differences in ego structures among people while the innermost world of all remains relatively constant and is the repository of man's need to care for others, to be cared for by others, to grow and to become a person of worth and dignity who needs the acceptance, respect and support of those around him.

Within the clinical process, empathy is conducive to making emotional and cognitive contact with the inner life of the client and for facilitating his attachment to and involvement with us in the therapeutic relationship. As we have already said, the ego function of empathy is the acceptance of our common humanity with the people we serve, the recognition that we are fundamentally no different from them at one level of existence, and the choice to feel within ourselves a semblance of what they experience because their needs and ours are linked in a common human existence. Empathy is, secondly, the humility to accept our differences as an accident of endowment and as a consequence of opportunities over which we had little choice or control. Finally, empathy is the realization that the most effective clinical resource we possess is our human commonality tempered and disciplined by the acquisition of knowledge and professional skill. At one level, the therapeutic relationship is characterized by empathic connectedness with the client, the prototypical experiences for which may be found in lower level processes of internalization. At another level, the relationship is characterized by separateness and respect for autonomy of the client, no matter how tenuous. At an intermediate level these two aspects come together in the working alliance as the client identifies with the therapist and joins with her in a mutually oriented process of exploration, confrontation and discovery.

Within the context of the therapeutic relationship, one goal is of generic importance regardless of setting or mode of intervention:

> to assist the client in freeing himself from the constraints which bind him to a level of personal and/or interpersonal functioning that interfere with his right to become more fulfilled as a human being

These constraints may be of a physical, psychological or social nature or a combination of the three. To suggest that the goal of fulfillment is contingent upon personal freedom is to refer to the potential within people to become responsible for themselves rather than dependent on others for supplies that may be undermining their psychosocial development. In ego psychological terms, people feel progressively more free and in control of their lives when their ego functions are intact and unimpaired by intrapersonal and/or interpersonal conflict. As a consequence they become more capable of making choices from inner convictions rather than out of needs to please or to conform to the inconsequential or unreasonable expectations of others. While therapy may be a vehicle for becoming aware of the reasons for impairment in one's sense of autonomy (which we have defined as responsible interdependence in social roles and relationships), therapy is also an opportunity of learning to experience choice and of learning to accept responsibility for the consequences of those choices.

Wheelis expressed the significance of this concept about the goal of ego-oriented therapy. In his essay on change, Wheelis reflected on the meaning of therapy as an opportunity for growth, a process of enabling people to become more than what they may be in the present. He said:

> Conflict, suffering, psychotherapy—all these lead us to look again at ourselves...more carefully, in greater detail, to find what we have missed, to understand a mystery; and all this extends awareness. But whether this greater awareness will increase or diminish freedom will depend upon what it is that we become aware of. If the greater awareness is of the causes, traumas, psychodynamics that 'made' us what we are, then we are understanding the past in such a way as to prove that we 'had' to become what we are; and, since this view applies equally to the present, which is the unbroken extension of that determined past, therapy becomes a way of establishing why we must continue to be what we have been, a way of disavowing choice with the apparent blessing of science, and the net effect will be a decrease in freedom. If, however, the greater awareness is of options unnoticed, of choices denied, of other ways to live, then freedom will be increased, and with it greater responsibility for what we have been, are, and will become. (Wheelis, A., 66, 1969).

THE FOCUS OF CLINICAL WORK

To clarify the focus of ego-oriented therapy, we will discuss three variables which collectively define this important dimension of the helping process:

—conflict
—time
—mode

One seeks help because he is in intrapersonal and/or interpersonal pain. Operationally, one is in a state of conflict when an imbalance occurs between internal ego systems and external social systems. The term *conflict* refers to those experiences which lead to a state of imbalance or upset which an individual feels unable to handle without professional assistance. Problems, on the other hand, refer to events which we all experience and are able to manage by use of available resources, either within oneself or within our immediate social environment. Inevitably, conflict will involve an upset in social roles and relationships which causes stress as well as upset in defensive, executive and adaptive ego functions. The two aspects of conflict occur simultaneously and have a transactional effect on each other. That is, an upset in social relationship will usually result in inner conflict and an upset internally will usually result in interpersonal conflict.

We have often thought of the applicant's initial presentation of his conflict as the "presenting problem" and then proceeded to discover the "real problem," the assumption apparently being that the presenting complaint can never be real enough to somehow account for the person's distress. In the ego-oriented model, the presenting problem is the real conflict and needs to be respected as the client's way, or more precisely, his ego's way of communicating to us how pain is experienced and understood. As the process of exploring the presenting complaint(s) unfolds, other dimensions of the conflict may be discovered and, of course, may become the focus of our interventive efforts. Until that occurs, however, we operate on the assumption that what the client is able to tell us is what troubles him. Once the therapist understands its significance within the context of getting to know the client as more of a whole person rather than as an applicant with a presenting complaint, action may be taken by the therapist to alleviate anxiety or to reduce stress associated with the presenting conflict. However, any action should be evaluated in relation to its adaptive benefit for the client and not as a diversion from getting to know the applicant as a person or from helping him to engage in the process of exploration. In that respect, information grounded on a solid base of fact about human behavior can often be helpful to the applicant in setting aside or ameliorating pressing issue(s) which may interfere with exploration of more critical matters.

The responsibility of the therapist throughout the helping process, but more particularly during the beginning phase, is to listen to the applicant and to evaluate the meaning of his conflict within a vertical and horizontal context. That is, to understand the person in terms of his current life situation and how his current concern about the conflict developed. Since we will discuss the process of clinical work later, let us focus here on the issue of who defines the focus of therapy and who sets the goals. The applicant does! The worker can only be available with her professional skills to assist the client in reaching goals that are the client's goals and not those of the worker. The identification of goals is a critical aspect of the beginning phase for the following reasons:

—goals provide structure for clients who may experience fragmentation in their lives;

—goals provide clients with a sense of control over a process that may be concerned with discovery of the unknown which is, by definition, not controllable and, therefore, provocative of anxiety;

—goals involve executive and adaptive systems in ego building experiences;

—goals convey respect for the autonomy of the client and hopeful expectation that he can be in charge of his life;

—goals establish boundaries between worker and client which help to define the client's responsibility for taking an active role in his own behalf;

—goals establish the reality that the means for resolving conflict, suffering and pain lie within the client and not in the therapist;

—goals are an essential part of a contract between therapist and applicant and offer the therapist an opportunity to decide whether she will accept the applicant as a client.

Goals may be negotiated and modified as part of the therapeutic process but they must remain as aspirations which the client wants for himself. While the goal aspect of the therapeutic contract may be renegotiated independent of other contractual aspects, the setting of at least tentative goals is an important part of the beginning of the therapeutic process. It is easy to drift into the ongoing phase of intervention without attending to this important aspect only to find powerful resistance as therapy unfolds. Resistance is a natural part of therapy but will be more manageable in an ego progressive sense if the client has been encouraged to set his own goals, has explored their significance with the therapist as part of the helping process and has a genuine sense that the therapist is with him in his struggle to realize his goals. Only when the applicant and therapist come together in a mutual understanding of goals does a therapeutic contract exist between them. At that point, the applicant for therapy becomes a client of therapy and the actual process of therapy begins.

Time is another variable that helps to define the focus of ego-oriented therapy. Although time has been an important element in the functional approach to social casework for decades, it has become a nodal issue in other approaches during the last two decades. Crisis intervention and planned short-term approaches make use of time in a deliberate and purposeful manner to enhance the potential for therapeutic success. Time has also been important in another respect. Some approaches to therapy focus on the "here and now" and either view historical time as inconsequential or not instrumental to the raison d'être of treatment. Although psychoanalysis has traditionally been associated with a vertical time perspective, that notion is not well understood or appreciated by those who have only a superficial or stereotypical understanding of the meaning of time in psychoanalysis. Regardless, time is an important aspect of any model of theory and requires clarification in that context.

The issue of whether we focus on the past or the present is easily resolved. We do neither! The focus of ego-oriented theory is always in the present and, when we explore the past, it is always within the context of the present. Awareness of history has no value to therapy unless it is related ultimately to present conflict(s) and used as a means to understand life as it is experienced today and how life can be better tomorrow. Historical awareness, as an end in itself, is limiting of more ego adaptive behavior and may be reinforcing of defensive hopelessness and abdication of responsibility for coming to terms with the person's "one and only life." In this model, the past is understood as always being "present in the present." History is utilized to deepen empathic understanding of the client and to help him become aware of the significance of the past to his current troubles. Thus, historical interpretation has a role in therapy but only if it pushes back the perimeters of current awareness so that the ego can function more adaptively. Understanding the past and integrating a cognitive and emotional appreciation of its significance may lead to a heightened sense of mastery and confidence in one's inner capacity to adaptively transcend historic events. One of the most obvious characteristics of the past is that it can never be changed. Its significance to present ego functioning and self-esteem can be modified, however, in relation to the cognitive and emotional aspect of the self and object representations.

Recent research supports the notion that a current focus is of value in assisting the client to function in a more ego adaptive way. Feedback studies on the value of therapy from the perspective of clients suggest clearly that therapy is most helpful when it focuses on current problems in psychosocial functioning and is supportive of the client's struggles to strengthen his adaptive capacities.

The helping process naturally moves from the present to the past. People are troubled by current conflicts and the therapist works to understand the manifest and latent dimensions of current conflict before exploring how the conflict developed over time. We have referred to that aspect of exploration as vertical exploration. To formulate an evaluative understanding of the client, the therapist needs to develop an appreciation of this person in time, which means an appreciation of how he came to be the person he is today. The historical perspective is indispensable to evaluation of who the applicant is at the present time. How that vertical perspective will be used in therapy will depend on how the client wishes to use therapy and how the therapist understands its value as an instrument to more effective ego functioning for the client. Historical material is elicited only as the applicant is ready to talk about the past. No rush need be imposed on the clinical process nor should clinical social workers impose an artificial structure on a relationship that gradually evolves between client and therapist as the former feels ready to share more intimate aspects of self, which may include memories of the past.

Therapy is a parsimonious process in relation to goals, modality, technique and time. Depending on the therapist's evaluation of the nature of the client's conflict and his level of internal organization, she will decide whether to explore or not to explore history. There is no value in pursuing historical data unless the client indicates a readiness to talk about his past and unless historic data will be relevant to the goals of therapy.

The mode of therapy is the third focus to clarify in this overview. The ego-psychological perspective is compatible with an individual or group mode of intervention whether that group be a marriage, a family or a therapy group. What the therapist chooses as a focus for her interventions will vary depending on the mode. Obviously, the dyadic nature of the individual mode restricts intervention to an intrapersonal focus although those interventions may involve the client in an exploration of his thoughts and feelings about himself, his perceptions and evaluations of others or his reactions to the therapist and their relationship. Nevertheless, the focus is limited to the client and his inner representations of self and his object representations of significant others. When two or more clients are involved in the therapeutic process, whether they are related to each other or not, the primary focus is on the interaction between or among them. While the skills employed by the therapist may be of a generic nature (such as support, confrontation and interpretation) the primary focus of the intervention will vary depending on the mode. Strict implementation of this parameter is neither realistic nor therapeutically desirable, however. Therapists do speak to individuals in an individual way even in groups but the primary frame of intervention in working with groups (defined as two or more clients sharing responsibility for the therapy) is on the interaction between and among them.

Although systems and group theory is indispensable to working with groups, the value of a base in ego psychological theory and skill is in the importance which that perspective attributes to the individual. No matter what the mode, clinicians are involved professionally with human beings: individuals interacting in social roles and relationships who experience suffering as human beings and not as elements in a social system or as actors in a social role relationship. To appreciate that reality is to see the individual in the context of social systems and not the other way around. Clinicians need to be trained in the theory and technique of family and group therapies but not at the expense of struggling with and mastering the complexities of individual therapy. Optimally, clinical social workers should be exposed to individual and group modes in professional training programs but be free to pursue the level of intervention that fits their individual interests and aptitudes.

The mode must also fit the conflict and interest(s) of the client. Social workers are frequently confronted with situations in which the optimal mode of intervention may be conjoint marital therapy or some form of family group therapy. Optimal conditions often seem to be the exception, however; practice may be characterized by working with who is available or not working with anyone. Thus, the client—or more precisely the client system—may determine the mode despite the most heroic efforts to reach out and involve other primary persons in the family. A distinction does exist, however, in the reasons for inviting participation of significant other(s) in clinical work vis-à-vis the concept of the helping process and its various phases. Family members who are asked to get involved at the phase of exploration and evaluation of the presenting conflict may be more receptive to the therapist's invitation than they would be if the purpose is not made clear or if there is a hidden agenda of entrapping them into family or marital therapy. Indeed, an entrée into conjoint and family therapy may be through the involvement of significant figures in the exploratory and evaluative process, but only when the parameters which we have outlined in relation to goals are respected.

THE CLINICAL PROCESS

The relationship between the applicant/client and the therapist is differentiated from other encounters of an interpersonal nature only in terms of its purpose, which structures the relationship and lends order to the clinical process. Systematically, the process has a beginning, middle and end which have no reference in this model, per se, to discrete number of interviews. In other words, the issue of open-ended or planned short-term intervention will be decided as a result of the exploratory/evaluation process in the beginning phase of clinical work rather than as a decision made independent of or imposed upon the applicant. During that phase, the therapist listens to the manifest as well as latent significance of time to the individual and explores the person's thoughts and feelings about time and time boundaries as the clinician would explore any important issue. The data now available about the meaning of time and the suitability of planned short-term intervention for many applicants indicate that these issues are to be explored during the beginning phase whether or not the applicant expresses concern about them.

Given the overall nature of therapy and the generic intent to be supportive of ego development and self-esteem, the clinical process symbolically resembles aspects of the internalization process. If psychosocial development is continuous, as we assume that it is, then the therapeutic relationship becomes a medium of development within the matrix of the helping process which parallels lower, mid and upper levels of internalization processes. The early work is to explore the conflict which the client shares with us and in so doing to involve the applicant in a relationship through which change may take place. While attachment is instrumental to involvement in therapy, it will be valued by the client in relation to the level of organization of his ego structures. The more impaired the ego, the more need there may be to attach to and depend upon the therapist while at the same time fearing a loss of separateness. During the middle phase of therapy the applicant, who has assumed the role of client as a result of the contract between him and the therapist, needs to identify with the therapeutic modus operandi and—to have any hope of realizing his goals—with the role of the therapist as a helpful person. This important dimension of clinical work will be explored in the next chapter.

In connecting with ego intact sphere(s), the therapist forms an alliance with the client through which goals may be mutually pursued by her use of purposeful therapeutic skills such as support, confrontation and interpretation.

During this middle or ongoing phase, the client must become more fully involved and identified with the potential of therapy as a means of change and become aware of its realistic limitations as a vehicle for resolving conflicts. In brief, he needs to accept the reality that only he can effect change within himself. As these values become a part of the client's own world in the form of new introjects, he experiences himself in a more differentiated way in the relationship as he begins to experience confidence in his inner ability to take care of himself. Bowen sees this change as an adaptive shift in the fusion of emotional and cognitive functioning with the latter becoming dominant over the former. This change is also understood as a strengthening of the self-representation, which brings about an enhanced sense of esteem for one's self. If the process moves along in this direction (which is contingent upon change not only in affect but in cognitive functioning and in behavior), the client will sooner or later experience diminishing need to hold on to the relationship and will look forward to letting it go. Separation will be influenced by the pleasure which the client can now experience in the practice of adaptive behaviors and in the success which he associates with more autonomous behavior in the real world, outside the therapeutic relationship.

THE ROLE OF THE THERAPIST

The generic role of the worker or therapist is to do, within the boundaries of the therapeutic relationship and as part of the clinical process, whatever she *thinks* needs to be done in order to be of assistance to the client—as long as her behavior conforms to ethical standards of the profession and is supportive of the client's ego development and self-esteem. The empathic use of professional skill integrated with an understanding of the developmental level of the client is a catalyst for change and the most powerful force for enhancing adaptive functioning via the clinical process.

Within that process, skills of focused exploration, dynamic evaluation and therapeutic responsiveness are employed as an integrated whole although each may be in ascendency at particular times. That is, one cannot communicate in a purposive and empathic manner without thinking about and evaluating the intrapersonal and interpersonal aspects of the situation with which the client is confronted. In exploring and evaluating that situation, the therapist is also responding or intervening in a potentially therapeutic way. Exploration may be more characteristic of and in ascendency during the early phase of the helping process, as the worker listens to the content of the concerns with which the client is confronted and tries to hear the feelings associated with those concerns. By listening and by trying to hear, the worker is responding purposively even if she uses no words at all. In fact, it is more important to the viability of their relationship and ultimately to the process itself that the client senses the empathic quality in the worker than to obtain a considerable amount of verbal feedback. Words themselves are less important than the meaning behind them.

Within this model of therapy, skills of focused exploration, dynamic evaluation and therapeutic responsiveness are generic in nature and indispensable to the various modes that one may employ in therapeutic work. Techniques, on the other hand, are more special or unique to a circumscribed type of intervention and are subsumed under the skill of therapeutic responsiveness; they include support, confrontation and interpretation. Their use, therapeutically, must be grounded in a differential understanding of the client's structural state, his level of ego development and the social-cultural context of his life including the nature of important roles and relationships, his social status, his ethnic and gender identifications. These elements of understanding constitute the dynamic evaluation.

Exploration is a two-dimensional process which involves concurrent and interrelated skills of listening and hearing. To listen is to be free enough within one's self to be open and receptive to accepting the significance for the client of what he is attempting to communicate. What meaning(s) does the client's behavior, whether verbal or nonverbal, have to him within the context of his life situation? For the client, that communication is most likely to be experienced and shared at a conscious level of the self. For the therapist, the effectiveness of the functional skill of listening depends on a sensitive perception of the client's physical environment, his familial background and his socio-cultural milieu. The second dimension of exploration, hearing, is more oriented to skills in "tuning in" to the feelings behind the more manifest behavior of the client. At that level, the therapist's investment in therapeutic work is oriented more to what she senses about the latent dimensions of the client's communication (about which the client may be unaware, partially aware, or temporarily aware). The skill of hearing is thematic in nature and is directed to current feelings which are unacceptable to the client's superego and/or to the developmental state of his ego.

The skill of hearing is connected to the evaluative function on the part of the therapist and is founded on the cognitive understanding of psychological and social dynamics associated with the structural and developmental state of the client. These skills involve an accurate awareness of one's self so that the therapist is able to distinguish between that which she may be hearing and that which the client may be saying. The intent here is not only to bring sound and reasonable knowledge to the therapeutic encounter with the client for the purpose of understanding him but also to understand one's self so that an appropriate degree of discipline may be exerted over those countertransferential tendencies which may interfere with the client's struggle to share parts of his life with the therapist.

Although the task of listening involves intuitive behavior, that of hearing involves more conceptual understanding of the vicissitudes in life and the dynamics of those behaviors on the part of the therapist which may promote the realization of the goal of clinical intervention. Refinement of the skill of hearing the less visible dimensions of the client's thoughts and feelings about his life differentiates the therapeutic relationship from that of a friendship or other relationships of a professional nature.

To promote integration of these two skills in the task of exploration, one must be able to evaluate the world of the client along several dimensions. This second skill is oriented to understanding the client as a psychological and social person. In contemporary practice, evaluation is complex because of the emergence of newer modalities of intervention which usually carry with them a special orientation not only for understanding people but also for implementing a particular strategy of therapy (e.g.: systems theory and its application to family therapy). Indeed, one of the values of ego-psychological evaluation is its potential for synthesizing strains of psychosocial theory which often appear conflictual or contradictory.

Because the next chapter details the skills of exploration and evaluation, only an outline of the variables included in evaluation are presented here:

A. Description of the locus of conflict
—intrapersonal
—interpersonal
B. Assessment of the current state of ego functioning

—defensive subsystem
—executive subsystem
—adaptive subsystem
—nature of internalized values and their affect on psychosocial functioning
C. Assessment of significant aspects in the familial and social worlds of the client which may have been assets or liabilities in his ego development and in his current roles and relationships
D. Tentative conceptualization of the level of intactness to impairment in psychosocial functioning of the ego based on an understanding of current functioning and on developmental experiences.

The initial evaluation, which is always incomplete and tentative, leads to a consideration of the implications of one's understanding for ongoing therapy. While this discussion of evaluation may seem to be associated with the beginning phase of the helping process, evaluation, in fact, is a part of the process from beginning to end; this is also true of the other skills discussed in this overview. The dynamic interrelationship of process and skill is important in clinical social work and helps to differentiate it from the traditional and lineal model of study, diagnosis and treatment.

As the interventive process unfolds, evaluation becomes increasingly more complete but never finished. As with ego development, evaluation is continuous. There will be qualitative differences in the substantive aspects of evaluation in the beginning, middle and end of the helping process. Aspects of evaluation will be useful to the therapist throughout the clinical process as she attempts to structure her intervention according to an empathic understanding of the client's communications to her. As a viable skill, evaluation is used parsimoniously throughout therapy. Periodically it is also useful to pull together a statement of the worker's evaluative thinking about the client. At those times, such as at the end of the beginning phase, the outline presented here may be useful for organizing one's thinking, for identifying areas that may need further exploration, for assessing the effectiveness of intervention up to that point and for reflecting upon future directions.

As the skills of exploration and evaluation become more fully integrated within the self of each therapist, intervention becomes increasingly more responsive to the needs of the client despite variability in style among therapists. Responsiveness, the third skill of clinical social work, is not a matter of style as much as it is a matter of using one's self in a way that will promote the inherent thrust of people toward growth, personal fulfillment and self-responsibility.

Responsiveness is defined as purposeful intervention which is tempered by what has been said (by the client) and what has been heard (by the therapist). It involves a consideration of the more technical options available to the therapist in communicating therapeutically to the client. This third aspect of intervention may involve the use of self by the worker in one or a combination of three ways:

Support

The technique of building upon those personal assets which the client brings to the relationship in order to assist him:

—to sustain a present level of ego functioning
                              or
—to move to a higher developmental level.

Confrontation

The technique of assisting the executive ego of the client to face currently unacceptable feelings within the self which may be at a conscious or preconscious level of awareness but which may have been previously unconscious.

Interpretation

The technique of assisting the ego of the client to become aware of the linkage of one level of feeling (conscious here and now) to another level (preconscious present, near present or past), with the intent of expanding the perimeters of conscious self-understanding.

Although one may be, and often is, supportive without being confrontive or interpretive, one may not be effective in the clinical process of confrontation or interpretation without first having developed a supportive working alliance with the client. Therapy as a process of ego development is, by its nature, always supportive, which involves an attitudinal-like stance or overall intent by the therapist in relation to this generic assumption. The technique of support is always congruent with that intent but not synonymous with it. There is a sequence to more intensive clinical intervention which must be based on a supportive relationship. Also, the use of confrontation and interpretation is oriented to assisting the ego of the client to make discoveries and connections by and for itself through an evolving process of exploration and reflection. Better that the client arrive at new awareness by himself than to have these offered by the worker.

While this discussion of the techniques involved in responsiveness has thus far been directed to individual work—as has the discussion of the skills of exploration and evaluation—these skills and techniques are also adaptable to working with a couple, a family or a group. I do believe that the learning of technique should be initially grounded in individual work, and the tone of this overview reflects that bias. However, I also believe that clinicians can master the skills of other interventive modes either concurrent with or by building upon the foundation of individual therapy. These skills and techniques offer a generic approach to clinical practice, regardless of mode. The focus of intervention will vary, however, depending on the mode. As we have already hypothesized, skills and techniques become more interpersonally focused as intervention shifts from an individual to a group mode.

The question of responsiveness is more accurately expressed as a question of what the worker empathically thinks the situation requires; responses must be tempered not only by what the client has said but also by what the worker has heard. On this third dimension of the clinical role, the question of intent and timing become germane as the therapist weighs the consequences of her responsiveness to the client. Here the technical aspects of clinical work and their inseparability from intent (which is derived from one's theoretical frame of reference in ego psychology) assumes primary importance in the helping process: that is, responsiveness tempered by an ego-oriented understanding of the readiness and capacity of the client to integrate new learnings about himself and/or his interpersonal relationship(s)—including his relationship with the therapist—which may be consciously unacceptable to him or unconsciously inaccessible to him at any point in time. The nature of the therapist's responsiveness, especially in relation to the use of confrontation and interpretation, is tempered as well by her readiness to assume the added responsibilities of working at a more intense level with feelings within clients and to contend with resistive forces which are inevitably associated with expectations and/or fears of personal and/or interpersonal change.

CONCLUSION

The ego psychological approach to clinical practice evolves out of the humanistic theory-building tradition of the social work profession.

Within a value orientation characterized by acceptance of the client as another human being and by respect for his right to self-determination (Hollis, 1981), that tradition has spawned several different approaches to practice which include the psychosocial, functional, ecological, behavioral and problem-solving models. This effort is a modest contribution to that tradition.

It focuses on the psychological organization of the human person, the most uniquely human part of which is the dynamic structure we refer to as ego, and derives from these understandings, skills and techniques of practice. Like the other models, it is oriented to the progressive and adaptive potential of the human being and to the development of interventive modes of therapy that will be responsive to that potential. This model is psychosocial in the sense that the focus of intervention is on enhancing the synthetic role of the ego as mediator between inner psychobiological forces and outer sociocultural expectations. Its functional aspects derive from the optimism of that school about human nature and its commitment to involving the client in a helping process through the medium of a therapeutic relationship in which change may take place. Its problem-solving aspects derive from the recognition "that life is an ongoing problem-encountering, problem-solving process" (Roberts and Nee, 1970, 139). Although this model does not purport to pay as much attention to the social aspects by direct intervention into social systems that affect the "interface between person and environment" (Germain and Gitterman, 1980, 12), it does recognize the importance of that dimension of practice. In a sense, the ego-oriented approach complements the ecological approach. While both acknowledge the importance of viewing the individual as a whole person, and of promoting his adaptive capacities, one approach emphasizes socially-oriented intervention while the other emphasizes psychologically-oriented intervention to realize that goal. While the ego psychological model might not appear to have much in common with the behavioral or task-centered approaches, it does draw significantly from learning theory and recognizes the inherent operant characteristics of any form of psychotherapy. That is, the specific techniques of dynamic therapy, as well as the general demeanor of the therapist vis-à-vis the client, has a powerful reinforcing effect on the latter. The significance of goals and contract within the ego psychological model also is derived, in part, from the behavioral approach to therapy.

Although these observations are not intended to be exhaustive, they do point up the commonalities between the model presented here and other approaches to clinical social work practice. This model of clinical practice is one attempt to grapple with the dilemma of understanding how people are put together psychosocially and how that understanding contributes to use of self in therapy. It focuses on the psychotherapeutic aspects of clinical social work and delimits the work of therapy to intrapersonal and interpersonal conflicts which are explored, understood and treated through a special human relationship oriented to change.

If theoretical orientation to understanding the meaning of behavior differs and techniques for facilitating change differ, as well, how is it that people change despite variability among therapists who treat them? Perhaps, as Burton suggests, the client has a strong need to believe in, have faith in, the efficacy of the therapist and her methods, which may become curative in and of themselves. As he says: "Faith is a part of every healing system and when faith is lost, healing stops" (Burton, 1976, 323). Perhaps it is in the healing power of a special friendship with another human being who cares enough to waste time with the client. Or, perhaps it is the optimism of the therapist that lends hope to another who experiences his life with little or no hope. On the other hand, it may be in the value of viewing therapeutic intervention within a dynamic systems context which places less emphasis on the target of specific interventions and more on the catalytic effect of change in one dimension of life on other dimension(s). At this state of our knowledge about the nature of humankind—of which there are as many notions as there are models of intervention—one must confess that no one knows why people change. In not knowing, we must continue to live with the paradox of believing in our ideas and our methods while grappling with the reality that we are, to a profound degree, dealing in mystery.

REFERENCES

Burton, A. (ed.) *What Makes Behavior Change Possible?*. New York: Brunner/Mazel, 1976.

Germain, C., and Gitterman, A. *The Life Model of Social Work Practice*. New York: Columbia University Press, 1980.

Hollis, F., and Woods, M. *Casework: A Psychosocial Therapy*. New York: Random House, 1981.

Mackey, R. "Generic Aspects of Clinical Social Work Practice," *Social Casework* 57: 10 (December 1976) 619-624.

May R., et al. (eds.) *Existence: A New Dimension in Psychiatry and Psychology*. New York: Basic Books, 1958.

Perlman, H. *Social Casework: A Problem-solving Process*. Chicago: University of Chicago Press, 1957.

Roberts, R., and Nee, R. (eds.) *Theories of Social Casework*. Chicago: University of Chicago Press, 1957.

Wheelis, A. "How People Change," *Commentary* (May 1969) 56-66.

7

EXPLORATION AND EVALUATION

In this chapter we will focus primarily on evaluation, a pivotal skill which organizes the process of psychosocial intervention. The term "pivotal" is used in the sense that evaluation is a skill around which revolves interventions of focused exploration and purposive responsiveness by the therapist. *Evaluation* is a "central, cardinal or crucial factor" in the helping process. Defined as the dynamic understanding by the therapist of the state of intactness/impairment in the client's ego functions, evaluation offers focus to exploration and purpose to therapeutic techniques of support, confrontation and interpretation. The access to psychosocial data upon which evaluative understanding is conceptualized within the mind of the therapist is the exploratory process. Before considering evaluation, therefore, we will discuss the skill of exploration which has received much attention in the social work literature. I do not intend to review or to repeat the theoretical or methodological work which has already been done. Those aspects of the literature most relevant to exploration are interviewing and psychosocial study. The reader is referred to the works of Garrett, Kadushin, Edinburg and Schubert for a review of interviewing techniques.

The works of Hollis, Perlman and Roberts are good sources for an understanding of the theory, content and method of psychosocial study.

EXPLORATION

Exploration, is a parsimonious inquiry on the part of the therapist into the thoughts, feelings and experiences of the applicant/client that are germane to understanding him as a person in conflict. Such inquiry is tempered by an empathic appreciation of the readiness of the other person to share various aspects of his life with the therapist. The state of readiness will vary according to the intactness of ego systems within the applicant/client and his faith or trust in the therapist. Because the development of a relationship always takes precedence over the development of evaluative understanding (both of which are ongoing and evolving aspects of the helping process from beginning to end), the nature of data which becomes available through the exploratory process is always contingent upon the therapist's respect for "meeting the client where he is" and for working with the client at his pace.

In this model exploration is, by its nature, a supportive skill which is intended:

—to elicit data upon which evaluative understanding will be grounded;
—to involve the applicant/client with the therapist in a relationship which is the vehicle through which change may be realized;
—to establish and then to reinforce the expectation that the primary source of change is within the client and only secondarily in the client-therapist relationship;
—to convey respect for the right of the client to engage in the process of therapy at a level that is congruent with his motivation and capacity for change; and
—to neutralize the natural human wish that change may come about without significant personal investment of the client in the process.

Although exploration may serve various needs throughout the helping process, it always has a relationship-building function. To encourage client relatedness with the therapist by way of empathic receptivity and responsiveness is to enhance adaptive behavior which may not only serve the needs of the therapeutic relationship but which may also facilitate more appropriate involvement of the client in human relationships outside of therapy.

Exploration in the beginning phase may be quite different from its use later in the helping process. In the beginning, the therapist tries to connect empathically with the way(s) in which the applicant is troubled. That connection usually begins with some definition of the conflict that triggered the request for help. As the applicant and therapist arrive at a beginning awareness of the conflict and its contemporary dimensions, the process naturally moves in the direction of considering how the conflict began and how it may affect ego functioning at the present time. As exploration focuses on horizontal and vertical aspects of the applicant's life, the therapist needs not only to listen to the more objective facts of the conflict but to hear the cognitive and affective themes associated with the applicant's experiences in the present and in the past. The timing and depth of beginning explorations must be tempered by the therapist's initial evaluation of the structural capacities and developmental level of the applicant's ego. Within that context, the process of exploration need not be encumbered by arbitrary time constraints. As Smalley has said:

> . . .most essential of all is the worker's sensitivity to what the other is experiencing in beginning and his response to that feeling, in a way appropriate to the particular situation, so that the other is freed to move through and beyond feelings which may be impeding his getting started. . .it is the worker's appreciation of the general promise and problems in beginnings, and his capacity to exploit this particular beginning for this particular client—to stay with the beginning, in all its inevitable awkwardness and tentativeness, rather than to rush to solve all the problems—that embodies skill in this aspect of the social work process (Smalley, in Roberts and Nee, 1970, 100).

Exploration in the beginning phase must also be concerned with helping the applicant to decide whether or not he wishes to become further involved in the helping process—that is, to become a client. The importance of distinguishing between the roles of applicant and client was originally identified by Perlman, who found that "continuance or discontinuance beyond intake may be affected by the understandings and agreements between applicant and worker as to what in the way of service and behavior is wanted, expected and realizable." She argued for a clarification of "at least preliminary ideas and expectations of reciprocal roles and working relationships" as part of the application process and suggested that an applicant did not become a client until there was a mutual understanding between applicant and worker of these issues (Perlman, 1960). We have referred earlier to the mutuality of that understanding as a *contract.* That aspect of exploration is a matter of clarifying what the applicant is seeking and how his goals fit with what the therapist has to offer. The process of exploration must not only be oriented to the applicant and his concerns but to the reciprocal aspects of the applicant-therapist relationship. In that respect, exploration should focus on (and a decision made about) whether or not applicant and therapist can work together within a mode(s) of therapy at which the worker is competent and within which therapeutic goals may have a chance to be realized. These contractual aspects of exploration are always part of the beginning phase in ego-oriented therapy although they may be renegotiated during the middle phase. Because they involve the applicant in decisions that affect his life and well-being, within a relationship that recognizes his suffering yet respects his autonomy, this aspect of exploration may well exercise ego functions and contribute to structuralizing. In other words, exploration in the hands of a skilled and empathic clinical social worker may be therapeutic in and of itself even when the helping process terminates in the beginning phase.

The following initial interview illustrates some of the ideas which we have been discussing. The applicant, a 21-year-old woman who was six months pregnant, had called the agency to request maternity home placement and to talk with someone about the personal and family conflicts which had occurred as a result of the pregnancy.

Ann arrived on time for her appointment. She is an attractive young woman with long red hair and a fair complexion. She seemed relieved to see me.

I told Ann that she could enter the maternity home six weeks before she was due and asked how that would be for her. She hesitated a moment but said it would be fine. She was concerned that they might still need her at work, but realized she will probably want to quit around that time anyway. Her supervisor told her it was up to her when she left; she could stay as long as she wanted. Ann explained that they think she is married. She said it's a good job because it's not too tiring. There aren't a lot of demands on her and she can rest. She hasn't been sick but the other day she really felt weak.

I asked Ann how life was for her. She told me not too well. She's getting pressure from her parents and Ed's parents. It's been a little better lately, but the pressure is still there.

She went on to talk about her mother. When mother became aware of the pregnancy, she insisted that Ann move out of her apartment to get away from her friends. Ann said this with some resentment. Her mother has tried to take over too much, in Ann's opinion. When they talk on the phone now, it almost always turns out to be upsetting. Ann feels this is her (Ann's) problem. "If they had let us get married when we had planned to, this wouldn't have happened." Her mother wants to know exactly what she's eating, but no matter what Ann tells her, mother says, "I know you're not eating properly." Ann tries to ask her mother questions about pregnancy, but mother told her she can't remember her own pregnancies.

After acknowledging the tensions between them, I asked Ann how she and mother had got along in the past. She said they were never very close. Ann had a governess when she was small. Her mother had her own activities; her father traveled quite a bit, and her brother and sister were quite a bit older than she. Ann was expected to behave in a certain way, and from what I can gather, she conformed to the parents' expectations.

Ann said that her parents never took her seriously. She told me of one occasion about a year ago when she tried to talk to them and they accused her of being drunk. "I had to be drunk because I was trying to be serious; I hadn't even had a drink; I didn't even drink at all then, not that I do much now."

Ann said that her father always had to travel a lot, and she never was close to him. She felt closer to her mother, although that relationship was not very comfortable. Apparently, Father has a good position and they are quite well off financially, but Ann feels he never paid much attention to her mother's and Ann's other needs. She offered an example: When Ann learned of her pregnancy, she wanted to tell her parents, but she didn't want to do so over the phone. She called her brother and told him about it, and he agreed that she should tell them in person. Ann called her father's office and spoke with his secretary who informed her that he was going to be out of town later in the week. He returned the call and asked Ann what the problem was, and couldn't they discuss it on the phone as he was going to be quite busy. "In other words, he didn't have time to fit me in." This made Ann angry. Father talked to her brother, who told father that he and mother should see Ann as it was rather important.

When Ann did tell them, she said the language that her father used was really bad. "He complains about the language Ed's mother uses, but you should have heard what he said when I told him! My mother didn't say much, but did accuse me of doing it to hurt her."

Ann began to talk of a maternal aunt. She explained that she had gone to the aunt's home for a weekend after telling her parents, and was "dying to tell her; I dropped hints all over the place, and she finally figured it out." My mother called me later and said, "well, I hope you're satisfied now." Ann is very close to this aunt. There apparently is some jealousy between her mother and her aunt. Ann's mother made some remark about Ann's telling the aunt to the effect that Ann was treating the aunt as if she were her mother.

We talked about these conflicts and then I asked Ann about Ed's mother, since she is another source of pressure. Ann started dating Ed when they were freshmen in college. During that summer, she was going to a wedding near Ed's hometown, and they planned to get together while she was there. A few days before the weekend, Ann wrote Ed a letter explaining when she would arrive. His mother opened and read the letter. Although Ann says there was nothing in the letter, his mother found something "between the lines" and was not in favor of her visit. She told Ed she didn't want Ann to stay with them. Ann said she arrived unaware of how his mother felt. She assumed they were expecting her. When she met his mother, Ann was not well received, and was told by mother that she didn't want Ann staying in her house. Ed's father, who is a very large man and of whom Ann says she is afraid, told Ed to do what his mother said. Ann explained that when Ed's mother is upset with him, she won't have sexual relations with her husband, who then tries to make Ed do what his mother wants. When Ed left for work, Ann went with him and did not return to the house. Ann views Ed's mother as a very disturbed person who is overly protective and attached to Ed.

Ed's mother has been very unreasonable and embarrassing to him at other times. Ed can't keep a roommate because his mother visits and "goes on one of her rampages." She has also been in contact with the school, trying to keep Ed and Ann apart.

Ed's mother also called Ann's parents on a couple of occasions, "collect," to talk with them about the situation. Her parents feel that she is crude, but as Ann said before, "my father used worse language when he found out I was pregnant." Ed's mother upsets Ann's mother when she calls, who then calls Ann. She has asked her parents not to accept calls from Ed's mother, and doesn't feel that the two sets of parents are honest with each other. She also dislikes the idea of their discussing the situation among themselves and not considering how she and Ed feel.

As Ann talked, she expressed concern that she was too cold and removed from the baby, that she didn't have any maternal feelings but said, "that's the only way I can handle it with all this going on around me." She expressed much guilt about feeling this way and connected it with her mother's insistence that she surrender the baby for adoption. I tried to reassure her that what she did was her decision, and no one else could make it for her. Ann says she knows that but "How do you politely tell your parents to go to hell?"

I commented on how upset she seemed. She replied by saying that all these things make her very angry, and she has no one on whom to vent all this hostility. She apologized to me for just coming in and getting all this anger out. I assured her that it was better to get her feelings out and to try to understand them. I was there to help her do that. She said, "I'll just save it up and come in and yell at you for an hour every week." She is experiencing a great deal of frustration, as evidenced by her whole manner; however, she can't be angry in a direct way at the people who make her angry.

Ann asked me if there was anything she hadn't brought up that she should bring up, since I should know what to discuss. I asked about Ed. She told me they had planned to get married at one point and that they had a date set. For some reason they didn't. They are still planning marriage but have no specific date. She had been seeing him frequently because he lives close to her. He doesn't want her to give up the baby. She has decided it's best if they don't see each other for a while, and hasn't seen him in about two weeks. It has taken a lot of pressure off her. She isn't now pressured as much by Ed or his mother, and it has appeased her parents to a certain extent. They have been better about the whole thing since she has stopped seeing him.

She told me about another boy whom she dated casually for a while. She felt funny about seeing him after she found out she was pregnant and kept putting him off. She finally decided she had better just tell him. She found this very difficult but finally did. He asked if she wanted him "to do anything about it"? She told him no, of course not, but he told her if she ever needed any help at any time to call him. She seemed relieved to have received support from him although she has never considered abortion as a solution.

Ann also expressed some concern about not telling friends. She has told a few people but most of her friends at school think she is home having an operation since she did not enroll this semester. She isn't concerned that they know she is pregnant because she feels if they are really her friends it won't make any difference, and if they aren't, "I don't care." Yet, she is concerned about not telling them the truth. She is also concerned that when she goes back to school they will find out that she lied to them.

We were at the end of the hour, so I arranged with Ann for another appointment. As she got up to leave, Ann remarked, "You know you're very good at your job. You just sit there and go uh-huh, uh-huh, and I go on and on." As we were walking to the door she said, "Well, now I'll go out and run in front of a car." I said, "I don't really think that'll be a solution, do you?" She answered, "I don't know, have you ever been pregnant?"

In this interview, the manifest or content aspects of exploration are quite clear. The initial request for help centered on two conflicts: maternal home placement and emotional upset, particularly with mother, as a consequence of the pregnancy. As the interview unfolds, it becomes increasingly clear that the troubled relationship between mother and daughter has a long history; the conflict between them is now more acute as a result of the pregnancy which, for mother, seems to be a catalyst of unresolved maternal guilt and for daughter a behavioral expression of her resentment toward mother as well as a way of dealing with her poor sense of self. As the therapist permits the applicant to express her feelings, Ann talks of her anger as deriving from a sense of having been cheated or deprived of mother's love and having never felt recognized or taken seriously by her parents. She experienced herself as always coming second to mother's other interests and father's career. We thus begin to see, although obscurely, the interaction of intrapersonal and interpersonal conflict through the process of horizontal and vertical exploration and how this young woman's current pain is part of a long-standing pattern of troubled family relationships.

We need not dwell further on the manifest aspects of this interview. My intent in discussing exploration is to identify its major dimensions and how exploratory skills fit into the helping process as a whole. I have not focused on techniques of exploration nor its content aspects in the beginning phase. For the reader who is interested in these topics, the references cited earlier in this chapter may be helpful. We will discuss the meaning of the content in relation to the process of the interview and the initial evaluation.

One of the striking aspects of this interview is how little the therapist talked and how much the applicant did. One may assume that the cathartic quality of the interview was related to the volume of pent-up feelings which the client stored in her preconscious internal world. While that inference may be accurate, it does not answer the question of why Ann responded as she did in this initial contact with *this* clinical social worker. To address that question, we must look beyond the current situation and examine the meaning of this interview within the applicant's vertical and horizontal life experiences.

To the therapist's neutral opening intervention of how life was for Ann, she responds immediately by complaining about her mother. The essence of her communication to the therapist is that mother has pushed her around, robbed her of what little autonomy she felt that she possessed and had no trust in Ann's capacity to make decisions for herself as a 21-year-old adult. We may ask why, of all topics, the client chose (albeit unconsciously) to begin this new relationship with this specific conflict. A tenable hypothesis is that she is not only acutely troubled about the relationship with mother but that she is also anxious about the new relationship with a stranger, who is also a woman with potential power over her. In a sense, the initial communication is an effort to test the power and control structure of this new relationship to see how the social worker will respond: Will she respond like mother or father, or will she respect my sense of autonomy? Will the therapist care enough to listen to me? It seems to me that initial exploratory interviews are inevitably characterized by this type of agenda although its manifest form will vary depending on the pain of the applicant and her association to the unknown stranger. We all deal with unknowns by attempting to introduce structure into the interpersonal vacuum. That structure will be related to the state of anxiety about applying for help and to the initial nature of one's internal representations of the therapist. Because the therapist is a neutral object not yet valued with goodness or badness, a non-structured other, the applicant will respond by attempting to structure the relationship with the only resources then available, object representations of significant figures who are inextricably tied up with the nuclear conflict with which the person requests help.

The response of the clinical social worker is critical to subsequent involvement of the applicant in the exploratory process. In this case, the therapist "read" the message accurately and permitted the client to share her conflict without introducing contaminating structure. She listened and by listening heard the need of the applicant to maintain a sense of control during the interview. Had the worker not connected with the underlying representation and responded in a more controlling way, the applicant may have responded as she had to mother and father by passive-aggressive manipulation or by acting out her anger. Because the perception of the worker within the mind of this young woman could not, at that point, be fully differentiated from fragments of past object representations, her only ego resource for defending against the situation would be by way of internalized patterns of avoidance and flight.

These observations raise the issue of the importance of empathic neutrality within a differentiated and real relationship in the initial exploratory interview. The welcoming acceptance of empathic connectedness and the nonjudgmental neutrality of the therapist are critical qualities in operationalizing exploratory functions within the interview. If the helping process parallels the internalization process, as I believe it does, the therapist needs to communicate those qualities that are instrumental to lower level process; that is, the therapist can create a holding environment within which she is empathically connected to the pain of the applicant while remaining a separate object of emotional support. Although realness will be shaped by individual styles among therapists, an understanding of the needs of the applicant should determine interventive behavior and not the idiosyncracies of therapists.

To temper style to the needs of the applicant is an important function of evaluation. Evaluative understanding informs therapeutic intervention so that use of self, although individual, may become responsive to the needs of the applicant and later the client. The social worker in this case was a naturally warm and empathic woman who had a knack for communicating those qualities without saying a word. Clients sensed her connectedness and responded to her much like Ann did. She had less problem with the empathic aspects of clinical work than she did with those aspects concerned with setting limits and maintaining boundaries with the client which involve a different, yet equally important, use of self in the exploratory process. Being with the applicant was less conflictual than helping her explore conflictual aspects of life, particularly her role in perpetuating the child-like relationship with her parents. Too much unconditional support and empathic connectedness with Ann may have reinforced her need to find and to hold on to the good mother of whom she felt deprived. Given the natural qualities of this therapist, that dynamic was a potential liability in the therapist-client relationship. Any potential to play out these unfinished aspects of development in the transference-countertransference were neutralized by an evaluative understanding of the therapeutic dynamics, which helped to clarify the structural state of this young woman vis-à-vis the social worker.

For the work of exploration to go forward, Ann needed to know that the good mother representation of the therapist would be there for her. Yet, the good mother, who created a holding environment within the parameters of the interview, could also help her face realities that were painful: would she keep or surrender the baby for adoption? Would she marry or sever her relationship with Ed? Would she become an adult daughter of her mother or remain enmeshed in a childlike relationship? Would she be able to exercise autonomy appropriate to her age and developmental level or would she continue to swallow her anger and differences from others, conform to their expectations out of object anxiety, and act out her frustrations in passive-aggressive ways? All these questions become foci of the exploratory process and required confrontation within the therapeutic relationship before they could become part of the contractual agenda of ongoing therapy.

This latter point raises an important dimension of exploration, which is the use of techniques such as confrontation and interpretation, particularly in the beginning phase. We will talk further about these techniques in the following chapter, but it seems important to comment on their use in the exploratory process of the beginning phase. We have already clarified exploration as supportive, but it also may become confrontive and interpretive, confrontive in the sense that exploration informed by evaluative understanding may lead to a therapeutic contract in which the applicant and therapist face matters that will become the objects of change efforts in the ongoing relationship of therapy. Unless therapy is purely a sustaining process oriented to the support and reinforcement of the status quo, it inevitably involves change, which means that the client must confront an aspect of self, or his self in interpersonal encounters, which he wishes to change. Those aspects of beginnings, which are the basis of therapeutic contracts, are among the most critical dynamics of that phase, yet ones that are most often avoided or neglected in our human desire to be helpful.

As Smalley has said, beginnings need to be tolerated, if not embraced, which means that a fundamental part of the therapist's role is "to stay with the beginning and let it be a beginning." In that process, some pulling together and formulation of the nuclear conflicts must be made upon which client and therapist will work together. The level of that interpretive work may be essentially conceptual or cognitive at that point. The interpretive work of exploration will be primarily in the interest of forming a supportive alliance within a goal-oriented relationship. This initial interpretive work may include a significant teaching component. The sharing of accurate and timely information at a cognitive level is not only a means of giving substance to the contract but may also have significant positive value as a resource in promoting integration and consolidation of ego structures and in compensating for developmental lesions. Indeed, cognitively-oriented interpretations in planned short-term intervention have become highly instrumental to goals in that mode of therapy. They may be of comparable value in open-ended therapy.

EVALUATION

Focused exploration is to evaluation what evaluation is to purposeful responsiveness. Taken as a whole, these three aspects of clinical work throughout the beginning, middle and end of the helping process refer to the use of self. Evaluation lends focus to exploration and purpose to responsiveness. Dynamic theory from ego psychology enables the worker to hear the underlying patterns and themes in the horizontal and vertical dimension of the client's life. Evaluative understanding suggests areas that need further exploration and sensitizes the therapist to the client's capacity and readiness to explore those areas so that her interventions are respectful of the integrity of the client's sense of autonomy and not intrusive of his defensive or adaptive boundaries. In brief, evaluation offers substantive understanding and empathic discipline to the therapist in beginning where the client is and staying with him throughout the helping process. Evaluation as understanding is a pivotal skill in the helping relationship.

Evaluation is a thinking process inherently linked with exploration and responsiveness. In that sense, evaluation refers to inferential hypotheses related to the meaning of physical, psychological and sociocultural dimensions of the client's life which the therapist formulates in her own mind. That notion of evaluation, commonly referred to as diagnosis, has a long history in social work theory. As far back as 1940, Hamilton observed that:

...the drawing of purposive inferences begins with the first interviews and observations and continues throughout the case...No interpretation of the living human event can be final, no diagnosis can be complete (Hamilton, 1940, 139)

The evaluative process begins as soon as we make any inference or raise any question about our understanding of the meaning of the other's behavior (verbal, nonverbal or experiential). These hunches, intuitions, spontaneous reactions and impressions are of value when accepted for what they are. They are hypotheses which must be assessed against potential countertransference responses to the client. They also need to be weighed against subsequent data about the client that emerge as exploration unfolds. The validity of our working hypotheses will be confirmed in the patterns and repetitive themes that become increasingly visible as the client becomes progressively able to be more open in sharing aspects of his life with us.

We have already utilized evaluation as process in discussing the initial interview with Ann. From that discussion, one can see the inductive character of the evaluative process, which is cumulative; evaluation may also be conceptualized in an organized statement of our understanding of the applicant or client at any point in the helping process. That type of evaluation is always a tentative or incomplete product which represents a synthesis of our understanding of the client and his conflicts.

The Blancks have argued that diagnosis, or what I prefer to call evaluation, should be based on an "appraisal of the structure of the ego" (Blancks, 1974, 92). Because structure may change as a result of therapy (as well as a result of extra therapeutic life experiences), evaluation is an evolving, conceptual understanding and remains an inherent part of the helping process from beginning to end. The organization of this understanding into a written statement is valuable to the therapeutic process early in the life of the applicant-therapist relationship and periodically after that time. In that respect, we agree with the thinking of Horner, who suggests that a "working hypothesis" of the therapist's understanding of the applicant be formulated by the end of the first session (Horner, 1979, 289). Of course, the early evaluation may raise more questions than it answers but that is the value of therapeutic hypotheses. They offer direction for future exploration and help the therapist to temper her intervention so that the therapeutic relationship may become an opportunity for enhancing structuralizing rather than a repetition or replication of conflictual relationships from which ego impairment has resulted. As the Blancks suggest, "the therapeutic climate must not repeat the pathogenic one" (Blancks, 1974,

104). Empathic understanding integrated with differential evaluation is the most valuable resource available for protecting the potential of the therapeutic relationship to promote a higher level of structuralization and to heal, at least partially, developmental lesions.

In contemporary theory-building efforts related to understanding clients through an ego-oriented framework, we are indebted to the diagnostic work of several people, especially Horner and the Blancks. Horner's approach to what she calls "assessment is a way of evaluating the extent to which there is a cohesive, reality-related, object-related self-structure and to what degree and in what manner these may be compromised" (Horner, 1979, 292). She suggests several areas in the form of questions that ask to be explored in order to formulate a "working hypothesis" about the patient. These areas include:

—the quality of attachment(s)
—the cohesiveness of the self-representation
—the quality of object representation(s)
—the level of differentiation of self
—the nature of the core, false and grandiose self
—the nature of the idealized self and the superego
—preoedipal and oedipal issues
—the state of other ego functions such as synthesis, autonomy, integration, thought, reality testing and defense

She also suggests several areas to be included in exploration so as to provide data to assess these areas. In particular, she identifies the importance of exploring the presenting problem, previous treatment, family processes, peer relationships, school and work history and reactions to beginning therapy (Horner, 1979, 292-302).

The Blancks introduce the concept of ego as "organizing process," a coherent coalescence of functions; they hypothesize that dysfunctional structures result "wherever the organizing process has begun to veer in a deviant direction" (Blancks, 1979, 65). They propose a developmental model of diagnosis

> with special stress upon the importance of the rapprochement crisis in determining whether development will proceed beyond it relatively normally or with organizational malformations, or whether development will be so impeded by subphase inadequacy that fixation in severe borderline pathology precludes neurotic formation (Blancks, 1979, 67-68).

To evaluate the developmental state and resulting structural impairment(s) in organization, the Blancks utilize an analagous "fulcrum" about which progressive and regressive struggles may be understood.

Rapprochement, as a fulcrum, is understood as a nodal phase within which

> higher levels of development bring about a turn inward, that is to say, when internalization and ego organization normally reach relatively stable levels which will continue in their onward progress but will no longer be so vulnerable to regressions to lower levels of the totality of organization (Blancks, 1979, 73).

They suggest that several variables are to be evaluated along a developmental continuum in the ongoing process of therapy in order to develop a more holistic diagnostic picture of the patient. Among those variables they include primary to secondary process thought, undifferentiated self-object to differentiated self with gender identity, organismic distress to signal anxiety, simple affect to full affective repertory, ambitendency to ambivalence, splitting of self and object images to whole representations, and replication of primary experiences with objects to capacity for transference (Blancks, 1979, 73-86). The organizational state of the ego, gradually revealed and understood within the process of therapy, is evaluated along a continuum from prestructure to structure with the rapprochement subphase of separation-individuation being a critical period.

In the model of evaluation which was outlined in the preceding chapter, the structural aspects of the ego require understanding in terms of the intactness to impairment of defensive, executive and adaptive subsystems. Impairment in any function within these subsystems may result in disequilibrium and conflict. This structural assessment is made by understanding the foci of current conflict and by exploration of the nature of current relationships, including the relationship with the therapist.

To more fully appreciate the nature of these conflict(s), exploration of the quality of internalization processes leading to internal structures is necessary but not at the expense of jeopardizing the building of a therapeutic alliance or of taxing the client beyond his current adaptive and defensive capacities, a principle which is well established in the Blancks' and Horner's models. A working hypothesis or diagnostic conceptualization of the level of ego functioning is formulated. That hypothesis reflects the therapist's thinking about the state of structuralization of the client's defensive, executive and adaptive subsystems and the level of intactness to impairment in ego functions. The following table summarizes the more salient characteristics of levels of impairment in ego functions.

Impairment may be mild, moderate or severe and have a contained effect on functions or a more pervasive effect on functioning in general and, as a consequence, on one's total sense of self. In clinical diagnostic terms, impairment at a neurotic level will usually be of a moderate nature and have a more sectoral effect on functions and on functioning in roles and relationships. That is, there will not be a complete shutdown of intrapersonal functioning or extensive withdrawal from involvement in or gross distortions about interpersonal relationships. Impairment at a mid-range level may be moderate to severe but more likely toward the severe end of the continuum. Conflictual impairment at that borderline level may be limited (i.e., contained) to specific relationships but will more likely affect intrapersonal and interpersonal functioning in a pervasive way. Impairment at a psychotic level, on the other hand, will almost inevitably have a severe and pervasive effect on the person, intrapersonally and interpersonally, particularly in its acute state. For a more detailed and refined presentation of characteristics by clinical diagnosis, the reader is referred to the *Diagnostic and Statistical Manual of Mental Disorders, DSM III.* Also, see Mac-Kinnon and Michels, *The Psychiatric Interview in Clinical Practice,* both of which are included in the references at the end of this chapter.

When viewed along an evaluative continuum from intactness to impairment in ego functioning, the neurosis would be found at one end and the psychosis at the other end. Distinctions between these two structural states tend to be more polarized than mid-range impairments. In contrast to the psychosis, neurotic structures reflect a relatively intact level of ego development. Moderate impairment associated with a neurotic level of organization is usually circumscribed to specific roles and relationships to which feelings and thoughts from previous conflicted relationships are transferred. Functions of cognitive mastery and reality testing are generally intact. Superego anxiety signals upper level defenses which protect the ego from affective guilt. Ambivalence, rather than polarization of affect, characterizes impairment. With the integration of self and object representations under the dominance of the self representation, the person tends to view himself and others in terms of cognitive and affective degrees of goodness and badness rather than as completely good or bad. The neurotically impaired person is generally capable of accepting responsibility for his actions and, in fact, is often plagued with a heightened sense of guilt for those thoughts, feelings and actions that may be incongruent with his ego ideal. In contrast, the psychotically impaired person experiences a general shutdown in ego functions. The ego may be overwhelmed with primary process thinking because of the failure of repression and the unavailability of higher levels of defense. Annihi-

Table 2 Ego Functions By Level of Impairment

Level of Impairment	Defense	Cognitive Mastery	Reality Testing	Emotional Sensitivity	Object Relations	Adaptation
Moderate	Ego and Superego Anxiety signals upper level defenses to avoid unpleasant affect; Flexibility in using defensive modes; Repression intact	Generally unimpaired; Level of intellectual functioning contingent primarily on constitutional givens and environmental opportunities	Unimpaired except for mild affective distortions of reality	Consolidation of sense of esteem for self permits empathic connectedness with object world although narcissistic needs may be conflictual in specific relationships	Impairment circumscribed to specific relationships to which feelings and thoughts from previous relationships may be transferred; Integration of object with self representations under dominance of the self representation	Roles and relationships are generally reality oriented and task centered; Flexible capacity to relate in symmetrical and complementary ways within relationships may be impaired with some people
Moderate to Severe	Object anxiety triggers fight-flight reac-	No gross impairment except in stressful situa-	Generally unimpaired; Contact with reality	Narcissistic needs overpower efforts	Relative differentiation of self and object	Task achievement may compensate for impair-

tions; Repression may break down in very stressful situations; Rigidity of defensive modes	tions which tax all functions; Cognitive achievements may compensate for impairment in other functions, particularly object relations	may deteriorate significantly in stressful situations	to become empathic with others; A laborious struggle to experience self as worthy of and separate from others	representations without integration; Relationships may become enmeshed or detached and associated with polarized feelings of good or bad	ment in object relatedness as long as relationship is not too symmetrical or demanding of emotional closeness; Relationships tend to be rigidly complementary to neutralize anxiety about separateness
Severe Repression fails; Ego is overwhelmed with primary process material; General breakdown of defensive system	Gross impairment in rational and logical thinking	Pervasive retreat from reality; Inability to differentiate inner chaos from outer reality	Minimal to no capacity for experiencing empathy toward others	Pervasive impairment in maintaining continuity of self in human relationships because of inability to differentiate self and object representations	Adaptive boundary grossly impaired; Withdrawal into fantasy from perception of real world as a dangerous place

lation anxiety triggers withdrawal from the real world while severe impairment in reality testing contributes to an inability to differentiate self from object representations and, as a consequence, to maintain adaptive boundaries with the external world.

Along the continuum are the mid-range impairments that are represented in the borderline, character and narcissistic disorders. There is considerable ambiguity in the professional literature in distinguishing among these structural states. The problem of reliability is most perplexing when categorical diagnoses are made on the basis of behavioral symptoms observed or reported in one or two interviews. This problem, particularly at the mid-range levels of impairment, is primarily a matter of qualitative interpretation which is contingent upon observations of the client's behavior interacting with the clinician's theoretical orientation. Since this model values the process of developing an understanding of the client within an empathic relationship more than categorical diagnosis, conceptual categorization is not a task to be pursued for its own sake but a potential outcome of evaluation. In other words, categorization is secondary to empathic understanding and is viewed as a conceptual abbreviation for evaluative judgments, which may remain inconclusive for some time.

Nevertheless, there are some structural characteristics that help to differentiate among mid-range states of impairment. People with narcissistic impairments tend to have developed a cohesive self-representation prematurely either because of deprivation of libidinal supplies or because of overindulgence of supplies which persist beyond developmentally appropriate levels. In either situation, there is a failure in empathic connectedness and mutuality of role reciprocity with significant others, a loss compensated by the persistence of a grandiose and omnipotent sense of self which continues to occupy "the center of the psychological stage" (Kohut, 1977, 74). As with other mid-range states, the narcissistically impaired individual experiences a strong fear of personal vulnerability and remains emotionally detached from significant others, whom he views as objects to satisfy his needs. He acts out of object anxiety since a benign superego, which would humanize objects, has not evolved sufficiently enough as an integral psychic structure. His relationships tend to be rigidly complementary and he is severely threatened by symmetrical involvements that may lead to sustained and egalitarian relations with others. Because of his self-centered mode of existence, there is little capacity for empathy except as a means of satisfying his own needs. Despite these features, the person suffering from narcissistic impairment may function remarkably well in specific social roles as long as he believes that he remains in control of the relationship(s) and as long as interpersonal feedback reinforces his fragile self-esteem.

There is considerable confusion about borderline and character disordered states. It seems almost as though the borderline concept has eclipsed the use of the character disorder concept in recent years. Differences between the two states may have more to do with superego aspects of ego structuralization and with prevailing contextual aspects of development that may be reinforcing of ego syntonic modes of defense. As with the narcissistic states, the defensive system of the borderline and characterologically impaired client is triggered by object anxiety which arrests the integrative process of forming whole self and object representations. Consequently, inner representations remain split between good and bad images. The primitive sense of shame and fear of consequences grounded in primary anxieties may inhibit the borderline person from acting on his projections, which is not necessarily the case with the character-disordered person. The client who suffers from borderline impairment tends to be in conflict internally as a battle rages between differentiated self and object representations while the client with a character disorder may be less inhibited in externalizing his conflicts, which may be reinforced, overtly and covertly, by the social environment. Even among sociopathic clients, however, there may be a significant self-defeating component to behavioral patterns which reflect a rudimentary yet available superego structure.

Although these dynamics may clarify some important variations within the moderate to severe level of ego impairment, they are by no means definitive and are often most difficult to make in actual practice. Frequently, these dynamics will cut across specific diagnostic boundaries and be manifested, as well, among clients at higher developmental levels. As already indicated, the primary raison d'être of evaluation is empathic understanding, not categorical classification. Definitive diagnosis, therefore, remains a secondary rather than primary objective of the evaluative process.

The following clinical summaries may help to clarify these points. Four examples are presented which illustrate impairment along the continuum from moderate to severe levels.

Maria, a 16-year-old adolescent of Hispanic background, was referred to the clinic by a physician affiliated with an adolescent medical clinic after an extensive physical examination had revealed no organic reasons for chronic headaches and bouts of crying. She had been seen at the same clinic two years before for heart palpitations shortly after the family immigrated to the United States so that they might be close to mother's relatives. Maria is the second oldest child with an older sister who attends college and younger brother and sister who live at home. Because of inability to secure employment, the father had moved to another area a few months before the referral. If his new job works out the family plans to rejoin the father in six months when the children will have completed the current school year.

Maria, who is of light black complexion, presented as a quiet, composed young woman who was troubled by "nerves" which she attributed to several factors. She was having difficulty in adjusting to school and to the community, where she felt isolated and ignored in contrast to her memories of her "real" home (i.e., former), where she had many friends. She also missed her father, whom she described as a warm and supportive person in contrast to mother, whom she depicted as a strict and rigid disciplinarian. To Maria, mother had always been that way but had become more strict after the father had left to secure employment in another state. Maria felt unsure about the future since there had been talk between her parents of mother staying with the older sister until she finished college and the younger children including Maria going to live with father at the end of the school year. In contrast, she recalled the stability and cohesiveness of her family before immigrating to this country and mentioned, specifically, that father was a buffer between mother and the children. From her description he was a strong figure in the family whom the children and mother looked to for support and direction.

As she talked about her concerns during the first two interviews, Maria seemed embarrassed and uncomfortable. She spoke with her eyes downcast and sat tensely in the chair. In contrast to typical teenage attire, she dressed in a very sophisticated, adult-like manner. Although she attributed her inability to make friends here as a result of her poor fluency in English, Maria had no difficulties in communicating to the therapist; in fact, her language was clear and articulate. She missed friends at home and wanted to make new friends but felt that people should come to her since she was a stranger in town.

Maria talked about the loss of father, whom she missed even more than her former community and friends. He now maintains regular contact with the family via telephone. She felt that she experienced more conflict about the separation than her siblings or her mother; they did not say much about how they felt. Although Maria expressed no anger at the father for being away, she expressed considerable hostility towards mother, whom Maria viewed as an infantilizing figure. To Maria, mother was trying to keep her a child and refused to let her become an adult. She felt that "everything would be alright" if her father was at home. Her grief at losing father and the anger at mother's lack of trust in her prevented Maria from having much empathy for mother's feelings although she was able to acknowledge that mother was also going through a difficult time. She thought that the parents had a "good marriage" and attributed mother's strictness to her cultural background, particularly the influence of the maternal grandmother, who was very protective of her children.

Maria engaged readily in the therapeutic relationship, which became a vehicle for exploring and neutralizing grief associated with father's absence. Although some remnants of splitting was evident (mother was all bad and father all good), this defense was not ingrained in an ego syntonic way into her character structure and was modified considerably as she verbalized her feelings about the loss of father and as she took initiatives to make friends in her community. Racism, which was a component in Maria's social isolation, did not prevent her from forming new friendships with peers who were mostly white.

Maria was suffering from the loss of a critical libidinal figure in her life, her father. Her symptoms were reflective of her grief and sadness at trying to adapt to disruption in a cohesive family group and a supportive social environment which she had known most of her young life. No significant pathology seemed to have pervaded her primary relationships prior to these losses. The intervention of choice was supportively and expressively oriented with a therapist who respected her autonomous strivings and adaptive strengths and who recognized the importance of collateral relationships within her sociocultural background. The therapist encouraged Maria's own desire to risk new initiatives in reaching out to peers while providing her with an accepting and structured atmosphere for verbalizing the underlying sadness and resentment toward important figures whom she held responsible for her situation. Verbal expression of her grief with an empathic therapist, who was attuned to her psychological suffering as a result of the loss of father and familiar sociocultural supports, freed up adaptive potentials to form new social relationships in what had been a strange and threatening environment. Mother was also involved in treatment; her need to shelter Maria appeared to transcend cultural traditions, and she was able to use therapy as a way of loosening her tight grip on Maria, which helped to neutralize intense conflict in their relationship.

Mr. and Mrs. Smith, a 24-year-old couple, applied for marriage counseling at the initiative of Mrs. Smith. She complained of interference by her in-laws, who were supporting Mr. Smith while he completed his college education. She was troubled by her husband's inability to settle down, finish school and become independent of his parents. Although feeling very angry with her husband about his inability to stand up to his parents, Mrs. Smith usually kept her feelings to herself and went along with him and his parents. To alleviate their financial dependency on Mr. Smith's parents, Mrs. Smith began to care for children in her home, where she could earn an income while remaining with her infant son. Mr. Smith recognized the difficulty of being dependent on his parents and acknowledged that their efforts to help were excessive. They not only had financed his education but had helped them purchase a house and gave them gifts for the house. Mr. Smith felt indebted to them, however, and did not share his wife's opinion that his parents interfered too much into their life. To him, they were good and well meaning people. His major complaint was directed at his wife's lack of interest and refusal to have regular sexual relations, which had been a source of conflict between them since the birth of their son.

This couple was seen primarily in conjoint interviews with some individual sessions throughout therapy. As they began to talk about their own backgrounds, the reasons for the differences in their relationship with their parents became more apparent. Mr. Smith was the older of two siblings. His sister was about to finish high school and planned to enroll in college. He described a very traditional family life with a mother who never worked outside of the home and a father who had become very successful in his own business. His mother was devoted to her husband and children and clearly played a nurturing and supportive role in the family. Father was very available, interested in his children, and an easy-going individual. Both parents valued a good education for their two children, and it was always assumed that each would go to college. In general, the family seemed to be a very cohesive and comfortable unit although there did appear to be significant and unspoken conflict with separation-individuation as Mr. Smith moved from adolescence to young adulthood.

Mrs. Smith came from a more conflicted family in which father had a violent temper and mother, seemingly the more competent of the two parents, placated her husband and appeared to play him off against the children. As the oldest of three, Mrs. Smith often felt caught between the conflicts of her parents and felt that her mother may have been responsible for much of her parents' marital unhappiness. She feared her father's potential violence although he was never physically abusive to anyone, yet tried to convince herself that he was a good person in spite of his anger. Her mother never got upset and appeared to play a quietly controlling and martyr-like role in the family. Although she remained on pleasant terms with her parents, she felt independent of them and able now to take care of herself in contrast to her husband, whom she saw as inappropriately dependent on his parents and unable to break away from them.

A prime focus of intervention was to support each spouse in becoming aware of his/her individual contribution to the conflicts between them and in accepting responsibility for changing patterns of behavior that perpetuated these conflicts. A supportive-confrontive approach with some reflective interpretive work was employed throughout therapy. Mrs. Smith was quite available psychologically for this level of intervention and moved more rapidly to confront issues than did Mr. Smith, who was more encumbered with guilt about unresolved separation-individuation.

The ego functioning of the Smiths, as with Maria, was at a moderate level of impairment. Unlike Maria, however, the Smiths were encumbered with some chronic separation-individuation issues which intruded into adult functioning and had an adverse effect on the marital relationship. Despite the more overt conflictual relationships in Mrs. Smith's background, she appeared more ready and psychologically available to confront her role in the marital conflict than was Mr. Smith. He had idealized his parents and resented any inference from his wife that might jeopardize his attachment to and involvement with them. In many significant ways, Mrs. Smith represented a continuation of the overindulgent mother who had always been there for him but who had evoked powerful feelings of guilt if he disappointed her. A part of Mrs. Smith complemented his need to be nurtured but she gradually came to resent the psychological price involved which led to increased marital conflict. Her object representations of men were tinged with mistrust and fear. She had significant conflicts in saying no and tended to maintain harmony by going along with what her husband wanted while sacrificing her own needs as her mother had done. As Mrs. Smith became more aware of her underlying fear of losing all that she had gained if she became more open and direct about her feelings, the Smiths went through a prolonged period of upset in their relationship. Gradually, Mr. Smith was able to set more reasonable limits with his parents, which contributed to separateness from them and more meaningful involvement in the marital relationship. After a long period of therapy both appeared to reach a more adult-like level of differentiation from their parental object representations and to accept personal responsibility for working toward a more symmetrical marital relationship.

James, a 20-year-old white man and the second youngest in a family of seven children, was referred to the clinic by a community outreach worker who had suggested that he see someone because he was "depressed." Initially, James denied feeling depressed and described himself as a bored and restless person with a bad temper who was occasionally abusive and assaultive toward others, particularly his siblings. He said that lashing out at others had occurred more frequently over the past four years, which he attributed to frustrations at finding and holding a job. When he worked, James was preoccupied with worries about his (work) performance and also acknowledged difficulties in getting along with people, which he blamed on his bosses and coworkers.

In initial interviews, James slumped in his chair, talked rapidly and communicated by talking concretely about events and behavior. He tended to isolate feelings about conflicts in his life by referring to experiences in a matter of fact way. James has lived his entire life in or near poverty, and his family has been dependent on welfare assistance since he was six years of age. At that time, his father was hospitalized because of a severe neurological impairment as a result of an accident which left him deaf and prone to violent outbursts. The father has remained in a chronic care facility to this day. Mother began to drink heavily after the father's accident and seemed to become a distant and shadowy figure in James' life. In the second interview, he shared a dream, which he had that week, in which he had gone to his mother because he was in some sort of trouble and had been told by her to leave her alone. In response (in the dream) he began pounding on the walls of their apartment, thought that he was going crazy and did not feel real. As he talked about his temper and fights in growing up, the tone of his voice changed as if they were a source of pride for him. In the same sequence he referred to himself as "weird, a loner and a strange person whom no one could understand." Although James had no previous therapy, his mother had been hospitalized several times for alcoholism, and two of his older sisters were hospitalized during adolescence for "nervous breakdowns."

His school experience was conflictual from first grade when he was apparently phobic about separating from his mother. Throughout elementary school, he could not keep up with academic work and was placed in special classes. He became involved in numerous fights with other students and experienced considerable difficulty in getting along with teachers. At age 16 (still in the sixth grade), James left school and has been sporadically employed since that time. He continues to live at home with his mother, a younger brother and an older sister. There has been no contact with father for several years.

His only long-term friendship has been with a neighborhood boy three years younger than he. He has had occasional relationships with girls but has not sustained involvement in any of these relationships beyond a fleeting and superficial level. Although James denied any suicidal ideation or feelings of depression, he described himself as accident-prone, particularly when he was employed, a trait along with his pugnacious manner that had resulted in his being fired from several jobs.

Although James insisted that he came to the clinic only because of the recommendation by the outreach worker whom he respected and did not initially verbalize any other reasons for therapy, he did report by the third interview that he found talking to the therapist helpful; he did not have any ideas why it was helpful. The more he talked about his chaotic family life and his pattern of resorting to defensive flight or fight whenever he became overwhelmed with anxious feelings, especially hostile ones, the more he appeared to experience therapy as an opportunity for dealing with his conflicts rather than as a threat to his tenuous self-esteem and psychic equilibrium. Because of his fragile impulse control and low tolerance for anxiety, therapy focused primarily on here-and-now issues within a relationship that allowed him enough psychological space to maintain a safe distance from the therapist.

James suffered from a moderate to severe impairment. His ego structure appeared to be highly fragmented and his self-esteem was of a helpless and hopeless nature. No doubt, the milieu of poverty within which he was raised, along with his repeated failures at school, contributed to his tenuous psychological state. Although James might be considered to have a character disorder because of his problem with impulse control and a propensity for acting out his angry feelings, he was also quite depressed and acutely sensitive to any sign of rejection, both of which reflected severe narcissistic wounds. His relationship with the therapist, who was a woman close to his age, tended to replicate his idealized fantasy of the good mother; it also had the potential of becoming eroticized as he became involved in ongoing therapy. For these reasons, the therapist structured the relationship by focusing on current issues in his life and by maintaining a careful balance between empathic support and professional distance.

As James gradually experienced the therapist as a real, separate, caring and dependable ally, he was able to initiate discussion of his troubled relationship with his mother, who had become increasingly seductive with him; he was able to talk, for the first time in his life, about father who, he felt, had abandoned him. Staying with him meant respecting his need to focus on concrete behavioral conflicts in his present life until he felt safe enough to share more intimate and powerful emotions associated with his chaotic psychological and social worlds.

Mrs. Ryan, a 26-year-old black woman, was widowed and lived at home with her five-year-old daughter and 58-year-old mother who was also a widow. She was the next to the youngest of four children and the only child still at home with mother. About six months after the birth of her daughter, Mr. Ryan was killed in an accident at work. Shortly after this death, she was hospitalized briefly for an acute psychotic episode. Approximately four months later Mrs. Ryan's father died after a lengthy illness. Since that time she has been troubled with hallucinations about seeing the ghost of her father in the figures of prominent entertainers on television, has heard voices telling her to kill herself and her baby, and has attempted suicide. Because of the severity of her symptoms, Mrs. Ryan has had several admissions to the inpatient unit of the mental health center and has been in continuous therapy for the past three years. Psychotic episodes were associated with stressful changes in her life, especially losses. Her ego functioning has been relatively stable over the past year as a result of the absence of change in her life, bi-weekly therapy with a clinical social worker and the faithful use of anti-psychotic medication which is monitored from month to month by a staff psychiatrist. With the social worker, Mrs. Ryan has talked about her illness as a "problem with hallucinations in which I am unable to tell reality from fantasy." Her goals for therapy were to regain her capacity to function so that she could return to finish her college education and to obtain a part-time job in order to feel more independent and self-sufficient.

Her memories of childhood were happy ones although she tended to idealize father as the perfect parent who held the family together. She reported that she had a good relationship with mother until she (Mrs. Ryan) became "sick." Since that time she has viewed mother as a meddling and intrusive figure who tries to run her life and has stolen her "baby" away from her. She now leads a very lonely and isolated life and has frequently tried to manipulate the therapist into hospitalizing her, her reasons for which are more related to her need for companionship with friends who, she believes, are still hospitalized in the inpatient unit, rather than to severe deterioration in her capacity to function outside of the hospital. For the last 18 months, Mrs. Ryan has functioned without being hospitalized. During that period she has been faithful to the therapeutic contract of twice-weekly 30-minute interviews and taking her medication. When the social worker who had been seeing her for the past two years left the clinic, Mrs. Ryan again requested hospitalization although she did continue to take her medication and to keep her therapy hours.

During initial contacts with the new therapist, Mrs. Ryan expressed some guarded feelings about missing the previous therapist, attributing her departure to anger at Mrs. Ryan for not making enough progress in therapy. She seemed to form an attachment with the new therapist very readily and after the initial interview said that she had forgotten her previous therapist. She related on a need-gratifying level, insisting that she be seen more frequently than twice each week. She complained that she needed more medication and that she was hearing voices again that told her to kill herself. As the therapist was firm about the treatment contract and focused on trying to understand with Mrs. Ryan the meaning of her demands, the client became less agitated and manipulative with the therapist. She expressed a wish that the therapist become a friend or a sister and said that she preferred to be addressed by her first name because "Mrs. makes me feel old." Because of the regressive significance of complying with such a request from this client, the new therapist was firm in addressing her as Mrs. Ryan and in refocusing their interaction on Mrs. Ryan's goal to become more autonomous in managing her life.

As was James, Mrs. Ryan was a moderate to severely impaired individual whose struggles with life revolved primarily around issues of psychological survival rather than in resolving conflictual feelings, which was the focus of interaction with Maria and the Smiths. We do know that the intactness of her ego deteriorated as a consequence of significant losses in her life which exacerbated a latent symbiotic involvement with mother. As therapy unfolded, it became increasingly clear that Mrs. Ryan had always felt overprotected and controlled by mother, which had been neutralized partially when Mrs. Ryan married but which emerged again with the deaths of her husband and father.

We do not know what constitutional predispositions may have been present and how they may have set the stage for prolonged involvement of the symbiotic unit, but we do know that severe impairment of adaptive functions and self-esteem was, at least partially, a consequence of the inability to separate and individuate. Her suicide attempts following the deaths of her husband and father may have been indicative of her hopelessness at ever being able to escape the symbiotic orbit. She had introjected the bad object and had turned her rage on herself. Her reality testing function was impaired severely as a result of fusion between self and object representations which made it impossible to differentiate rage toward others from self-hatred. The intervention of choice was a supportive-protective relationship with a real person who could be empathically attuned to Mrs. Ryan's suffering yet provide enough distance through a reality-oriented use of self so that a fused replication with the therapist as a maternal object was avoided. The use of medication was important as it helped to restore her reality testing capacities and thus made Mrs. Ryan more available psychologically for therapy. Efforts to involve the mother in therapy were not successful.

HISTORICAL AND SOCIOCULTURAL ASPECTS OF EVALUATION

A danger in using dynamic theory is that we may attempt to reduce the evaluative process of understanding structural impairment to a developmental lesion that occurred at a specific point and attribute to that event or relationship a causal significance which may be disproportionate to the complexities of interacting etiological factors. Events that take place within primary relationships in the early formative years are critical to ego structures in subsequent periods of development. Rather than view these primary relationships as isolated happenings, we must see them as the critical beginnings of patterns that may persist unless corrective shifts occur in subsequent relationships. In other words, early experiences should be evaluated within the context of the history of the client's relationship with primary and secondary figures who may perpetuate or offer corrective experiences for impairment in ego development. Rather than assess events, as such, we need to evaluate the meaning of primary and secondary experiences with important figures over time and to evaluate their significance in shaping internal structures.

For example, in the case of Ann, we may initially hypothesize an impairment in object relatedness to mother, the current manifestation of which appears to reflect a long-standing pattern of polarized differentiation between enmeshment and pseudo-separateness in their relationship. There is an estranged involvement between Ann and mother, no doubt exacerbated by the meaning of the pregnancy for each, which suggests a conflict in the rapprochement subphase of separation/individuation. Although data is based on tentative impressions, Ann does not appear to be functioning now at a borderline level and may have compensated for hypothesized deviations in development by relationships with significant others such as her aunt. Perhaps, as well, libidinal supplies in the mother-daughter relationship were more plentiful than she is now able to acknowledge. Clinically, she appears to be more of an acting-out adolescent who is angry with her parents for perceived inadequacies in their empathic relatedness to her, which may be exacerbated by her guilt about the pregnancy. Further exploration of her current thoughts and feelings as well as more detail of earlier experiences would be necessary to clarify the evaluative picture.

The critical notion here is that early developmental experiences lead to internal ego structures which include the shaping of self and object representations that persist, over time, in concert with the responsiveness of significant others. The overly available or unavailable maternal figure of the first rapprochement subphase may continue to be overly available or unavailable as a figure of rapprochement in subsequent phases of development. If she happens to change by becoming more appropriately responsive to the dependent child or adolescent or if compensatory figures become available to neutralize the original loss, the individual may be able to work through some of the important issues associated with this critical developmental process. If not, moderate to severe impairment may result and have a pervasive impact on one's capacity to integrate goodness and badness with self and object representations and to eventually consolidate a nuclear sense of self. These conflicts were clearly apparent in the internal worlds of James and Mrs. Ryan, and to a lesser extent in the Smiths.

As we begin to understand the client in the light of new data that evolves as the result of a deepening therapeutic relationship, evaluation becomes more complete and refined. In that respect, evaluation serves the relationship; relationship never serves evaluation except in those situations where evaluation is the explicit raison d'être of intervention.

Processes of internalization leading to the organization of ego subsystems into a state of relative equilibrium (i.e., structuralization) proceed from an undifferentiated symbiotic-like level with significant other(s) to a consolidated sense of the autonomous self. Since no one emerges from these developmental experiences without at least some remnants of unfinished intrapersonal and interpersonal business, ego structures and a cohesive sense of the nuclear self is impaired in some respects among all people even when developmental experiences have been optimum. The Blancks have observed, for example, "that all sorts of symptoms, even those traditionally regarded as psychotic, are found in normal and neurotic structures as well." (Blancks, 1974, 94). As we have suggested in Chapter Two, that generic quality of the human experience is the basis of empathy which is indispensable to the process of ego-oriented evaluation. We are thus dealing with qualitative differences among people who in their progressive attempts to become autonomous are struggling to escape the narcissistic entitlements to their own egos of powerful, residual, child-centered needs while reaching to become more compassionate, sensitive and accepting adults.

The struggle toward integration and consolidation of ego functions is tempered and shaped by the social environment. Processes of internalization and the configuration of ego systems that result from them need to be understood within the context of the sociocultural milieu. Culture is to a social system what the superego is to the ego. That is, cultural values of a reference group have a tempering effect on the interpersonal relationship of people just as patterns of internalized values shape ego structures. The character of internal structures that result from human relationships will be influenced substantially by the values transmitted through processes of internalization, particularly via identification within the context of primary groups, the most important of which is the family of origin.

Values may be defined as the expectations of desirable or preferable behavior for a particular group. In their more generalized form values, or more precisely, value orientations, represent the pattern of beliefs, which have a powerful yet subtle effect on the nature of human relationships. In their more specific forms, values may be expressed explicitly as norms which regulate or control specific patterns of behavior within and between groups and subgroups. Values have their most powerful effect on the shaping of internal structures during the earliest years of life when the preconceptual ego of the child relies primarily on an assimilative mode of identification rather than an accommodative mode. Capacity for choice modifies considerably as the individual resolves mid and higher levels of internalization, when identification with group expectations becomes progressively more selective. Although the paradigm developed in this monograph for understanding the structural and developmental aspects of the human ego is a generic one in the sense that processes of internalization may be found across ethnic, class, gender and racial lines, the social context will temper the form that each process will take and, as a consequence, the shape of internal structures. The superego dimension of each process may thus be understood as the internalization of values from the reference groups with which the individual identifies.

Several people have contributed to our understanding of the influence on development and on ego functioning of value orientations (Kluckhohn, 1968; Papajohn and Spiegel, 1975; and Pinderhughes, 1979; Gilligan, 1982). Papajohn and Spiegel, as well as Pinderhughes, adopted the system for clarifying value orientations developed by Kluckhohn, who assumed that there were not only ''a limited number of common problems for which all people. . .must find some solution,'' but that the solutions, although variable, were not limitless and could be identified among all societies in both dominant and variant forms (Kluckhohn, 1968). Five problems common to all human groups (including families) were hypothesized together with a range of preferred solutions:

—the intrinsic nature of the human being: evil, good, or a mixture of good and evil;
—the relation of humans to nature: subjugation, harmony or mastery;
—the temporal orientation to life; present or future;
—the preferred mode of human activity: being, being-in-becoming or doing;
—the orientation to human relationships: lineal, collateral or individualistic.

Depending on patterns of thoughts and feelings associated with preferred solutions to these common human problems, various family groups may value specific processes of internalization in different ways. For example, separateness and autonomy may vary in meaning, cognitively and emotionally, and be manifested in different behaviors depending on lineal, collateral or individualistic orientations to human relationships within specific family groups. Since internalization refers primarily to internal, psychological states, one does not have to experience biological or social distance from primary figures to value one's self as separate and relatively autonomous. The meaning of being or becoming an autonomous person will vary, however, depending on the values associated with collaterality and individualism of the family and the modes through which these values are communicated to the person within lower-and mid-level processes of internalization, particularly by way of identification.

Traditionally, the dominant belief system in the United States (as represented in the upwardly mobile middle class) has valued mastery over nature, including human nature, by means of individual achievement especially in relation to a future goal(s). These ''preferred solutions'' may result in individualistic and competitive behavior which tend to become normative for this segment of American society. Other reference groups may value variant solutions to these problems whether or not they share similar social class status. In fact, identifications along ethnic, and religious lines may have as powerful an effect on value orientation as does social class. As Gilligan has pointed out, one's values will also be shaped by gender, particularly in relation to processes of attachment and separation, with men associating danger with connectedness, and women with separateness (Gilligan, 1982).

For example, collaterality and connectedness in Maria's culture was highly valued and their loss, both in relation to the familiar community and father's separation from the family, had a powerful impact on her sense of psychosocial continuity during the separation/individuation challenge of adolescence. Her depression and somatic symptoms reflected the sadness and sense of estrangement associated with the perceived unavailability of familial rapprochement figures and the loss of familiar communal supports. The conflict in differentiation and separateness of Mrs. Ryan from her mother, which became increasingly apparent as therapy unfolded, may have been reinforced by the effects of racism on the mother-daughter relationship. Pinderhughes observes that "overfunctioning" of the black mother may be a consequence of the lack of support and perceived dangers for the child in society. Mother may become a controller and regulator of relationships in order to protect the child, rather than a facilitator of separation/individuation. If, as Bowen suggests, the mother carries within her significantly unresolved issues with her own differentiation, the child may become an object of her projections. With the Ryans, the tragic losses experienced by both mother and Mrs. Ryan led to regressive tugs to reestablish the symbiotic-like mother-child relationship which appeared to be shaped, in part, by socio-cultural forces to which Pinderhughes refers. The cultural context of chronic poverty within which James was raised no doubt contributed to his sense of subjugation and hopelessness. Although we do not know what constitutional factors may have affected his function of cognitive mastery, it became apparent, as the therapist got to know him, that he was somewhat impaired in his ability to think through and to understand even the most mundane issue in daily living. The losses associated with father's severe handicap and mother's subsequent alcoholism created an environment in which he had minimal support for mastery in school and almost no limits on his deviant behavior. As a consequence, the familial and communal environment fed his sense of inferiority and undermined any potential for building self-confidence essential to learning. With the Smiths it appeared that middle-class values of mastery and accomplishment of individual goals actually fueled arrest of separateness and individuation. In the interest of helping their son achieve a college education, a strong value of the parents, they actually fueled prolonged dependency into adulthood. A striking feature of the parenting role in this family was the value placed on gratifying the needs of the children, thus preventing their frustration and resulting conflict. When Mr. Smith reported that he felt no anger toward his parents' intrusiveness, he was telling the therapist of important familial values introjected as part of his object representations (of the parents).

Value orientations with which people identify and subsequently internalize may vary in complex ways between and within groups even when there may be homogeneity on specific attributes such as class, ethnicity, gender or race. To classify people by a single sociocultural trait is as potentially dehumanizing as categorizing them by a single psychological variable. The skill of evaluation is served most adequately by attending to the multidimensional and interacting effects of inner and outer forces that are mediated by the ego rather than relying on stereotypical generalizations formulated from observations of unidimensional attributes, whether the latter be in the psychological structure or in the sociological context. Because we are concerned in evaluation with the individual ways by which external values become internal regulators of ego functioning, it is important to integrate that dimension of the client's life into our empathic understanding of him as a psychosocial being. Discussion of clinical illustrations here and elsewhere in this book have tried to address that concept.

SUMMARY

Evaluative skills play a pivotal role in the helping process. Evaluation as dynamic understanding serves the therapeutic function of focusing intervention on aspects of the client's life, present and past, which encumber his sense of ego autonomy and interfere with adaptation. Dynamic understanding also enables the clinical social worker to become empathically attuned to the developmental state of current functioning, so that her intervention may be responsive to the capacities and readiness of the client to engage in therapeutic work at the optimum level of intensity to promote a progressive move toward ego integration and consolidation. While theory about ego structures and processes of internalization—the vehicles through which structures evolve—is useful for understanding people in general, evaluative hypotheses are best formulated within the context of the client's developmental experiences. Internalized values from these experiences integrate as part of the self as they regulate ego functioning and temper self and object representations in very individualized ways. Finally, evaluation is a dynamic process which evolves as an inherent dimension of the therapeutic relationship. In that new context, evaluative understanding of the client changes as the client changes; evaluative understanding then is a continuous process.

REFERENCES

Blanck, G., and Blanck, R. *Ego Psychology: Theory and Practice.* New York: Columbia University Press, 1974.

———. *Ego Psychology II: Psychoanalytic Developmental Psychology.* New York: Columbia University Press, 1979.

Diagnostic and Statistical Manual of Mental Disorders, Third Edition (DSM III). Washington, D.C.: American Psychiatric Association, 1980.

Edinburg, E., et al. *Clinical Interviewing and Counseling: Principles and Techniques.* New York: Appleton-Century-Crofts, 1975.

Garrett, A. *Interviewing and Counseling: Principles and Techniques.* New York: FSAA, 1942.

Gilligan, C. *In a Different Voice: Psychological Theory and Women's Development.* Cambridge: Harvard University Press, 1982.

Hamilton, G. *Theory and Practice of Social Casework.* New York: Columbia University Press, 1940.

Hollis, F., and Woods, M. *Casework: A Psychosocial Therapy* (3rd Edition). New York: Random House, 1981.

Horner, A. *Object Relations and the Developing Ego in Therapy.* New York: Jason Aronson, 1979.

Kadushin, A. *The Social Work Interview.* New York: Columbia University Press, 1972.

Kluckhohn, F. "Variations in Basic Values of Family Systems," *A Modern Introduction to the Family* (Revised Edition). Edited by N. Bell and E. Vogel. New York: The Free Press, 1968, 319-330.

Kohut, H. *The Restoration of the Self.* New York: International Universities Press, 1977.

MacKinnon, R., and Michels, R. *The Psychiatric Interview in Clinical Practice.* Philadelphia: W. B. Saunders Company, 1971.

Papajohn, J., and Spiegel, J. *Transactions in Families.* San Francisco: Jossey Bass, 1975.

Perlman, H. "Intake and Some Role Considerations," *Social Casework,* April 1960, 171-177.

———. *Social Casework: A Problem-Solving Process,* Chicago: University of Chicago Press, 1957.

Pinderhughes, E., et al. "The Effect of Ethnicity Upon the Psychological Task of Separation-Individuation: A Comparison of Four Ethnic Groups." Paper presented at 56th Annual Meeting of The American Orthopsychiatric Association. Boston, April 1979.

Roberts, R., and Nee, R. *Theories of Social Casework.* Chicago: University of Chicago Press, 1970.

Schubert, M. *Interviewing in Social Work Practice.* New York: Council on Social Work Education, 1971.

8

THERAPEUTIC RESPONSIVENESS

Therapeutic responsiveness refers to the intentional behavior of the therapist toward the client based on her evaluation of the structural resources of the client and her empathic connectedness with him. In a broad sense, exploratory skills may be considered within the perimeter of this definition. However, we are thinking more precisely of those actions that have a therapeutic intent of supporting, confronting or interpreting defensive, executive or adaptive functions of the client. Exploratory interventions are an inherent aspect of these intentional actions on the part of the therapist since exploration provides access to data which, by way of evaluative thinking, orients therapeutic responsiveness. When we talk of interventions whose content is oriented toward behavioral change or maintenance of adaptive strengths, we are referring to purposive options which the therapist may exercise in the interests of promoting integration and/or consolidation of ego functioning. These options are always preceded by exploration of the affective and cognitive meanings associated with the client's past, present or anticipated behavior. Thus, clinical interventions may be understood as:

—exploratory
—exploratory→supportive
—exploratory→supportive→confrontive
—exploratory→supportive→confrontive→interpretive

Regardless of how we may intervene, our generic orientation is to respond to the client with the intent of promoting his adaptive thrust toward ego autonomy. In that respect, there is a sequence to clinical intervention such that one may be supportive without being confrontive
or interpretive but one may not be effective in a confrontive or interpretive sense without first having developed a supportive alliance
with the client. Clinical work, like human development, is contingent
upon an empathic relationship oriented toward building up ego functioning and enhancing self-esteem.

This chapter will explore therapeutic responsiveness by first examining the contributions of others in conceptualizing typologies of
clinical social work interventions. The second section will then discuss
more fully the techniques of support, confrontation and interpretation
within the ego-oriented perspective. That discussion will draw on clinical vignettes to illustrate these ideas. The latter part of this chapter
will discuss the matrix within which the helping process evolves—the
therapeutic relationship.

To put the discussion of therapeutic responsiveness into perspective, a review follows of the assumptions upon which the ego-oriented
model of clinical social work is grounded:

1. The Generic thrust of clinical social work within this ego-oriented
   perspective is always adaptive in the sense that our raison d'être
   is on the side of growth which, depending on social supplies, is continuous and progressive from birth to death;
2. The clinical process is client-oriented in the sense that one begins
   where the applicant is and works with him toward goals that are
   of value to his sense of well-being;
3. The method of clinical work is carried out through a process which
   has a beginning, middle and end within which skills of exploration,
   evaluation, support, confrontation and interpretation are the means
   for facilitating development and enhancing structuralization;
4. The working alliance evolves from conflict-free executive and adaptive functions within the client and worker and becomes the contractual vehicle for working toward mutual goals;
5. The therapeutic relationship is not egalitarian in terms of the power
   and control of the therapist over the helping process;

6. The respectful, consistent and empathic way in which the therapist carries out her role vis-à-vis the client is the sine qua non of effective clinical work and many of the features may resemble a holding environment;
7. The focus of clinical work is primarily in the present although past and future may become foci in the interest of supporting increasing differentiated, integrated and consolidated functioning in the client's psychological and social life;
8. Purposeful intervention is tempered by what the client has shared within the therapeutic relationship and by what the therapist has heard, such that empathic understanding determines the use of self rather than any à priori assumption about time or technique.

These assumptions provide the basis of a framework for integrating clinical practice with the theoretical paradigm discussed in chapters two through five of this book.

DEVELOPMENT OF TYPOLOGIES IN CLINICAL SOCIAL WORK

The following outline presents the principal efforts of social workers to conceptualize and categorize their clinical skills. These efforts began with Mary Richmond in 1917 and culminated in the work of Florence Hollis in the 1960s.

1917-Richmond (*Social Diagnosis*)
Direct: "mind on mind"
Indirect: environmental intervention

1940-Hamilton (*Theory and Practice of Social Casework*)
administration of practical service(s)
environmental manipulation
direct treatment (counseling)

1947-Bibring ("*Psychiatry and Social Work*")
suggestion
emotional relief
manipulation (emotional relief)
clarification
interpretation (insight)

1948-Austin ("Trends in Differential Treatment in Social Casework")
Social Therapy
    influencing factors in the environment
    use of social resources
Psychotherapy
    supportive
    experiential (intermediary)
    insight

1949-Hollis ("The Techniques of Casework")
environmental manipulation
psychological support
clarification
insight development

1958-Maas ("Social Casework")
environmental modification and ego support
clarification of the effects and meaning of behavior
uncovering the forgotten causes of behavior

1958-Community Service Society of New York
(*Method and Process in Social Casework*)
    supportive treatment method
    modifying treatment method

1964-Hollis (*Casework: A Psychosocial Therapy*)
    sustaining procedures
    procedures of direct influence
    catharsis or ventilation
    reflective discussion of current person-situation configuration
    reflective discussion of dynamics of client's response patterns
    reflective discussion of development of client's response patterns

Except for Richmond's dyadic classification of casework into direct and indirect methods and Hamilton's triadic distinctions among administrative, environmental and counseling modes, relatively little was published about typologies of intervention until the late 1940s. Historically, casework had been identified with socially oriented modes of intervention to ameliorate the dehumanizing effects of poverty, which was reflected in the writings of Mary Richmond.

By the time Hamilton published her casework text in 1940, practice had changed considerably. While concern continued with the social aspects of intervention, which continued to be directed primarily to the poor, social work practice was becoming increasingly identified with psychological methods of helping people. During the 1930s new formulations in psychoanalytic theory focusing on the ego became available and served as theoretical underpinnings for the development of clinical typologies in social work during the 1940s, 50s, and 60s. Except for the functional school of practice which identified with Rankian theory, clinical social work identified with psychoanalytic theory as social workers searched for answers to explain the complexities of human behavior that they confronted in practice. There never developed a social work theory of human behavior and, as a consequence, social workers have adapted analytic theory and technique to our approach. The adaptation had to be stretched to fit the realities of social work practice.

By the 1940s four themes in theory building (as represented in the writings of Bibring, Austin and Hollis) were apparent. There was recognition that *the caseworker continued to have a responsibility for social intervention in situations where her actions might ameliorate adverse environmental factors or where an awareness of social resources would be helpful to the client.* (The exception was Bibring, who was contributing to social work technique from her perspective as a psychoanalyst.) In addition to the administrative function of linking clients to social resources, Hamilton talked about the responsibility of workers to intervene into the social world of the client to modify adverse attitudes of significant others (toward the client). Austin and Hollis referred to the responsibility of workers to change the environment to make it more favorable to clients. Although they did not refer to roles such as advocacy, brokerage and coordination, which appeared frequently in the professional literature during the late 1960s and early 1970s, these authors were referring implicitly to these types of interventions. All three believed, however, that assisting the client to cope with environmental forces by himself was preferable to direct action by the worker.

A second theme, related to the prominence of supportive intervention as a primary modus operandi of the worker, viewed support as *a way of reinforcing adaptive strengths* within clients through accepting and nonjudgmental attitudes, emotional relief of tension via ventilation within a permissive atmosphere and protective relationship, reassurance and guidance via suggestion and the use of appropriate social resources. Since the birth of the profession early in the century, social workers had already accumulated a repertoire of supportive skills of a nonconceptualized nature which were responsive to the needs of clients confronted with overwhelming conflicts. Until the late 1930s, psychoanalytic theory (upon which social workers leaned) was based on uncovering and interpreting techniques—these were not appropriate to the majority of clients served by social workers. In their efforts to fill this gap, practitioners had accumulated much "practice wisdom" in responding empathically. Hollis and Austin, in particular, seemed to be tapping that wisdom in their conceptualization of ego-supportive interventions.

A third theme concerned the realities of practice which could not be accounted for by the concept of support. Workers had become masters of support but were also utilizing other techniques which were not purely supportive either by intent or by anticipated consequence. Austin referred to these techniques as intermediary between support and insight, the latter being considered a form of psychotherapy traditionally reserved to psychoanalysis. This intermediate level of intervention was identified by Austin as experiential therapy, which seemed to be similar to the notion of manipulation discussed by Bibring, who viewed that technique as a benign use of the relationship to evoke behavioral and/or attitudinal change in the client. Their notions of experiential therapy and manipulation appeared to have much in common with the "corrective emotional experience" of Alexander, who utilized the "here-and-now" experience of the relationship as a vehicle for redirecting cognitive and emotional energies into behavioral change (Alexander, 1948). Insight via interpretation of dynamic or genetic factors was generally not considered instrumental to this means of change by social workers.

A fourth theme related to the recognition that social casework had become a significant resource for people who were suffering from psychological conflict which might be ameliorated *by use of clarifying and interpretive techniques in addition to supportive measures* and the experiential use of the professional relationship. By the 1940s there was recognition that clarification, as a way of helping clients think through and sort out subjective reactions from objective facts, was a legitimate technique of the social caseworker. Not so with interpretation or insight which was considered to be the principal technique of psychotherapy. Interpretation went beyond clarification to uncover dynamic forces in the personality of the client (dynamic interpretation) and to link current difficulties with their unconscious source in past developmental experiences (genetic interpretation: Bibring, 1974). The question was whether or not the worker was qualified to engage in that level of intensive therapy. Although the nature of interpretive work was (and is) clearly different between social casework and psychoanalysis, the use of interpretation was becoming a recognized technique of the worker, parallel with appropriate safeguards (e.g.: special training, supervision, consultation). Austin and Hollis were particularly instructive in viewing insight within the context of supportive, experiential and clarifying processes while Bibring illuminated the dynamic interface of internal and external factors which may facilitate psychological change apart from the use of interpretation.

Although Hollis and Austin had made connections between the use of specific techniques and the nature of differential diagnosis, that aspect of clinical work was a significant focus of the theory building efforts of Maas and the Community Service Society in the 1950s. When viewed along a continuum with supportive interventions at one end and uncovering/modifying interventions toward the other end, support was considered appropriate for the client whose adaptive resources were temporarily impaired as a result of imbalance between his inner and outer worlds. Impairment, as we have defined it in the preceding chapter, was of a moderate nature and confined to circumscribed aspects of psychosocial functioning.

Support was also considered the "treatment of choice" for clients who were severely impaired. With these folks, support was to be grounded in a reality oriented and protective relationship with the worker, who would provide concrete supplies to assist in neutralizing further impairment to the client's ego. Included in this set of techniques was direct intervention into the environment to effect change in stressful realities as well as reassurance, information, logical discussion, advice, suggestion, setting realistic limits and ventilation (Community Service Society, 1958). As one moved along the continuum in the direction of modifying work, Maas identified a set of intermediate techniques which were clarifying in nature and helped people understand the current dynamics of their behavior. His notions of these intermediate techniques were similar to those identified later by Hollis with reflective discussion of client response patterns. The use of clarifying and modifying techniques was considered appropriate for clients who were moderately impaired in ego functioning as a result of intrapsychic blocks which affected social adaptation. These blocks were thought to be confined to a sector of the ego (namely, the use of certain defenses which interfered with adaptation) where there were no severe distortions in the executive function of reality testing. Of course, the use of these techniques was contingent upon the interest, motivation and readiness of the client to engage in this self-reflective mode of treatment. Clarification was considered the predominant technique in this uncovering/modifying mode, which consisted of the following steps:

—confronting the client with the stereotypical patterns in his current behavior;

—enabling the client to separate his subjective feelings from the objective reality of his situation;

—encouraging the client to understand the inappropriate influence of his past experiences on current behavior;

—helping the client use this understanding to control stereotyped patterns in current and anticipated relationships. (Community Service Society, 1958)

The evolution of practice in the direction of counseling and psychotherapy was clearly apparent by the 1950s. Family counseling agencies, child guidance and psychiatric clinics were investing their professional resources into the diagnosis and treatment of intra and interpersonal conflicts of their clientele. The MSW social worker, referred to as a psychiatric social worker and then a clinical social worker (in the 1970s), became the backbone of these programs. By the 1960s, most of the clinical services in these settings were being delivered by social workers.

Based on her empirical studies of practice in several of these settings during the 1950s, Hollis published a new typology of therapeutic techniques in 1964. Up to that time, we tended to assume that a relatively clear distinction could be made between supportive and modifying techniques and that the intent of such interventive efforts would be congruent with their consequences for clients. That is, support was not conceptualized as a mode of intervention in which psychological or social change was either intended or expected. In contrast, clarifying and interpretive techniques were by theoretical definition intended to accomplish that objective. In analyzing her data, Hollis found:

> ...that there seemed to be *no sharp dividing line* between supportive and clarification cases...casework can best be described on a continuum, beginning with cases in which no clarification whatsoever was used, going on to those in which snatches of it were used from time to time, proceeding to others where it played a considerable part in treatment....in most cases treatment moved through phases in which the balance between supportive work and clarification was constantly changing (Hollis and Woods, 1981, 97).

Hollis's contribution was highly significant for several reasons She was the first social worker to undertake an extensive empirical investigation of the actual behavior of social workers as they interacted with clients. In that respect, she was able to document the process of clinical work by examining the content of one hundred cases across a range of settings. In several respects, her findings confirmed the implicit beliefs of the profession—commonly referred to as practice wisdom—and also clarified the developmental and dynamic nature of the client-worker relationship. Her ideas had a profound effect on my own growth as a social worker and served as a conceptual beacon for the development of this ego-oriented model of clinical practice.

Hollis' discussion of sustainment, direct influence, ventilation and reflective discussion of environmental, behavioral, affective and relational aspects is subsumed within the process of support in the current model. When the therapist is conducting herself in such a way as to engage the client in an exploratory, expressive, clarifying and reflective discussion of current and historical material, she is responding supportively to the client. Of course, there are critical boundaries to the supportive use of self, which Hollis and others have pointed out, particularly with the client whose ego and sense of self is so narcissistically grounded, fragmented or fragile that unlimited positive regard and an ambiguous permissive atmosphere may have debilitating consequences. In these situations the worker may have to assume a more protective role and introduce structure into the process in order to contain irrational or harmful expression of affect and to neutralize acting-out, rather than verbalization, of that affect. Notions of lending the ego and guarding autonomy address that aspect of the supportive role.

As we have said, exploration is tempered by focus, which is determined by the therapist's evaluation of the state of structuralization within the client and his developmental capacity to take care for himself. Reflection of dynamic factors is a confrontive process once the therapist has heard and has been able to engage the executive ego of the client in a process of considering, cognitively and emotionally, those aspects of his current life that repeatedly cause him pain. Thus, confrontive use of self is responsive to affective themes and behavioral patterns which transcend specific reactions to people in horizontal and vertical relationships. Reflective consideration of developmental factors is an uncovering and interpretive process in which the client is engaged in affectively recognizing and cognitively linking his current patterns to current or past significant relationships. Hollis's contribution was to help us recognize the wholeness of these therapeutically responsive techniques as well as the fundamentally supportive orientation of the clinical social worker. We do not talk of interpretation or confrontation as interventions separate from support but as technical means through which we attempt to enhance the development of internal ego structures. The integrated use of these techniques is, thus, expressed as *supportive confrontation* and *supportive interpretation* rather than as simply confrontation or interpretation.

SUPPORT

Support is one of the technical options available to the therapist and is oriented primarily to conscious thoughts and feelings which the client has been able to share. It is defined as the therapeutic process of building upon those personal assets which the client brings to the relationship in order to help him sustain a present level of ego functioning or to assist him to move to a more adaptive level. Support is oriented to executive and adaptive functions and may include sustainment, direct influence, ventilation and much of reflection discussion of the person-situation gestalt as discussed in the Hollis framework of psychosocial therapy. Although the therapist may tolerantly respect and benignly accept defensive behavior within the concept of support, she should never support defenses as such. Rather, therapy can support adaptive attempts within the client to cope with his situation, which attempts may have a beneficial affect on the disabling consequences of his defensive functions. In that respect we "search out, diagnostically, those areas in which [the ego] has reached its highest points of development" (Blancks, 1974, 346), and lend our efforts to reinforcement and/or enhancement of adaptation. This notion of the supportive use of self by the therapist is the foundation of the helping process from beginning to end and is an inexorable component of any other technique including confrontation and interpretation.

Support is of value (to clients) when the therapist has heard and connects empathically with cognitive and affective themes associated with the client's suffering and communicates that awareness through an accepting and understanding psychological posture. Support is thus as much a matter of attitude as it is a matter of technique. Kohut suggests that the client's sense of being empathically understood is an essential therapeutic prelude to other forms of intervention which include confrontation and interpretation. He also suggests that this type of understanding may thematically replicate for the client the original empathic merger with significant others (the self object) and their need-satisfying actions (Kohut, 1977).

While empathic attunement to the client is essential to effective clinical work, it is seldom sufficient. Support may also involve the reality-oriented use of the therapeutic self in providing structure for the client who needs to experience, not only a sense of being heard, but a sense of purpose and boundaries to the helping process.

Mrs. Young—a 40-year-old extremely religious, white single parent—lives with her four-year-old daughter Helen in the home of her 65-year-old mother, who is a widow. The family is supported by Aid to Dependent Children, and Mrs. Young works, part time, as a nurse's aide. When Mrs. Young was eight months pregnant with Helen, her husband left one day to do an errand and never returned. The only contact he has had with her in the past four years has been occasional phone conversations about child support payments. Otherwise, there has been no personal contact either with his wife or with Helen. Mrs. Young says that she does not know why her husband abandoned them. Although acknowledging bitterness, she displays no affect in discussing his actions.

Although she shared little information about her background, Mrs. Young described her childhood as happy. She was particularly fond of a younger sister who died about one year before her application for therapy. Her father had died five years before that loss. She blamed both deaths on the incompetence of medical treatment and felt that their physicians had not prescribed proper medication. The sister had died of a traumatic shock which her physician attributed to an overdose. In discussing these losses, Mrs. Young's affect was flat as it was in relation to the desertion of her husband.

She was referred to the clinic by her welfare caseworker for evaluation of Helen, who had trouble sleeping, experienced considerable difficulty in being away from mother at nursery school and had temper tantrums, which Mrs. Young told the worker were hard for her to handle.

Her initial contact with the clinical social worker was guarded and full of apprehensive mistrust. Although she wanted Helen to attend school and was bothered by Helen's reluctance to separate from her, Mrs. Young seemed to experience her involvement in the evaluation and the subsequent recommendation for therapy (for both her and Helen) as a threat to her symbiotic-like involvement with her daughter. Mrs. Young expressed fear that the worker's concern for Helen's independence might lead to the clinic's taking her daughter away from her.

The present family relationships are characterized by a lack of differentiation between Helen and her mother as well as between Mrs. Young and her mother. Mrs. Young denied any anger toward her mother for criticizing her parenting of Helen and seemed to be unable to separate her feelings from those of Helen. She reported that she was happy when Helen was happy and was bothered only by Helen's unhappiness in attending school. Separateness from Helen was associated with concern about environmental dangers which appeared to become more pronounced after her sister's death one year ago and now focused on Helen's being away from her at school. Her world centers around her daughter and her mother; her only friend was her sister, whose death increased Mrs. Young's social isolation, which appeared to foster an already intense symbiotic involvement with her daughter. In other aspects of her life, Mrs. Young functioned well as a nurse's aide and as a religious teacher. She expressed a strong desire to be a good mother to Helen.

Initial evaluation suggested that Mrs. Young was suffering from a moderate to severe impairment in ego functioning, particularly in object relatedness to her four-year-old daughter. Although therapy needed to focus gradually on assisting Mrs. Young to help Helen negotiate the process of separation-individuation (by helping Mrs. Young talk about her own separation anxieties), this goal could not be addressed immediately or directly as it would be too intimidating to her fragile sense of self. In order for separateness to occur, it was hypothesized that Mrs. Young would have to develop a better sense of self and have some of her needs met through the relationship with the therapist rather than the relationship with Helen. The development of a protective and supporting relationship for her alone was seen as the primary tool to realize therapeutic goals. Because of significant ego distortions manifested in borderline characteristics, the empathic and structural aspects of the therapeutic relationship were considered critical to these goals. The therapist, as a real object, oriented her interventions to education on child management issues, exploration of anxieties related to separation, strengthening of the self-representation and building self-esteem by recognition of Mrs. Young's achievements and improvement of her reality testing.

The following interview took place after Mrs. Young had been in therapy several months:

Mrs. Young: How are you today?

Therapist: I'm fine, thank you. I was thinking of our session last week (Mrs. Young had described herself as the "Rock of Gibraltar" and said at the end of the previous interview that she needed no one or nothing to survive. She took care of other people's needs and not her own. The therapist had commented that Mrs. Young seemed to have difficulty in doing things for herself, which Mrs. Young wanted to discuss in their next session.) You talked about not wanting to buy things for yourself or to give yourself anything. We talked about how important it was to be good to yourself as well as to Helen; I think that it's important for us to discuss this.

Mrs. Young: I don't want to buy myself anything but I know you think I should.

Therapist: How does that make you feel?

Mrs. Young: We are each entitled to our own opinion.

Therapist: Yes. How do you feel about my suggesting something that you may not feel comfortable with?

Mrs. Young: I don't mind. I have my reasons.

Therapist: Last week you said that there was a time when you felt O.K. about buying things for yourself. I wonder what is different for you now.

Mrs. Young: Financial! (She then elaborated on how difficult life was now that she had to depend on welfare compared to a few years ago.)

Therapist: You are in a difficult situation which makes being good to yourself hard but I wonder if there may also be other reasons.

(Silence)

Therapist: What's it like when other people give you something or do something for you?

Mrs. Young: I don't like it. I'm usually touched but I don't like to show my feelings or emotions. I've been hurt. My marriage didn't hurt me; it makes me bitter. But I've been hurt in other ways. (When the therapist inquired how she had been hurt, Mrs. Young talked about a man to whom she had been engaged before meeting her former husband. He was killed in an accident. She also mentioned a boy of whom she was fond during her teens who was also killed). I've been hurt, so I built up this wall. I don't show my feelings and I don't get hurt. When my sister died, I was very hurt but I didn't show it. (Mrs. Young related this material without much affect and with her eyes downcast and then she was silent).

Therapist: You have had a lot of big losses which have really hurt and created a lot of strong feeling within you.

(Silence)

Therapist: It is difficult to talk about this, isn't it? But I can hear why you have built up a stone wall. I wonder if you think that it prevents you from reaching out and getting to know others.

(Silence)

Therapist: Would you like to understand why there is a stone wall and why it's difficult to share your feelings? That's something we can work on here, if you wish.

Mrs. Young: I guess so. I don't care but I don't like talking about myself. You ask me a lot of questions.

(Silence)

Therapist: I do ask lots of questions but you also share a lot of information about your thoughts, feelings and experiences even when I don't ask you questions.

Mrs. Young: You are good at what you do.

Therapist: What do you mean?

Mrs. Young: You want to be a good social worker, but not for your own ego. I can tell you're sensitive, not like some social workers my group talks about (client is also in group therapy with other mothers who have children about Helen's age).

Therapist: Well, thank you. I realize that you may not like some of my questions, and I'm glad that you can tell me and let me know that it may make you angry.

Mrs. Young: Don't take it personally. It's not you. It's just people.

Therapist: It's alright to be angry with me. We can talk about it and try to understand what makes you angry.

This vignette shows the struggle of the client in becoming involved in therapy and how vulnerable she feels abⱺut a relationship in which another human being can connect with her inner self and know her as she fears to be known. The therapist's patient use of self enabled this woman to gradually feel more comfortable and less frightened in sharing her thoughts and feelings. Resistance to involvement in therapy was a prominent theme throughout therapy and continued to be a nodal issue, particularly at those times when Mrs. Young had shared very painful and personal parts of her self with the therapist. Although the therapist was empathic and supportive, she also served as a real person to this woman whose internal object relations were at a need-satisfying level and whose self-representation was fragmented and diminished.

Working with parents who are seen because their children have problems is usually a delicate process. Since parental involvement in therapy may confront the projective defenses of scapegoating and may be interpreted by them as indictment of their adequacy, the function of empathic support and protection of autonomy is critical to involving them in a therapeutic relationship. This mother, no doubt, experienced these ubiquitous reactions but also had to contend with overwhelming anxieties about her sense of differentiation and separateness from people. The consistency of the therapist in gently, yet firmly, keeping the therapeutic agenda before the client while respecting her need to maintain distance and to protect her fragile sense of autonomy cannot be emphasized enough in this type of work. Support is fundamental to that effort. Premature confrontation or interpretation may be received as an attack and overwhelm the ego of the client. With a person like Mrs. Young who suffers from object anxiety, differentiation of self from others and fear of involvement in meaningful relationships (that have always been destroyed), gradual involvement with a real object that becomes progressively more humanized (to Mrs. Young) is the intervention of choice. For clients whose object relatedness is polarized between good and bad, the therapist as an object becomes humanized as the harshness of the self-representation is modified. The means toward achieving that superego shift is the empathic relationship with another person who consistently treats the client better than she can treat herself by tolerance of her need for emotional distance, acknowledgment of her strengths and respect for her worth as a human being.

Support may be instrumental in neutralizing anxieties associated with confrontations that occur within the client as a consequence of progressive involvement in the therapeutic relationship. We are talking about anxieties that may trouble the client as he becomes more aware of forbidden thoughts and feelings even though the therapist has remained empathically protective of the client's need to defend against such material. In other words, supportive intervention may lead to self-awareness even when the intent of the therapist has been to respect defenses. Indeed, some of the most effective work of a confrontive and interpretive nature occurs within therapeutic relationships where the therapist has assumed a consistently supportive role. Resistance is a natural response to change and must be confronted in a supportive yet firm manner.

Several weeks after the above session, Mrs. Young began an interview by complaining about the lack of communication with Helen's teacher and by confronting the therapist with a question about the need for weekly appointments. In previous weeks she had gradually talked more about herself and her inner feelings although she avoided any direct expression of her ambivalence toward therapy or the therapist. These feelings were externalized (outside of their relationship), a need which the therapist respected while empathically nudging the client to express her reactions to their work together. Although Mrs. Young had mentioned her concern about the need for weekly sessions, she dwelled on complaints toward the school and responded to the issue of her therapy only after the therapist had twice picked up on her concern.

Mrs. Young: I don't know why you feel that I need to come every week. Helen has no problems now and she has improved at home and at school.

Therapist: That's good, but we have not just been talking about problems but ways in which you can help Helen grow up.

Mrs. Young: Yes (silence) but I think Helen is getting too independent. (In response to the therapist's inquiry, Mrs. Young elaborated on what she meant and cited several examples of Helen's attempting to do things which are dangerous and beyond her capabilities. Projective identification was evident in her description as were her anxieties about the threat to her symbiotic involvement with Helen. The therapist asked how Helen's becoming independent was a problem to Mrs. Young).

Mrs. Young: It's not a problem for me. It's a problem for Helen!

Therapist: What do you think about using this time to work on ways to help Helen with this problem?

Mrs. Young: Fine, but why every week?

Therapist: Can you tell me what it's like for you to come every week and why you feel every other week would be better for you?

Mrs. Young: Why should I come every week if I don't feel different after I leave? It's like a sermon—not to compare you to a minister—but if I don't feel better, why should I come?

Therapist: Have there been times when you've felt better after leaving here?

Mrs. Young: Yes, there have been a few times. I bet you didn't expect that answer (with a rare smile on her face). The last two times I was here were good. Then there were the times when I talked about my sister's and fiance's deaths. I felt relieved to talk about those things and to get them off my chest. It was the first time that I've talked with anyone about these things. (Silence)

Therapist: I can see what you mean and understand what you are saying. Sharing like that is often scary for people and involves risks.

Mrs. Young: Well, life is made up of risks. That's part of life.

Therapist: How was it for you to take those risks here?

Mrs. Young: I just don't think about it. It was a relief.But why must I come every week? What does it have to do with Helen? Helen has improved and now wouldn't miss school for the world. I wouldn't do anything to take that away from her even if I have to come to see you every week.

Therapist: Whether or not you come to see me will have no effect on Helen's staying in school. (The therapist then reviewed their original agreement to meet every week and reinforced the importance of continuity in the therapy by weekly sessions).

Mrs. Young: A lot of the things that bothered me in the beginning are no longer big problems–like getting Helen off the baby bottle and getting her to go to school.

Therapist: Have you thought about areas that you would now like us to work on? Perhaps you can think about this question and we can talk about it next week and then talk further about how often you may need to come.

Mrs. Young: You tell me what the goals are and I'll be happy.

Therapist: We need to work on that together. I'll see you next week.

This vignette illustrates the process of staying an empathic inch ahead of the client while hearing and respecting the need to move at his own pace. While the client relates on a need-satisfying level of ego development and tends to act out of object anxiety, the therapist is consistently on the side of helping Mrs. Young to exercise a higher level of function and as a consequence to build ego resources and to neutralize her impulse toward flight. The matter of the spacing of interviews was symptomatic of more nodal issues that needed to be explored through encouraging verbalization. To put into words her thoughts and feelings was a way of supporting the ego to exercise its latent capacity for synthesis and integration of experience rather than defensive flight.

Once change begins to occur, the tendency of clients to pull back from therapy is not uncommon, especially if they are very need-oriented in their relationships. While one responds in the interest of protecting autonomy, no matter how tenuous, one must reach out to these clients and attempt to involve them in exploration of their reactions. Firmness is critical—but even more critical is the focus on enlisting the executive ego of the client to reflect upon goals and to base any change in therapy on reevaluation of his situation. Frequency of interviews thus becomes another means of fitting the intervention to the evaluation and in the process to encourage the exercise of executive functions and to promote more adaptive behavior. With Mrs. Young, her resistance may have had defensive (avoidance) as well as adaptive (separation) value. As it turned out, the resistance at this phase of therapy was also related to Mrs. Young's anger at the therapist for what she perceived as loss of symbiotic gratification with Helen. While her progressive side could enjoy and take satisfaction in the achievement of more age-appropriate separateness between her and Helen, she mourned the loss and was trying to avoid facing her anger at the therapist. Her regressive side was attempting to preserve the symbiotic-like perception of the therapist as a soothing object that would always be available but at a safe distance.

Support can also be manifested in more directive and educative interventions which combine exploratory, clarifying and teaching skills. The level of structuralization within the client will determine his capacity to assimilate cognitive supplies and to use information in the interest of adaptation rather than defense. These clients will often be struggling with remnants of more disabling impairments in object relations although the overall character of ego development may be relatively intact.

Mr. Wade called to request an appointment for his wife. He said that they were in the process of ending their marriage and he had recently moved out of the house. He was concerned about her "mental state" and worried that she might not be able to manage her life and to care for their five-year-old daughter who continued to reside with mother. Although reluctant, Mr. Wade accepted an appointment to explore his concerns with the clinical social worker.

During the interview, Mr. Wade maintained his perception of the problem as a concern for the well-being of his wife and daughter. Although acknowledging that he felt badly about the situation, he insisted that he was coping with the separation without unusual difficulty, was not interested in therapy for himself and only wanted to be sure that everything would be O.K. at home. The therapist offered to see him again and also to see his wife if she wished help. However, she would have to decide that for herself and contact the therapist if she wanted help. Mr. Wade refused additional appointments and said that he would pass on the information to his wife.

A few days later Mrs. Wade called to request an appointment. During the initial interview, she was composed and appeared to be adapting to the separation without overwhelming anxiety. There was no impairment in executive functions. She seemed relatively open about the pain of going through a divorce which she had requested because of her unhappiness with the marriage. She, too, did not see a need for therapy for herself but did express concern about the disrupting effects of separation on their five-year-old daughter, who had become very moody and was giving her mother a "hard time" about going to school.

The following vignette took place during the latter half of the initial interview:

Therapist: Tell me about what it's like at home now for you and Liz (her daughter).
Mrs. Wade: She's more withdrawn and spends a lot of time alone in her

room. In the morning when I'm busy trying to get ready for work, she complains of stomachaches and does not want to go to school. When I'm firm, she dawdles and cries about attending school. I'm sure she is feigning illness to stay at home. So I do not let her and often end up driving her to school, which interferes with my work schedule. I don't mind, however, because I think that it's good for her to be at school with other people to keep her mind occupied.

Therapist: To keep her mind occupied?

Mrs. Wade: She was close to her dad, being the only child, and I'm sure that she misses him.

Therapist: Have you and Liz talked about dad's leaving and the reason for the separation?

Mrs. Wade: No, not really. I'm sure that she is aware of how unpleasant our life together was this last couple of years but she never mentions anything about it or the separation.

Therapist: You said that these difficulties with your daughter began after your husband left (about one month ago).

Mrs. Wade: Yes, but . . .

Therapist: What do you make of that?

Mrs. Wade: I guess that I haven't thought too much about it. You mean that her behavior now may have something to do with our problems (i.e., marital problems).

Therapist: Well, you said that her weepiness and difficulties in getting to school began only after Mr. Wade left. I take it from what you've told me that it's a difficult time for everyone in the family. What do you think the separation may mean to her?

Mrs. Wade: I assumed that she misses her father and will eventually get over it. Do you think there may be more to this than that?

Therapist: Yes. How do you think kids of five may feel about conflicts which they observe in their parents' marriages?

Mrs. Wade: We did sometimes have arguments about Liz. He was very permissive about things like bedtime, correcting her, etc. Usually, I was the only one who would discipline her. But we did not separate because of those difficulties. They were a minor, even insignificant, part of our troubles.

Therapist: Do you think a five-year-old sees life in the same way?

Mrs. Wade: I hadn't thought about it. I guess that I've been too preoccupied getting through this mess and haven't been too sensitive to Liz's feelings. (Begins to cry.)

(Silence)

Therapist: Perhaps you're being very hard on yourself now. After all, this is a tough time for you as well. You know it's not unusual for kids to feel responsibility for their parents and to blame themselves if something goes wrong. In fact, it's a common and very normal reaction. I wonder how you would feel about inviting Liz to talk about her reaction to the separation with you.

Mrs. Wade: You don't want to see her?

Therapist: Let's talk about whether or not that's going to be necessary after you've had a chance to talk with her.

Mrs. Wade: O.K. I never thought that she might feel responsible for our problems.

In the next interview, Mrs. Wade reported that she had sat down with Liz and both had talked about the separation. She was surprised to find out that the therapist had been correct; indeed, Liz had felt responsible for causing them to end the marriage. Mrs. Wade reported that both of them had cried a little and felt much better after their talk. She thought that it had been helpful to Liz but also felt relieved herself to be able to openly and honestly discuss what was "really going on" with her daughter. To her surprise, she even acknowledged in their discussion that she too missed her husband but was firm about her decision. Mrs. Wade was able to reassure Liz that the trouble in their marriage was between her daddy and mommy and had nothing to do with Liz. She also felt good about being able to tell Liz that both of them loved her and were not going to leave her alone.

This vignette illustrates the supportive use of clarifying and educative interventions which were also tinged with benign confrontation. Mrs. Wade was able to use this type of therapy constructively because the structural level of her ego was intact enough to respond adaptively rather than defensively to fairly direct interventions. To have focused only on her feelings of loss and guilt may have increased her own preoccupation with self and left her even more out of touch with the pain of her daughter. She was able to hear the therapist and to take empathic action on her own to assist Liz in coming to terms with her suffering. In the process, the mother was helped to feel better about herself and to feel renewed confidence in her parenting role. This illustration shows how people's internal thoughts and feelings and their sense of self-esteem may shift in a positive direction as a result of constructive behavior. Reinforcement for behavioral change, along with sound information grounded in an accurate understanding of human dynamics, may be a powerful tool for enhancing ego functions and in promoting a more positive sense of self.

The Murphys were a family of five children who lived together with their mother and father. Mr. Murphy worked two jobs to support the family, who resided in a small home in a well-kept urban neighborhood which consisted primarily of Irish Catholic families like the Murphy's. Mr. and Mrs. Murphy had been involved briefly with the clinic two years before the current contact. At that time, their oldest child, a daughter, had become involved with a black young man whom she wished to marry. The news had caused turmoil in the family and led to the parents' involvement in brief therapy. Although the daughter was seen once, therapy was not recommended for her but for her parents to help them cope more constructively with the situation.

Mr. and Mrs. Murphy had not changed noticeably from their last contact with the clinical social worker (two years ago). Early in the interview they reported that life was going well for Cindy, who was now a junior in college. Although she still dated Ralph (her black boy friend) the parents thought that the relationship had "cooled off," which they attributed to their "growing up." Because it had been helpful to talk with someone about their strong reaction to Cindy's involvement with a black person (which they later found out was similar to his parents' reaction to her), they were hopeful that we might help with their 18-year-old son Bob, the second oldest. According to the parents, Bob was always a good boy who "everyone" expected would some day become a priest. Since his senior year in high school, he had become more aloof from the family. They had suspected that he was using drugs and mother tried to talk with him. Bob became quite upset, accused her of trying to run his life, and then announced that he was a homosexual. He was not going to become a priest, nor was he going to college that year.

These parents did well by their children until late adolescence when they seemed to get bogged down in the (second) separation-individuation struggle of their children. The available mother reacted to the struggles of their oldest daughter and son to separate and individuate by an overprotective reaction which was inappropriate to late adolescence development. The family was deeply religious and cohesive. Their cherished values related to religion, their strong prejudices about race, and their rigidity about sexual conduct were being dramatically challenged by the behavior of Cindy and Bob. In a real sense, the two children had confronted the value system of the culture (as represented in the values of their parents) in a way that would provoke conflict and perpetuate object ties with the parents.

Although mother was the dominant parental figure and seemed to rule the roost by retaining intense involvement with her children even when they needed room to test out independent strivings, she functioned well in other areas. Albeit intrusive, Mrs. Murphy was not unworkable in the sense that she was able to make some rather significant shifts in her own behavior around the separation conflict with Cindy. Mr. Murphy was more passive and tended to go along with his wife, whom he referred to as "the boss." He tended to neutralize her emotional intensity toward the older children with humor and stroking although he himself remained on the periphery of the battle. Given the cultural identification of these parents, their moralistic and rigid reactions to the behavior of Cindy and Bob were understandable and more an indication of residual conflict in coping with the second separation-individuation phase than an indication of severe impairment in ego functioning. Their use of therapy and the relationship with the clinical social worker (who showed a similar background) resembled brief contacts with a parish priest whom they felt too embarrassed to consult about these issues.

Toward the end of the first interview, the therapist picked up on a theme of disappointment in Bob which had pervaded the latter half of the interview although the parents could not put their feelings into words.

Therapist: What is it like for you to now have to contend with Bob's struggle to grow up, which is not unlike your reaction to Cindy's behavior two years ago?

Mother: I was very hurt by Cindy and I think she knew that she hurt us. With Bob, I don't know but I am upset because he has changed so much. I don't feel as though I can trust him alone in the house with the younger boys. I don't know what he might do.

Therapist: You're not sure of anything any longer?

Mother: I'm not sure of anything any longer. It was so much easier when the kids were small.

Father: Maybe we're the ones who have the problem! Maybe we should come for help.

Mother: What do you mean? (angrily)

Father: We don't have problems with our kids until they reach this age; then all hell seems to break loose. The other kids are alright but so were Cindy and Bob when they were younger. I wonder if all parents have these problems. God knows we tried.

The parents are struggling here with the disequilibrium that is characteristic of the second separation-individuation process of adolescence (Blos, 1967). The protectiveness of the family and the cohesiveness of the culture which sustained them in coping with the limited manifestations of earlier separation-individuation struggles begins to break down as the parents experience progressively less control over their older children. One wonders how trapped these kids may feel within a tight, symbiotic-like network and whether their dramatic gestures of nonconformity reflect their progressive strides to break away while, at the same time, provoking a reaction in their parents that prolongs object ties (Loewald, 1962).

Guilt is a powerful affect in this family for insuring conformity, and when it appears to no longer work as effectively as it once did, the parents feel lost and seek help in order to reestablish control over their children. A supportive alliance with these parents (and with any applicant for therapy) is achieved by reaching out to them in an empathic and accepting way. However, because of the rigidity of their response to their young adult offspring, who continue to be "children" within their object representation of them, the therapist must be unusually sensitive to the sociocultural aspects of their reactions. Their difficulties in differentiating between childhood separation-individuation and that of adolescence is a nodal issue which must be heard and confronted without feeding their sense of guilt and failure. The importance of empathizing with the struggles of these parents—within the context of their internalized value orientations—is important for all clients but particularly so when the clients may not fit with prevailing culture mores which may be a part of the therapist's value system. This notion of support is particularly important with various ethnic groups—women who value equality with men, and the poor who may be responding from values that are foreign to the therapist. The importance of listening with tolerance and hearing within a cultural, as well as psychodynamic, context are not only instrumental to making empathic contact but critical to the supportive foundation of the therapeutic relationship.

As therapy evolved with these parents, they became less encumbered by superego anxiety and more responsive to the therapist's invitation to look at their parenting roles and how they could help their children grow from adolescence to young adulthood. The primary thrust of interventive efforts was to strengthen their empathy for Bob and to reduce the irrational force of their guilt, which prevented them from letting go of their oldest son. As the father became more aware of his wife's lonely struggle to bear the responsibilities of parenting, he was able to take a more active role in helping with management of the children and in supporting his wife. This shift was somewhat painful for Mrs. Murphy because of her need to retain control and also because of Mr. Murphy's harshness and use of corporal punishment with the children. She felt a need to protect the children from his aggression. As they explored the parenting patterns which had evolved in the family, it became increasingly clear that he withdrew from an assertive role as the father because of his own fear and resulting guilt about his aggression. By removing himself from an active part in matters of discipline, Mr. Murphy could maintain his self-representation as a "good guy" whom everyone loved. Gradually, he was able to learn about putting his angry feelings into words rather than acting on them. Family interviews with Mr. and Mrs. Murphy and Bob were also instrumental in helping them to integrate change in their relationships and to promote more openness in their communication patterns.

At one point, Bob had stolen a car with some friends in order to joy ride. He was arrested and the mother called in a panic to request an immediate session. She feared the worst; he might be sent to jail. After exploring the situation, the therapist decided not to offer an extra session and conveyed confidence in the parents' capacity to deal with the problem. He would see them all at their regular time in two days.

Mother: I was so upset about this incident. It seemed to set us back–like undoing all the progress we've made.
Therapist: Can we look at what did happen?
Bob: We (two friends and himself) took this car from a parking lot on a dare. We didn't mean anything by it. We just rode around. I was driving because I was the only one with a license (perverted sense of fair play). I guess that

I was a little scared and worried that we shouldn't have done it.

Father: Tell him what a stupid thing you did.

Bob: We had been riding around for a couple of hours when I spotted a police car at an intersection. I stopped and then started up slowly and drove in such a cautious way, I guess, that the cop followed us. We pulled into a driveway and the cop followed and asked for identification. I said that my brother lived in the house and could verify who I was. The cop looked at my license and then went to his car to check on the registration; we all ran like hell. I was scared, I guess, and stayed out all night and when I tried to sneak in after my father went to work (at 6 A.M.), my mother caught me and threw a fit. They're making a big deal out of this whole thing. My mother's over-reacting again.

Therapist: How come you got caught?

Father: That's what I wonder too. I think he wanted to get caught.

Therapist: What about that?

Bob: I got scared. Maybe I did want to get caught. I don't know and don't give a damn. Nobody gives a shit around here anyhow!

Therapist: What about that? How do you all feel?

The family then went on to talk about how the event had affected them. Bob was eventually able to confront his mother with his feeling that she overreacts to him and doesn't listen unless he says or does something dramatic, which then makes things worse. He recalled saying to her that he may be a homosexual and told her of his decision not to attend college. He isn't gay but he thought it might get her off his back. It only accomplished the opposite.

Bob: You don't listen to me (to mother) and dad doesn't care. I only want some time off from school to think about my future. That's all. You made a big deal out of it. It's nothing. I need time to think.

Therapist: How do you all feel about the changes that you have been able to make in the family?

Father: I thought things were going smoother.

Mother: Yes, they were.

Therapist: How about you, Bob?

Bob: It was good but I was waiting for my mother to pounce on me again. It was too good to last.

Therapist: Change is difficult isn't it? I wonder if you're not expecting too much and being hard on yourselves again?

The family was then able to focus on how they felt about the changes that had occured in recent weeks and how disappointed they were in what the parents interpreted as a setback. Bob was gradually able to put into words his need to test the change and accept responsibility for provoking what the parents viewed as an undoing of gains that had been achieved in therapy. While the father stood by Bob, both parents were firm that he would have to be responsible for the consequences of his actions. Father planned to accompany him to court but insisted that Bob would have to speak for himself.

This vignette demonstrates the value of helping clients to learn about their current reactions in significant relationships and through that process to effect shifts in patterns of relating to each other. In this family, the shift occurred in the parenting relationship as the father became less disengaged in his relationship with the children (Minuchin, 1974). As he became a mutual ally of mother in the parenting process, she felt less burdened by loneliness of having total responsibility for the children and of being bearer of all parental guilt. As a consequence, mother became less enmeshed in their lives and more tolerant of their need for differentiation and separateness. The crisis of the stolen car incident was a temporary detour in their journey toward these goals and one from which they were able to profit. Bob was confronted with his need to take responsibility for the consequences of his actions, while the parents were able to see that even a minor setback could evoke old patterns of sealing off newly discovered patterns of openness in their relations with their children. This form of support was oriented to an educative mode of enhancing parenting skills by way of understanding their current patterns of relationship and incorporating into their parenting roles a balance of empathic supplies with firmness.

A critical variable in the therapy was an appreciation of the sociocultural forces at play in this Irish Catholic family. Respect for this dimension of the evaluative process enabled the therapist to temper his interventions to the value orientation of these parents. A supportive, educative use of self oriented to behavioral aspects of current relationships was the treatment of choice. Some confrontive techniques were part of the intervention but no interpretive work, either of a dynamic or genetic nature, was attempted.

CONFRONTATION

Confrontation is a process of assisting the ego of the client to face currently unacceptable thoughts and feelings toward himself or toward his object representations of significant figures in his interpersonal environment. Support is part of the confrontive process in the sense that the therapist must be empathically attuned to those unacceptable thoughts and feelings (which the client's defensive system keeps from consciousness) before attempting to engage the client in a process aimed at openly facing them. Support also provides the trustful matrix through which these affects and thoughts may emerge into preconsciousness or even into consciousness. Supportive interventions, in themselves, may lead to the type of intrasystemic confrontation to which we refer. In fact, "to help the observing part of the ego look at the experiencing part and confront itself" is the most viable form of this technique (Blancks, 1974, 353). The more the ego of the client can be supported to do for self, the more effective the outcome of clinical work. In that sense, confrontation of the client by the therapist may be considered a secondary option when attempts to engage the client in intrasystemic confrontative work has failed.

No matter what its mode, intrasystemic or extrasystemic, confrontation always involves a loss. In facing the unfaceable, the client is sacrificing or separating himself from accustomed characterological patterns which always involve the defensive system's interaction with executive functions such as thought patterns, object relations, insensitivity to the feelings of others or ways of testing reality. Either the therapist or the client is taking something away that has served a useful purpose in the past. Although that behavior may not have been adaptive in the sense of promoting realistic modes of problem solving, it will have contributed to intrapersonal and/or interpersonal equilibrium. Depriving a person of defensive functions that contribute to equilibrium requires rather thorough understanding of the client as a whole human being and empathic attunement to the meaning of his suffering. Otherwise, confrontation runs the risk of being an expression of our counter-transference reactions and, because of the inherent aggressive component involved in confrontive work, will be a means of punishment rather than a means of liberating the client from those irrational forces that encumber his autonomy.

Because the intent of confrontive work involves an aggressive element in its focus on separating the executive ego from habitual patterns of defensive behavior, the importance of self-awareness of the therapist in utilizing techniques to promote this type of horizontal awareness cannot be overemphasized. Myerson observes that

> . . .however meticulously we try to think out what we are doing, once we are in the real, emotionally charged situation where we are trying to modify another human being's behavior and are confronted ourselves with our patient's reluctance to change, we cannot avoid being somewhat influenced by the way we have resolved our own problems about forcing, being forced, hurting, and being hurt. Moreover, our patient will be influenced in one way or another, not just by our conscious intentions, but by the way we react to the way he reacts to us, by our irritated concern at his resistance or by our apparent patience in the face of this resistance filtered through his correct and not so correct perceptions of our motives for behaving the way we do." (Adler and Myerson, 1973, 30)

In discussing extrasystemic confrontation (i.e., by the therapist), Welpton identifies two forms:

1. the angry confrontation in which the therapist is annoyed by the behavior of the client either because she dislikes the client or is impelled to change his behavior, and
2. the empathic confrontation in which the client is accepted while his current behavior is questioned or challenged (Welpton, in Adler and Myerson, 1973).

In the empathic confrontation, there is an inquiring and reflective posture on the part of the therapist, which is captured well in Hollis's discussion of therapeutic procedures oriented toward reflective consideration of dynamic factors (Hollis, 1981). We have already observed that the therapist listens to content while trying to hear themes. Confrontation tries to help the client become aware of incongruence or discrepancy between what is said by the client and what is heard or observed by the therapist.

Confrontation resembles dynamic interpretation. Both often seem to be used in the literature synonymously. The distinction is similar to the one between clarification and interpretation—that is, a matter of depth. As we have defined confrontation, it may involve a dynamic interpretive aspect, the intent of which is to make ego-systonic behavior, thoughts or feelings ego dystonic. Since the process inevitably creates disequilibrium, the therapist must evaluate carefully the structural capacity of the client to tolerate involvement in this form of learning. Generally, confrontive techniques have been considered more appropriate for clients with moderate levels of impairment whose ego-integrative capacities are intact. However, confrontation is most useful and, according to Kernberg, the treatment technique of choice—along with dynamic interpretation—in working with the borderline client who falls within a moderate to severe level of impairment (Kernberg, 1980).

Impairment in the client at a borderline level of development involves failure of integration of self and object representations although they are differentiated sufficiently to offer the client a sense of ego boundaries and separateness from others. Representations of self and other may be split and each may be imbued with an all-encompassing sense of aggression or idealization which impairs integration or a sense of inner wholeness. To enable the ego to achieve a higher developmental level of integration, the client needs to be helped to explore and to eventually confront the split-off representation(s) as they manifest within the relationship with the therapist and in other current relationships. A strictly supportive orientation to therapy may perpetuate the developmental arrest while genetic reconstruction may overwhelm tenuous ego boundaries and reality testing. Thus, we see that confrontation, which is always directed to current dynamics rather than past experiences, may be very useful with a wide range of clients who are suffering from moderate to severe impairment in the functioning of their egos.

With the client who is impaired severely (at a psychotic level), confrontation may be therapeutic when it is focused on the reality testing function. The expression of "lending the ego" to these severely impaired people may be another way of expressing this intervention. In lending the ego, the therapist serves as a real object to the client and, in the process, supportively confronts him with the discrepancies between his inner representations of reality and the external world as it really is.

The following vignettes illustrate two aspects of confrontation. The first shows what Welpton refers to as the angry confrontation, when the therapist is acting out of negative counter-transference motives which have interfered with empathic attunement to and supportive connectedness with the client. The therapist has not heard the underlying themes behind the client's behavior and uses confrontive interventions to "hit" the client with his perception of her irritating behavior. The intervention is isolated to a feature of behavior rather than integrated within a supportive process of working with the client toward facing feelings unacceptable to her representation of self.

Mrs. Rowe applied for therapy because of marital conflicts, which she vaguely described as a lack of communication with her husband. Although she expressed a desire to be seen conjointly with her husband, he refused to become involved. Efforts to reach out to him were unsuccessful; as a consequence, Mrs. Rowe was accepted for individual therapy.

Mrs. Rowe is a 30-year-old white woman, who said that their marriage was poor from its beginnings, not unlike her parents' marriage, which ended in divorce when she was 13. In describing her perceptions of mother and father, she depicted the father as an "evil" person who, she felt, was responsible for mother's unhappiness. The object representation of mother was of a decent and kindly person who put up with a lot of suffering until her husband deserted the family for another woman. Although she did not appear to be aware of the similarities, many of her recollections of father were identical to her current description of Mr. Rowe.

The Rowes had been married for nine years and had two preschool children. The pregnancies were consciously planned but appeared to be an unconscious attempt on her part to breathe life into a marital relationship in which she felt her husband was cold, distant and uncaring. Since the birth of their second child two years ago, Mrs. Rowe had felt increasingly hopeless about the marriage. She tends to keep her emotions locked up inside, as her mother did, and reports feeling more depressed over the past year and occasionally crying for no apparent reason.

Except for the disequilibrium fed by disappointment in an unhappy marriage, Mrs. Rowe functions reasonably well. She talks positively about her relationship with her children and seems attuned to their needs. She has friends who are a source of social support although she does not talk with them about her unhappiness out of a sense of loyalty to her husband. Although some impairment is evident in integration of self and object representation as these relate to her mother and father and her current thoughts and feelings about the marital relationship, no pervasive splitting of representations is evident. No doubt the intensity of her feelings about the marriage has been exacerbated by the gradual resignation to its demise, which has troubled her increasingly over the past several months.

In the third interview, Mrs. Rowe had been talking about her courtship and the fact that she and her husband married only five months after they met. Although he had pursued her and repeatedly proposed marriage during the brief time in which they knew one another, Mrs. Rowe took the initiative to plan the wedding, which she viewed as an opportunity to test out her independence from her mother. In this interview, she had been expressing her ideas about her concept of marriage as an open partnership in which husband and wife could be honest and supportive of each other.

Therapist: That is a very ideal notion of marriage.
Mrs. Rowe: It would have worked out if he (Mr. Rowe) was not such a jerk. He'd never talk to me and even if I got irritated and tried to tell him, he'd pull away more and more. It's hard for me to tell people how I feel and I'm sure that I must have gotten under his skin but he never said anything. Now he tells me that he doesn't love me anymore and he wants to leave. I have to push him to do anything except going to his company's parties. He never invites me but he tells me about his friendships with female coworkers.
Therapist: You sound like a jealous wife.

The client responded with denial and appeared offended by the therapist's remark. She observed that Mr. Rowe was no "Don Juan" and then began to talk about her poor housekeeping skills which Mr. Rowe obliquely criticized. Rather than pick up on the questionable theme of jealousy, the therapist needed to explore further Mrs. Rowe's feelings about her role in the relationship. Was she saying, for example, that her assertiveness drove him to other women? How did she feel about her own aggression and what was it like when she tried to speak up for herself? Can aggressive assertiveness drive people away and ruin one's dream of a happy marriage?

In a later session, Mrs. Rowe was describing how one of her friends, a woman, reacted to finding out that Mr. Rowe was a scoundrel. (Mrs.

Rowe had confided in this person, which was the first time she had expressed her feelings about the marriage to anyone beside the therapist.) The friend wanted to have a talk with Mr. Rowe and to let him know how much he was hurting his wife. She then described how lonely and frustrating it was to live with a man who ignored her.

Mrs. Rowe: He comes home from work, says nothing to me, reads the paper and then fools around with that goddam stereo set. I turn it off, and he just sits there like a jerk!
Therapist: You sound like a real nag.

The therapist again missed an opportunity to explore Mrs. Rowe's feelings and is apparently acting out of negative counter-transference. His intervention here is a clear example of how confrontation without empathic attunement may be a punitive action. To the therapist, Mrs. Rowe is a nag but we do not know how she views herself and what her assertive behavior may mean to her.

(later)
Mrs. Rowe: He's become intolerable to live with. He surprised me the other day by suggesting a separation. He'd move in with his parents for a while. I thought it was a good idea so I ironed his shirts, packed his bags and even offered to drive him to his parents' place. It's been a lot more peaceful since he left. He and I are even more civil to one another.
(silence)
Therapist: Perhaps he saw this as an outright rejection.
Mrs. Rowe: Maybe, but I still love him.
Therapist: Does he know that?
Mrs. Rowe: He ought to know. After all, I show him by taking good care of the children and I've even become a better housekeeper to prove that I love him.

The therapist is out of tune with the client's feelings. What needs to be explored is how Mrs. Rowe feels and thinks about this rather monumental event, but we get no idea what the behavior of Mrs. Rowe in promoting the separation means to her. Is she scared, proud, relieved? Rather than empathically identifying with the client, the therapist takes the side of Mr. Rowe through a process of projective identification. Despite these technical errors, Mrs. Rowe remained in therapy although her initial motivation appeared to be related, to a considerable extent, to her masochistic need to suffer the consequences of her actions at the hands of the therapist (not unlike the reaction of her mother when her marriage failed). As the therapist was able to confront his own counter-transference reactions, his approach mellowed and he was able to assume a more exploratory and supportive role with Mrs. Rowe.

Mr. Bourne, a 38-year-old Vietnam veteran, was referred to the clinical social worker after applying to the clinic for therapy. He said that he needed someone "to keep me honest" by helping him to stop drinking and using drugs.

During the initial evaluation, Mr. Bourne was personable and engaging despite his unkempt appearance. He talked about himself with little emotion and described his conflicts as if he were talking about someone else. Except for alcoholism and drugs, his concerns were nebulous. He conveyed the impression of being helpless and of wanting the therapist to assume responsibility for taking care of him.

Although reluctant to discuss his experience in Vietnam, he dated his current problems to that period in his life. He expressed bitterness toward the government, viewing it as manipulative and corrupt. He wanted nothing to do with it or with society; refused to work so he would not have to pay taxes, yet expressed no conflict in the paradox of accepting a government stipend to pursue his college education. Despite a strong academic record, he was bored and had made up his mind to drop out of school. In the last two years since being enrolled as a full-time student, Mr. Bourne has lived with a woman whom he described as a "roommate." While she has worked to support the two of them, he describes her as a "clinging vine type" who depends on him too much. He wants to get out of the situation, especially since he now views her as an alcoholic and a bad influence on him.

His family background was quite chaotic. He was the oldest of six from a poor background. He described his mother as a "good person" and his father as an alcoholic who was a "good and bad" father. He expressed no feelings toward them or toward his siblings except to say that he felt sorry for his father and did not hate him. The parents separated when he was 12 and divorced when he was 18. He then lived with a sister before being "sucked" into the Army with the promise of special training. As with his descriptions of people in general, Mr. Bourne tends to view others as objects who are there to meet his needs, a state of ego development which suggests that introjected images of significant others have not been humanized by identification with them as people. When they can no longer meet his needs, objects are discarded, just as he felt discarded by his parents.

Evaluation of Mr. Bourne suggests that he is suffering from a moderate to severe level of impairment. Although no gross distortions are evident in reality testing, this function begins to deteriorate in stressful situations, particularly within relationships that involve an ongoing commitment or expectation that he assume a more responsible or egalitarian role. His interpersonal relations appear shallow and distant and tend to be polarized as good or bad depending on how effectively they satisfy his needs. He appears to be quite bright and gifted in cognitive endowment, which has served as a compensatory resource to impairment of reality testing and object relations. However, his intellectual capacity is also used in the interest of defense as he retreats into introspective fantasy or engages in philosophical projections of paranoid thoughts on to the world in general.

The interventions of the therapist were oriented to three foci:

—reinforcement of adaptive strengths;

—use of self as a real object to confront the reality of current relationships; and

—use of the therapeutic relationship as a means of integrating split-off representations.

Early in therapy Mr. Bourne, as we have pointed out, related in a passive and indifferent manner, looking to someone outside himself to change his behavior; he was terrified of closeness and feared an ongoing relationship with the therapist. His behavior suggested the need for contractual structure within which he might feel less vulnerable.

Mr. Bourne: What's so bad about drinking all day? At least I'm not hurting anybody and I feel good!

Therapist: To a certain extent you are right, but what about the fact that you're hurting yourself?

Mr. Bourne: So what! If I feel like doing it then that is my business, isn't it?

Therapist: If you really feel that way, I find it hard to understand your reasons for wanting my help.

Mr. Bourne: Yeah, I know. I just wanted to see what you'd say.

(Later)

Mr. Bourne: I'm probably going to be leaving the area soon.

Therapist: I didn't know of your plans. That will make for difficulties in our working together, don't you think?

Mr. Bourne: I hadn't thought about it. I don't know. Maybe you can keep me honest quicker.

Therapist: Well, you know there are responsibilities for both of us in this relationship. You have to try to tell me what is troubling you and I have to try to understand your troubles and then see if we can figure out what you can do about them. I want to help you but I really can't keep you honest. Maybe as we understand how you are troubled, you can learn to do that for yourself.

This form of confrontation in the beginning of therapy is almost inevitable with most people no matter how supportively we may do it. In a sense, any contract for therapy involves a confrontation and need for clarification of goals, norms and roles of therapist and client. With Mr. Bourne, several interviews were necessary to explore and clarify his interest in becoming a client. He also needed time within the relationship to test the therapist—to assure himself that she was safe enough to trust and someone who was there to help and not to hurt.

Later in therapy, Mr. Bourne was castigating society and government for its abuse of people.

Mr. Bourne: . . . you know judges are no damm good either. I wonder if you can possibly understand what these ideas mean to me. You're very career and money oriented by virtue of being a social worker. Not like me. Can you understand?

Therapist: You don't like to be judged. Neither do I. I'm here to explore your concerns with you and to try to understand what they mean to you. Unless you tell me, I have no way of understanding what you think and feel because I am not you.

The testing quality of Mr. Bourne's behavior is an expression of his anxieties about ego boundaries and becoming engulfed in the relationship. He also uses this form of communication and these topics as a means of establishing and maintaining contact with the therapist, whom he finds difficult to differentiate within his paranoid projections onto the external world. The consistent realness of the worker as a separate and attuned object helps to neutralize this severe impairment in object relations. This reality-oriented use of self, balanced with support and confrontive nudges to change current thoughts and feelings, is the intervention of choice. As Kernberg observes, historical interpretations are ineffective because of the difficulty which the client experiences in integrating memories of self and object and in differentiating them from current realities. Given his cognitive abilities, Mr. Bourne dealt with any attempt to obtain history by producing his own intellectual interpretations disassociated from their painful affective significance to him. An introspective and philosophical person by character, he had already made all the cognitive connections between his current behavior and their etiological origins. When asked how he felt, he would respond by shrugging his shoulders and saying that he guessed the painful experience(s) must have bothered him but he was a child then and it didn't bother him now.

Mr. Bourne: When I was a small child, I overheard my parents arguing and my father said that he (the client) was the reason they got married. If my mother hadn't been pregnant with me, they never would have married. I guess that's why my father never liked me and that explains why he started drinking. I was the original sin that started everything downhill. That's why I have a problem with self-esteem.

Therapist: How do you feel?

Mr. Bourne: I guess that I was pretty mad with my parents and damm well ought to be (with a smile).

Therapist: You're smiling as you say that.

Mr. Bourne: I'm telling you what you want to hear. Is that what I'm supposed to feel?

Therapist: Let's take a look at that.

Mr. Bourne was not able to tolerate feeling badly and would project his badness on to external objects, thus preserving at least a tenuous sense of inner equilibrium. To him, the world was a bad and dangerous place where one had to be extremely careful. To trust was to become vulnerable to annihilation. His projection of the bad self on to evil objects produced a tinge of pervasive paranoia to all his representations. His superior cognitive resources, which were invested in constructing philosophical rationalizations for the state of his world along with a well-ingrained capacity for blatant denial, helped to preserve his fragile hold on reality.

Later in therapy the worker had responded to Mr. Bourne's denial of any anger within himself by commenting that everyone feels bad from time to time and it's very understandable for all of us to experience anger. Mr. Bourne then began to expound on the corruption of government and society, which he had come to recognize as a way he used to avoid uncomfortable material.

> *Therapist:* You're rambling again about things that bother you. I wonder if you're also bothered by my saying that you too, like me and everyone else, feels anger from time to time.
> *Mr. Bourne:* Well, yeah. I do that without even thinking.
> *Therapist:* What do you make of it? How do you understand your need to do this?
> *Mr. Bourne:* I know that I do it. I guess that I'm not sure what parts of me I can trust you with.

This interaction illustrates the healing power of the existential aspects of the therapeutic relationship when confrontive interventions are grounded in an empathic understanding of structural impairment and developmental lesions. As Blanck and Blanck have pointed out, "Behavior is altered . . . by dynamic interaction between the patient and a therapist who, in effect, constitutes a new and presumably more benign environment" (Blancks, 1974, 4). What we may perceive as a slight modification or shift is for this man (and many of the clients with whom we work) a giant step toward trusting the human world in which they feel so frightened and vulnerable. It is also a good example of what we mean by the observation that ego-oriented therapy always focuses on the present and the past in the present. The relationship with another human being who is attuned to and accepting of the client's unfinished business in human development is the supportive and protective matrix within which important confrontive work may proceed.

INTERPRETATION

Interpretive interventions, like confrontive ones, may never be isolated from their supportive base. One critical aspect of support as it relates to interpretation is the safe therapeutic environment which may permit the client to explore parts of self which were previously off limits to consciousness. These thoughts and feelings were so potentially threatening to psychic equilibrium that they were relegated to a level of nonawareness. Within this orientation, the client is invited to take responsibility for engaging in his own interpretive work so that the therapist does not become an object for the playing out of intrasystemic resistances that are ubiquitous to personal and interpersonal change. In other words, the clinical social worker never does for the client what the client can do for himself.

Interpretation is defined as a process of assisting the ego of the client to become aware of the linkage of one level of conscious experience to another level within the preconscious with the intent of expanding the perimeters of self-understanding. To think of interpreting unconscious material is presumptuous since it does not exist, by definition, within close enough proximity to consciousness. For the client, the unconscious exists not at all except as a conceptual figment which may derive from an intellectual awareness of psychoanalytic theory. The process of supportive work may, indeed, loosen unconscious themes, which may become more accessible to awareness and thus a focus of our interpretive efforts. Until that accessibility evolves, the client is not ready to have his hidden world exposed. Prior to that time, interpretation of the unconscious is a narcissistic exercise for the therapist which is not in the interest of promoting structuralization and of enhancing ego development for the client.

While confrontation is primarily an emotional process which involves loss, interpretation involves a significant cognitive gain. In understanding the connection between present functioning and its correlates in dynamic or developmental processes, new learning becomes available to the executive ego in its task of integrating and synthesizing past and present experiences. The emotional impact of interpretive work will be proportionate to the intensity of involvement of the client in taking responsibility for his own therapy. All the therapist can do is to serve as a vehicle or a catalyst for conceptualizing the thematic linkages. While interventions of that nature may be empathically delivered to the client, only the client can truly experience their affective meaning. As a consequence, the more he is encouraged to take a responsible role in the interpretive process, the greater the potential

for synthesizing the cognitive and emotional dimensions of his connections. To optimize the potential for integration and synthesis, a reflective posture by the therapist (as discussed by Hollis) toward interpretive collaboration with the client is an instrumental part of this aspect
of therapeutic responsiveness. The use of the empathic question and
comment directed to hidden themes which the therapist has heard is
probably more effective than our stereotypes of interpretation as
declarative wisdom springing from the head of the therapist.

Generally speaking, the same evaluative parameters apply to the
use of interpretation as apply to confrontation. Enough internal structure must be available so that the ego is capable of exercising integrative and synthetic tasks. Usually, clients with a mild to moderate impairment in ego functioning are structurally available for this level of
therapy. Structural availability does not, in itself, insure psychological readiness to engage in this type of clinical work, however. Indeed,
much interpretive work is focused on helping the client understand
the nature of his resistances to therapy and as a consequence to make
a more informed choice about the nature of his involvement in the
therapeutic relationship.

Mrs. Parker, a married woman in her late thirties and the mother of three
teenage children, was of an ethnic background where children, particularly females, were to be seen but not heard. Standards relating to emotional expressiveness, sexuality and independence were harshly suppres-
sive, especially for female children. Although she never experienced
physical punishment and was considered a perfect child, Mrs. Parker had
felt smothered by mother's overprotectiveness and ignored by father's in-
difference to her, which she attributed to her sex. Although he appeared
to be a detached and aloof figure in the family, Mrs. Parker felt that father took some interest in the achievements of her brothers but none at
all in her achievements. No matter how good she was as a person or as
a student, he ignored her. Mother, on the other hand, was an overly-
involved and libidinally overwhelming figure in her life but never seemed
to be satisfied nor respectful of the client's autonomy. To Mrs. Parker,
mother had subtle yet powerful ways of reminding Mrs. Parker of her incompetence no matter how successful the accomplishments. Within this
atmosphere, she developed a very harsh superego which permitted no imperfections and an ego ideal of womanhood and motherhood which was
impossible to realize.

The clinical social worker became acquainted with Mrs. Parker when
she was referred to a women's therapy group which he was leading. The
patient had been in individual treatment for three years, which consisted
of weekly sessions along with medication for depression. She had originally applied for therapy because of depressed feelings which she associated with a belief that she was sexually frigid. The client joined the therapy group after it had been in existence for two years and remained a

member of that group for two additional years, when it disbanded as members terminated. A major termination issue for many of the other members was their guilt for leaving Mrs. Parker behind. They felt that they had profited from the group experience and were conflicted that she could not "get her anger out" and continued to insist that her husband was perfect and that she, unlike them, had nothing about which to be angry. In retrospect, these confrontations were instrumental in confronting Mrs. Parker's affective realities which she assiduously avoided in her previous therapy and in her life. She was also anxiously puzzled by what she perceived as the mystery of women getting better by saying that they had faced and worked through angry parts of themselves which they had previously disowned.

Once the group terminated, Mrs. Parker was interested in continuing therapy and was accepted as an individual client by the former group leader. The following vignette occurred several months after individual therapy began. One of the prominent themes up to that point was her puzzlement and fear of being crazy because she could never become angry, which was a carryover from the group. She cognitively recognized the inappropriateness of this fear but continued to worry that she might be more seriously disturbed than she had ever realized.

Mrs. Parker: I always find it hard to begin because you never say anything, but I was thinking of last week's session and I think that I learned something. (Silence)
You know how angry I've been feeling lately, but it's just all over the place and no place. I just feel angry for the first time in my life but it's not directed to anyone in particular. Maybe I'm angry with myself. I was thinking of something you said that made a lot of sense when I thought about it later, but I didn't know what you were talking about at the time. You said that people get angry when they don't get what they want. Somehow I don't think that I ever got what I really wanted.

Therapist: What are your thoughts about that?

Mrs. Parker: What I really think is that I'd like to find out what I want from people. But that is difficult now. Everyone has always taken me for granted and assumed that I was this all-giving, kind and gentle person who loved everybody and was loved by everybody. Now that I'm trying to be myself and show people my other side, they don't like it. I'm saying "no" more to my husband and he tells me that I ought to stop coming here because I'm getting worse rather than better. I guess he must be upset to see that I have needs too and can also be annoyed when he just assumes that I'll always be smiling and happy. Then my sister-in-law who, I think, has always taken advantage of me (babysitting, etc.) thinks that I ought to see a psychiatrist. I can't stand her saying that I've changed just because I told her that I would no longer watch her kids. She really tried to put the old guilt trip on me so I told her to cut it out. Then she tells my husband that I need a psychiatrist rather than a social worker. Sometimes I wonder if being honest is worth the price of upsetting people and losing their friendship.

Therapist: How do you feel about the work we've done together in trying to help deal with your angry feelings.

Mrs. Parker: I don't understand what you mean.

Therapist: You don't understand?

Mrs. Parker: Well—you're a good listener but you don't say too much.

Therapist: Uh-huh.

Mrs. Parker: See what I mean?

Therapist: Yes, I do. What's it like for you?

Mrs. Parker: It's nothing like it was with my other therapist, whom I saw before the group. He told me a lot of things and gave me medication. You don't say anything. You can't even prescribe pills for me. I know what you're getting at. You think I'm angry with my father who never said anything and gave me nothing.

(Silence)

Therapist: It's really not important how I feel. Let's try to understand how you feel.

(Later)

Mrs. Parker: You remember how I wanted to feel refreshed after coming back from that vacation with my mother last summer. She is so good and generous. We couldn't afford a vacation unless she paid for it. And she does it for me every summer for a week. But this year I felt disappointed and the more I thought about it, the lousier I felt. And then the old guilt started to haunt me. How could I be so ungrateful. I still feel ashamed of myself. I could never tell her how I really feel. It would kill her.

Therapist: No wonder you are so afraid of your anger. It can kill!

Mrs. Parker: It can also get me hurt, especially with men more than women. My mother makes me feel trapped and smothered but men scare me. My father scared me because he never said anything and seemed so mysterious.

Therapist: You also have said that I don't say enough.

Mrs. Parker: But you seem to care about what goes on with me. You listen. Nobody ever cared in my family so I guess I stopped thinking because it didn't matter to anyone how I felt (begins to cry).

With this woman as with many clients who are neurotically impaired, interpretive work often is oriented to the current remnants of pre-oedipal experiences which perpetuate into post-oedipal life. Separation/individuation for Mrs. Parker is a nodal issue yet she appears to have more inner structural resources available than do many clients who are suffering with borderline conflicts. Somehow, her ego has been able to compensate and she has been able to extract from the human environment libidinal supplies that have facilitated differentiation and integration of important ego functions. Despite the mother's smothering presence, she seemed to care, and the client at some level heard that message. Qualitatively, the internalization of that message is quite different from the borderline client who has felt abandoned and completely rejected during separation/individuation.

The transference-countertransference aspects of the therapeutic relationship were very important in helping Mrs. Parker reach her goals to become a more complete and whole human being. As she was able to experience anger with the therapist and to discover that he would not be damaged nor would he retaliate by rejecting her as a client, Mrs. Parker was able to gradually transfer that learning to her life in the real world. As often happens in a family system, Mr. Parker became very anxious and upset about the change in his wife, interpreting it for a long time as a regression; subsequently he entered therapy. After Mrs. Parker had terminated her individual therapy, the couple were seen conjointly, which helped to stabilize and consolidate the gains which Mrs. Parker had made. Conjoint therapy also helped Mr. Parker to adapt to these changes and to use therapy as a vehicle for looking at his role in their relationship and making some changes, himself.

Her ego impairment was tied up with social expectations about the traditional status and role of women in her subculture, which had become internalized as part of her superego (Gilligan, 1982). These internalized values, related to subservience and passivity, were questioned as she became involved with other women in the therapy group who once shared similar values but who were questioning and challenging the repressive pull of those standards on their sense of autonomy. That experience was catalytic in upsetting Mrs. Parker's intersystemic equilibrium and supportive in encouraging her to risk involvement in individual therapy. In a sense, this client, as with all clients, had to become disillusioned with her state in life before she was ready to choose a different path. The supportive-interpretive therapeutic relationship was the vehicle through which she was able to free her innate potential toward ego autonomy and more adaptive functioning.

RELATIONSHIP

The helping process takes place within a human relationship which is the medium through which therapeutic skills of exploration, support, confrontation and interpretation are employed to assist the client toward more adaptive functioning and a more autonomous level of human existence. This notion of the relationship has been implicit in our discussion of clinical social work throughout this book and frequently the explicit focus of attention. As with values, I have tried to integrate ideas about relationship into the discussion of clinical skills because relationship is an inherent and inextricable aspect of the therapeutic process. There is need, however to underscore certain aspects of relationship before closing this chapter.

Historically, the concept of relationship has received extensive attention in the social work literature. For the reader who is interested or wants to become familiar with this concept from the social work perspective, the works of Hollis, (1981); Perlman (1979); Ferard and Hynnybun (1962); and Biestek (1957) are recommended. My focus here will be on several important features of the interaction between client and therapist within the ego-psychological perspective which serves as the theoretical framework for this model of clinical social work practice.

Within any human relationship, there is always a present or existential dimension and an historical one which I have referred to as the past in the present. Traditionally, we have regarded the latter (dimension) under the general notions of transference (McNees, A., 1973). In recent years, there has been increasing interest in the concept of "object replication" as another form of the past intruding into the present, particularly among moderately to severely impaired clients (Blancks, 1979). The more severe the structural impairment(s) as a result of insufficiencies in processes of internalization (particularly during lower level processes), the more the client may relate through a need-satisfying mode and unconsciously attempt to replicate unresolved aspects of primary relationships. The more moderate the impairment(s) (particularly if they occur during mid or higher levels of internalization), the more the client will feel confidence in his structural representation of self and will displace relatively discrete affect(s) associated with significant object representations on to the person of the therapist. The former state has been referred to as object replication in which the client's relatedness is motivated from a need to experience again the incompleteness of primary experiences in order to acquire the external supplies that will contribute to a sense of inner wholeness. The latter state is now considered by many theorists within the phenomena of transference. In our discussion of therapeutic responsiveness, Mrs. Young and Mr. Bourne were people who related pervasively on an object replicating level within the therapeutic relationship while the Murphys and Mrs. Parker tended to transfer or displace affect associated with internalized object representations of significant others.

The distinction between the ideas of object replication and transference is a qualitative one which is contingent upon the level of structuralization. In the moderately to severely impaired client, social supplies have not become internalized sufficiently and transmuted into psychological structures. As a consequence the person continues to seek out social relationships that he perceives will satisfy his unmet needs and sense of incompleteness. Because the self-representation has not been built up to the point at which it becomes dominant over object representations, this person suffers from a chronic sense of devaluation of self and tends to form relationships with significant others that may resemble his object representation(s) of the original need-satisfying experience(s). In Mahlerian terms, these people have not achieved self or object constancy because of subphase inadequacies either during rapproachement or during an earlier phase(s) of development. People who suffer from structural impairment of this nature may have significant difficulties in differentiating between self and object representations. Even if the process of differentiating has been partially resolved, the sense of self may be so tenuous that these people tend to gravitate toward external figures who they assume will complement their need to be cared for and nurtured. Such relationships seldom remain in a relatively steady state since equilibrium is contingent upon the preservation of polarized complementarity in roles of ego and alter. Sooner or later, complementarity begins to break down because the demands for replication exceed the reasonable expectations of current interpersonal realities. Complementarity also tends to deteriorate into interpersonal conflict because of overwhelming anxiety associated with the perceived threat of and vulnerability toward fusion of self with other.

Within the therapeutic relationship, these dynamics confront the clinical social worker with a unique challenge. Mrs. Young, for example, had to be helped to use the therapist not only as a separate object but as a humanized one. In other words, Mrs. Young needed someone who would empathically connect with her structural deficiencies while remaining a differentiated and caring human being who accepted her as she was and was willing to work with her without intruding precipitously into her fragile psychological world. The therapist was oriented to creating a therapeutic environment which would protect Mrs. Young's hold on reality while enhancing her potential ego capacities to use the relationship as an opportunity for the development of inner structure and enhancement of self-esteem. By putting into words her acceptance of the client's struggles to avoid hurt and by acknowledging the split-off or disowned feelings associated with critical losses, the therapist was using the relationships as a corrective experience (for Mrs. Young). Rather than explore transferential feelings (i.e., therapist = mother) which may have overwhelmed this woman's fragile sense of intersystemic equilibrium at that point in the therapy, the therapist refocused the work in order to engage the ego of Mrs. Young on how difficult it was to share her underlying struggles, which had been sealed off from consciousness. With clients such as Mrs. Young, this form of intervention may promote integration and at least partial healing of painful developmental lesions which interfere with more age-appropriate functioning as a mother and as an adult woman.

With Mr. Bourne, the therapist was confronted with similar dynamics, although this client's rage—projected on to the world in general, and on to the therapist in particular—required a delicate balance of empathic respect and protective distance. In both situations the therapists needed to connect with the underlying sense of sadness (in Mrs. Young) and hostility (in Mr. Bourne) while maintaining enough objective realness to remain outside of the need-satisfying orbit which these clients wished, yet feared, to replicate within the therapeutic relationship. The consistency of these therapists in recognizing underlying suffering, in providing a protective environment within which overwhelming fears could be gradually explored and in communicating respect for each client's autonomy (no matter how tenuous), were essential supplies in building a therapeutic relationship. In Adler's terms, they were offered "good enough therapist(s)" whose use of self was on the side of progressive rather than regressive developmental forces (Adler, in Mack, 1975).

We have said that the notion of transference refers to the displacement of relatively specific affective fragments of object representations on to the person of the therapist. As a phenomenon of the therapeutic relationship, transference has been differentiated from object replication by some theorists primarily in the quality of intactness of ego structures within the client. The capacity for transference presupposes an inner sense of separateness and autonomy within which the client is able to differentiate self from object representations and where the self-representation generally eclipses that of object representations. As a consequence the person is capable of tolerating object ambiguity within a relationship because intersystemic equilibrium is grounded primarily in a relatively stable nuclear sense of self and only secondarily in the acceptance and approval of external figures. Signal anxiety, rather than object anxiety, shapes the form of defensive and adaptive responses within the client's ego.

The work with Mrs. Parker offers an example of transference and illustrates how that concept is manifested in the "working through" aspects of supportive-confrontive-interpretive modes of therapy. Although the structure of the therapist's inner world, shaped by her own past, is the primary determinant of the counter-transference, the current interaction between therapist and client has a significant influence on the emergence of particular transference reactions within the client. That is, one's style in responding along the therapeutic continuum from gratifying-supportive interventions to frustrating-confrontive ones will have a shaping effect on the quality of transferential responses within the client. Of course, the reverse is also true. The countertransference is shaped by the client's current behavior within the therapeutic relationship. The notion of the "blank screen" or complete objectivity is impossible and, indeed, undesirable in clinical social work with any client, regardless of his level of impairment, a notion which we shall return to later.

With Mrs. Parker the therapist was empathically in touch with the client's suffering and supportive of her struggles to free herself from the bondage of distorted object representations; at the same time, he was partially frustrating of her unconscious attempts to retain him as an object of gratification. The balance between support and frustration was compatible with the developmental level of this client and others whose egos may be intact enough to tolerate that sort of therapy. In a sense, he permitted the client to experience anger at him as a depriving object, a derivative representation within the client of the original depriving figures in her life. Acceptance of those feelings by the therapist was a new experience for Mrs. Parker. Gradually, she was able to see the link between her response to the therapist and the ways in which she defended against similar responses to others in her real life both in the present and in the past. As Mrs. Parker was accepted and respected for who she was, a person with human thoughts and feelings which deserved to be understood, she began to relate to others more adaptively and less defensively. In other words, she was able to free herself (considerably) from stereotypical, affective modes of reacting to people, to become more accepting of her inner sense of self, and to acknowledge her worth and adaptive strengths. One instrumental vehicle for that change was the living out within the therapeutic relationship of those parts of herself to which she never felt entitled and for which she felt excessive guilt, the geneses of which were in her early primary relationships.

No matter how much of the past intrudes into the present, whether in the form of object replication or transference, the actual process of clinical work always takes place within an existential encounter between two human beings. The power of the need for replication or transference may exert enormous pressure on the therapist to adopt roles that are ultimately not in the interest of the client's well-being, but essentially she can only offer a new experience with a real object, albeit a humanized one, who is available to work with the intact executive ego of the client in its journey toward greater autonomy. As we have said, the unimpaired ego of the therapist is a resource for restoring impaired functioning and for enhancing the integration of

new learnings about current reality. Regardless of the level of impairment, we can be for the client only what we have become up to that
moment for our self. The most effective clinical work is done by people who value themselves as beings in the process of becoming and
who are open to new learnings about current realities. In essence, we
may ask no more of our clients than we ask of ourselves. For many
who hold to that value, it means that they too need to pursue their own
psychotherapy or psychoanalysis in order to be more fully with clients
in their struggles to achieve greater autonomy and adaptive functioning in their daily lives.

We have suggested that the therapist has no other choice than to
be herself regardless of the level of structural impairment within the
client. But what does it mean to be one's self, which Adler defines as

> the quality of therapist activity rather than the extent of self-revelation that
> is required by the [client] in order to feel the holding, support and con-
> cern of his therapist instead of a sense of abandonment and rejection
> (Adler, in Mack, 1975, 35-36).

To be real, then, implies a use of self (or more precisely, the therapeutic self) tempered by genuine regard for the well-being of the client,
empathic contact with and acceptance of his suffering, and a congruence of respect within the therapist for the integrity of the client
as another human being equal in spirit to her yet different in ego assets and liabilities. These qualities, in one form or another, have been
identified as essential attitudes of therapists in developing effective
working alliances with clients. Rogers has identified warmth, genuineness, empathy and congruence as indispensable qualities of effective
therapists within helping relationships (Rogers, 1962). Truax and Carkhuff (1967) talk of the genuineness, nonpossessive warmth and accurate empathy of therapists. Ferard and Hunnybun (1962) discuss the
importance of honesty, humility and inner peace of therapists. Sharing a part of the self within the context of these humanistic values,
which shape the therapeutic superego, should be aimed toward the
generic goal of supporting the client's potential for more adaptive functioning. As the therapist becomes more of a real person in an explicit
sense, the potential for transference or object replication tends to be
neutralized, which may be instrumental to therapeutic goals, especially
with people whose inner structures may be poorly organized and
whose hold on reality may be tenuous.

A critical aspect of the notion of realness in the therapeutic use of
self is related to the intent of our behavior, which is to be profession-

ally supportive of more adaptive functioning, ego autonomy and self-esteem (without imposing ourselves on the client as a "model" of more desirable behaviors). The contemporary emphasis on modeling appears misplaced in that it seems to be based implicitly on a presumption of superiority rather than empathic respect for individuality. That clients may imitate us and even adopt what they perceive to be our ways of adapting to conflict is well established. However, modeling as an intent of therapy is quite different from the client's identifying with what he perceives to be a better or more effective means of coping with life. The latter is a byproduct of the therapeutic process and one over which the client may exercise choice rather than a primary raison d'être imposed on the process by the clinical social worker.

A final aspect of the existential dimension of the therapeutic relationship is what Greenson refers to as the "working alliance," which he viewed as "the relatively non-neurotic, rational relationship between patient and analyst which makes it possible for the patient to work purposefully in the analytic situation" (Greenson, 1967, 46). Despite the level or extent of impairment, enough intact ego functioning must be or become available for the client to ally with the humanistic values underlying the therapeutic process as these values are communicated, verbally and non-verbally, by the clinical social worker. In this encounter between two human beings, the more intact, observing ego of the client needs to be free enough from impairment to connect with the conflict-free ego of the therapist in a shared effort toward realization of mutual goals. To engage people whose ego is severely impaired, such as Mrs. Young and Mr. Bourne, the therapist's task is to seek out and to connect with whatever intact ego is available in order to build, no matter how slowly, a viable contract with the client.

The therapeutic relationship in clinical social work is a complex gestalt within which past and present converge in a special kind of human encounter. Although the relationship has many elements of a true friendship, it is shaped primarily by the offering of one person of her self, her knowledge and her skills to support the adaptive potentials of the other(s). Empathic acceptance of individuality and genuine respect for personal integrity are the fundamental values upon which the process of clinical work is grounded. These existential values along with the clinical skills outlined in this essay serve as parameters for the practice of ego-oriented clinical social work. These parameters leave enough room for the individual style (of the therapist) to be expressed in ways that are unique to the personality of each therapist. Indeed, the individual nature of style tempered by knowledge, skill, values and by empathic contact with the suffering of the other person whom we call the client is the foundation upon which this model of clinical social work practice is grounded.

REFERENCES

Adler, J., and Myerson, P. (editors) *Confrontation in Psychotherapy.* New York: Science House, 1973.

Alexander, F. *Fundamentals of Psychoanalysis.* New York: W. W. Norton & Company, 1948.

Austin, L. "Trends in Differential Treatment in Social Casework." *Social Casework.* 29 June 1948, 203-211.

Bibring, G. "Psychiatry and Social Work," in *Social Casework.* 28 June 1947, 203-211.

Biestek, F. *The Casework Relationship.* Chicago: Loyola University Press, 1957.

Blanck, G., and Blanck, R. *Ego Psychology: Theory and Practice.* New York: Columbia University Press, 1974.

———. *Ego Psychology II: Psychoanalytic Developmental Psychology.* New York: Columbia University Press, 1979.

Blos, P. "The Second Individuation Process of Adolescence." *The Psychoanalytic Study of the Child,* XXII. New York: International Universities Press (1967) 162-182.

Community Service Society. *Method and Process in Social Casework.* Staff Committee Report. New York: FSAA, 1958.

Ferard, M., and Hynnybun, N. *The Caseworker's Use of Relationship.* London: Tavistock Publications, 1962.

Gilligan, C. *In a Different Voice: Psychological Theory and Women's Development.* Cambridge: Harvard University Press, 1982.

Greenson, R. *The Technique and Practice of Psychoanalysis* (Volume 1). New York: International Universities Press, 1967.

Hamilton, G. *Theory and Practice of Social Casework.* New York: Columbia University Press, 1940.

Hammer, E. *Use of Interpretation in Treatment: Technique and Art.* New York: Grune and Stratton, 1968.

Hollis, F. "The Techniques of Casework," in *Social Casework,* Vol. 30, June 1949, 235-244.

Hollis, F., *Casework: A Psychosocial Therapy,* New York: Random House, 1964.

Hollis, F., and Woods, M. *Casework: A Psychosocial Therapy.* (3rd Edition). New York: Random House, 1981.

Kernberg, O. *Borderline Conditions and Pathological Narcissism.* New York: Jason Aronson, 1975.

———. *Internal World and External Reality: Relations Theory Applied.* New York: Jason Aronson, 1980.

Kohut, H. *The Restoration of Self.* New York: International Universities Press, 1977.

Loewald, H. "Internalization, Separation, Mourning and the Super-ego," in *Psychoanalytic Quarterly.* 31, (1962): 483-504.

Maas, H. "Social Casework." *Concepts and Methods of Social Work.* Edited by W. Friedlander. Englewood Cliffs: Prentice-Hall, 1958.

Mack, J. *Borderline States in Psychiatry.* New York: Grune and Stratton, Inc., 1975.

McNees, A. "The Understanding of Transference by Social Workers in Clinical Practice." Boston College Graduate School of Social Work, 1973, Unpublished paper, 65 pp.

Minuchin, S. *Families and Family Therapy.* Cambridge: Harvard University Press, 1974.

Perlman, H. *Relationship: The Heart of Helping People.* Chicago: University of Chicago Press, 1979.

Richmond, M. *Social Diagnosis.* New York: Russell Sage Foundation, 1917.

Richmond, M. *What is Social Casework?: An Introductory Description.* City: Russell Sage Foundation, 1922.

Rogers, C. "Characteristics of A Helping Relationship." Special Supplement #27, *Canada's Mental Health,* March 1962.

Simon, B. *Relationship Between Theory and Practice in Social Casework.* City: NASW, 1960.

Truax, C. and Carkhuff, R. *Toward Effective Counseling and Psychotherapy: Training and Practice.* Chicago Aldine Publishing Company, 1967.

BIBLIOGRAPHY

Ables, B. *Therapy For Couples*. San Francisco: Jossey-Bass, 1977.

Ackerman, N. *The Psychodynamics of Family Life*. New York: Basic Books, 1958.

Adler, G. and Myerson, P. (editors). *Confrontation in Psychotherapy*. New York: Science House, 1973.

Ainsworth, M. "Object Relations, Dependency, and Attachment: A Theoretical Review of the Infant-Mother Relationship." *Child Development* #40 (1969):1025.

Alexander, F. *Fundamentals of Psychoanalysis*. New York: W. W. Norton & Company, 1948.

Anthony, E. J., and Benedek, T. (eds.) *Parenthood: Its Psychology and Psychopathology*. Boston: Little, Brown and Co., 1970.

Aptekar, H. *Basic Concepts of Social Casework*. Chapel Hill: University of Carolina Press, 1941.

Argyris, C., and Schon, D. *Theory in Practice: Increasing Professional Effectiveness*. San Francisco: Jossey-Bass, 1974.

Austin, L. "Trends in Differential Treatment in Social Casework." *Social Casework*, June 1948, 203-211.

Bandura, A. *Social Learning Theory*. Englewood Cliffs: Prentice-Hall, 1977.

Bardill, D., and Ryan, F. *Family Group Casework*. Washington, D.C.: Catholic University Press, 1964.

Beck, D., and Jones, A. *Progress on Family Problems: A Nationwide Study of Clients and Counselors' Views on Family Agency Services*. New York: FSAA, 1973.

Bell, A., Weinberg, M., and Hammersmith, S. *Sexual Preference: Its Development in Men and Women*. Bloomington: Indiana University Press, 1981.

Benedict, T. "Parenthood As a Developmental Phase: A Contribution to the Libido Theory." *Journal of the American Psychoanalytic Association*, vol. 7 (1959):389-417.

Bettelheim, B. *Freud and Man's Soul*. New York: Alfred A. Knopf, 1983.

Bibring, G. "Psychiatry and Social Work." *Social Casework*, June 1947, 203-211.

Biestek, F. *The Casework Relationship*. Chicago: Loyola University Press, 1957.

Bion, W. *Experiences in Groups*. New York: Basic Books, 1961.

Blanck, G., and Blanck, R. *Ego Psychology: Theory and Practice*. New York: Columbia University Press, 1974.

———. *Ego Psychology II: Psychoanalytic Developmental Psychology*. New York: Columbia University Press, 1979.

———. *Marriage and Personality Development*. New York: Columbia University Press, 1968.

Blos, P. "The Second Individuation Process of Adolescence." *The Psychoanalytic Study of the Child*. New York: International Universities Press Vol. XXII (1967):162-182.

Boehm, W. *Objectives of the Social Work Curriculum of the Future*. New York: Council on Social Work Education, 1959.

Bowen, M. *Family Therapy in Clinical Practice*. New York: Jason Aronson, 1978.

Bowlby, J. *Attachment and Loss, Vol. 1: Attachment*. New York: Basic Books, 1969.

———. *Attachment and Loss, Vol. 2: Separation, Anxiety and Anger*. New York: Basic Books, 1973.

Brazelton, G. "The Infant as Focus for Family Reciprocity." In Harvard Seminar Series, *The American Family* (cassettes): Cambridge, 1980.

Breger, L. *From Instinct to Identity: The Development of Personality*. Englewood Cliffs: Prentice-Hall, 1974.

Briggs, R. "The Problem of Dependency." *Proceedings, First National Conference of Catholic Charities*. 1910.

Burton, A. (ed.) *What Makes Behavior Change Possible?* New York: Brunner/Mazel, 1976.

Chadorow, N. *The Reproduction of Mothering: Psychoanalysis and the Sociology of Gender*. Berkley: University of California Press, 1978.

Cohen, N. *Social Work in the American Tradition*. Hinsdale: Dryden Press, 1958.

Cohen, S. *Social and Personality Development in Childhood*. New York: MacMillan Publishing Company, 1976.

Coleman, J., Janowicz, R., Fleck, S., and Norton, N. "A Comparative Study of a Psychiatric Clinic and a Family Agency." *Social Casework*, Vol. XXXIII, Nos. 1 and 2, January-February, 1957:3-8 and 74-80.

Community Service Society. *Method and Process in Social Casework*. Staff Committee Report, New York: FSAA, 1958.

Council on Social Work Education. *Socio-cultural Elements in Casework*. New York: 1955.

Diagnostic and Statistical Manual of Mental Disorders, Third Edition (DSM III). Washington, D.C.: American Psychiatric Association, 1980.

Edinburg, E., Zinberg, N., and Kelman, W. *Clinical Interviewing and Counseling: Principles and Techniques.* New York: Alppleton-Century-Crofts, 1975.

Edward, J. Ruskin, N., and Turrini, P. *Separation-Individuation: Theory and Application.* New York: Gardner Press, Inc., 1981.

Edwards, D. *Existential Psychotherapy: The Process of Caring.* New York: Gardner Press, Inc., 1982.

Epstein, N., and Vlok, L. "Research on the Results of Psychotherapy: A Summary of Evidence." *American Journal of Psychiatry,* 138:8 (August 1981): 1027-1035.

Erikson, E. *Childhood and Society.* New York: W. W. Norton & Company, 1950.
———. "Identity and the Life Cycle." In *Psychological Issues,* Vol. 1, no. 1 (Monograph 1). New York: International University Press, 1959.
———. *Identity, Youth and Crises.* New York: W. W. Norton & Company, 1968.

Evans, R. *Dialogue with Erik Erikson.* New York: Harper and Row, 1969.

Ewalt, P. (ed.) *Toward a Definition of Clinical Social Work.* Washington, D.C.: National Association of Social Workers, 1980.

Ferard, M., and Hunnybun, N. *The Caseworker's Use of Relationship.* London: Tavistock Publications, 1962.

Final Report of the Joint Commission on Mental Illness and Health. *Action for Mental Health.* New York: Basic Books, 1961.

Fischer, J. *The Effectiveness of Social Casework.* Springfield: Charles C. Thomas, 1976.

Ford, D., and Urban, H. *Systems of Psychotherapy: A Comparative Study.* New York: John Wiley and Son, 1963.

Fraiberg, S., Adelson, E., and Shapiro, V. "Ghosts in the Nursery: A Psychoanalytic Approach to the Problems of Impaired Infant-Mother Relationships." *American Academy of Child Psychiatry,* #14 (1975):387-421.
———. *Every Child's Birthright: In Defense of Mothering.* New York: Basic Books, 1977.

Frank, V. *Man's Search for Meaning.* New York: Washington Square Press, 1963.

Freud, A. *The Ego and The Mechanisms of Defense.* New York: International Universities Press, 1946.

Freud, S. *An Outline of Psychoanalysis.* New York: W. W. Norton & Company, 1949.
———. *The Ego and the Id.* New York: W. W. Norton & Company, 1960.
———. *The Ego and The Id.* Translated by Joan Riviere. New York: W. W. Norton & Company, 1962.
———. *The Complete Introductory Lectures on Psychoanalysis:* New York: W. W. Norton & Company, 1966.

Garrett, A. *Interviewing: Its Principles and Methods.* New York: Family Welfare Association of America, 1942.

Germain, C. and Gitterman, A. *The Life Model of Social Work Practice.* New York: Columbia University Press, 1980.

Goldberg, A. (ed.) *Advances in Self Psychology.* New York: International Universities Press, 1978.

Gilligan, C. *In a Different Voice: Psychological Theory and Women's Development.* Cambridge: Harvard University Press, 1982.

Gordon, W. "Basic Constructs for an Integrative and Generative Conception of Social Work." In *The General Systems Approach: Contributions Toward an Holistic Conception of Social Work.* Edited by G. Hearn. New York: Council on Social Work Education, 1968, 5–11.

Greenson, R. *The Technique and Practice of Psychoanalysis.* (Vol. 1) New York: International Universities Press, 1968.

Hamilton, G. *Theory and Practice of Social Casework.* New York: Columbia University Press, 1940.

———. *Theory and Practice of Social Casework.* (2nd edition, revised) New York: Columbia University Press, 1951.

Hammer, E. *Use of Interpretation in Treatment: Technique and Art.* New York: Grune and Stratton, 1968.

Hartman, H. *Ego Psychology and The Problem of Adaptation.* New York: International Universities Press, Inc. 1958.

———. *Essays on Ego Psychology.* New York: International Universities Press, 1964.

Hoffman, M. "Empathy, its Development and Prosocial Implications." In *Nebraska Symposium on Motivation, 1977: Social Cognitive Development.* Edited by C. B. Keasey. City: University of Nebraska Press, 1977.

Hollis, F. "The Techniques of Casework." *Social Casework,* June 1949, 235-244.

———. *Casework: A Psychosocial Therapy.* New York: Random House, 1964.

———. "Evaluation: Clinical Results and Research Methodology." *Clinical Social Work Journal,* Vol. 4, No. 3 (Fall 1976):204-222.

Hollis, F., and Woods, M. *Casework: A Psychosocial Therapy.* (3rd edition) New York: Random House, 1981.

Horner, A. *Object Relations and the Developing Ego in Therapy.* New York: Jason Aronson, 1979.

Jacobson, E. *The Self and the Object World.* New York: International Universities Press, 1954.

———. "The Self and the Object World: Vicissitudes of Their Infantile Cathexes and Their Influence on Ideational and Affective Development." *The Psychoanalytic Study of the Child,* Vol. IX. New York: International Universities Press, 1954, 75-127.

Kadushin, A. *The Social Work Interview.* New York: Columbia University Press, 1972.

Karpel, M. "Individuation: From Fusion to Dialogue." *Family Process,* Vol. 15, No. 1 (March 1976):65-82.

Kasius, C. (ed.) *Principles and Techniques in Social Casework: Selected Articles, 1940-1950.* New York: Family Service Association of America, 1950.

Kernberg, O. *Borderline Conditions and Pathological Narcissism.* New York: Jason Aronson, 1975.

———. *Object Relations Theory and Clinical Psychoanalysis.* New York: Jason Aronson, 1976.

———. *Internal World and External Reality: Object Relations Theory Applied.* New York: Jason Aronson, 1980.

Klein, D., and Lindemann, E. "Preventive Intervention in Individual and Family Crisis Situations." In *Prevention of Mental Disorders in Children.* Edited by G. Caplan. New York: Basic Books, 1961, 283-306.

Kluckhohn, F. "Variations in the Basic Values of Family Systems." *The Family*. (Revised Edition). Edited by N. Bell and E. Vogel. New York: The Free Press, 1968, 319-330.

Kohlberg, L. "Development of Moral Character and Moral Idealogy." In *Review of Child Development Research*. Edited by M. Hoffman and L. Hoffman. New York: Russell Sage Foundation, 1964, 383-431.

Kohut, H. *The Analysis of Self*. New York: International University Press, 1971.

———. *The Restoration of Self*. New York: International Universities Press, 1977.

Krill, D. *Existential Social Work*. New York: The Free Press, 1978.

Laurie, H. "The Development of Social Welfare Programs in the United States." *Social Work Year Book*, 1957, 19-45.

Lazare, A. "Hidden Conceptual Models in Clinical Psychiatry." *New England Journal of Medicine*, 288 (February 15, 1973):345-351.

Levinson, D. "The Mid-Life Transition: A Period in Adult Psychosocial Development." *Psychiatry*, Vol. 40 (May 1977):99-112.

Lieberman, F. (Editor) *Clinical Social Workers as Psychotherapists*. New York: Gardner Press, Inc., 1982.

Loewald, H. "Internalization, Separation, Mourning and the Super-ego." *Psychoanalytic Quarterly*, Vol. 31 (1962):483-504.

Lowell, C. "The Economic and Moral Effects of Public Outdoor Relief." *National Conference on Charities and Corrections*. City: 1890, 81-91.

Lidz, T. *The Person: His and Her Development Throughout the Life Cycle*. (revised edition) New York: Basic Books, 1976.

Lynd, H. *On Shame and the Search for Identity*. New York: Harcourt, Brace and World, 1958.

Mack, J. *Borderline States in Psychiatry*. New York: Grune and Stratton, 1975.

Mackey, R. "Professionalization and the Poor." *Social Work*, Vol. 8 (September 1964): 108-110, 119.

Mackey, R. Taschman, H. and Ryan. C. "Periodic Surveys of Community Resources: A Project to Improve Referrals for Direct Service." *Community Mental Health Journal*. Vol. 3, No. 4 (Winter 1967):331-334.

Mackey, R. "Crisis Theory: Its Development and Relevance to Social Casework Practice." *Family Coordinator*, Vol. 17, No. 5 (July 1968):165-173.

———. "Personal Concepts of the Mentally Ill Among Caregiving Groups," *Mental Hygiene*, Vol. 53, No. 2 (April 1969):245-252.

———. "Views of Caregiving and Mental Health Groups About Alcoholics," *Quarterly Journal of Studies on Alcohol*, Vol. 30, No. 3 (September 1969):665-671.

Mackey, R. Taschman, H. and Kisielewski, J. "An Analysis of Requests for Help to a Mental Health Study Center," *Public Health Reports*, Vol. 84, No. 10 (October 1969):923-928.

Mackey, R. "Generic Aspects of Clinical Social Work Practice," *Social Casework*, Vol. 57, No. 10 (December 1976):619-624.

———. "Developmental Processes in Growth-oriented Groups," *Social Work*, Vol. 25, No. 1 (January 1980):26-31.

MacKinnon, R., and Michels, R. *The Psychiatric Interview in Clinical Practice*. Philadelphia: W. B. Saunders Company, 1971.

Mahler, M., Pines, F., and Bergman, A. *The Psychological Birth of the Human Infant*. New York: Basic Books, 1975.

Mahler, M. The Selected Papers of Margaret S. Mahler, M.D., Volumes 1 and 2. New York: Jason Aronson, 1979.

Maier, H. *Three Theories of Child Development.* New York: Harper and Row, 1965.

Malucci, A. *Learning from Clients: Interpersonal Helping as Viewed by Clients and Social Workers.* New York: Free Press, 1979.

Mangold, M., and Zaki, E. *Annette Garrett, Interviewing: Its Principles and Methods.* (3rd edition) New York: FSAA, 1982.

Mass, H. "Social Casework," *Concepts and Methods of Social Work.* Edited by W. Friedlander. Englewood Cliffs: Prentice-Hall, 1958.

May, R., Angel, E. and Ellenberger, H., (Editors). *Existence: A New Dimension in Psychiatry and Psychology,* New York: Basic Books, 1958.

Mayer, J., and Timms, N. *The Client Speaks: Working Class Impressions of Casework.* New York: Atherton Press, 1970.

McNees, A. "The Understanding of Transference by Social Workers in Clinical Practice." Graduate School of Social Work, Boston College, 1973.

Minuchin, S. *Families and Family Therapy.* Cambridge: Harvard University Press, 1974.

Muson, H. "Moral Thinking: Can it Be Taught?" *Psychology Today.* February 1979.

Northern, H. *Clinical Social Work.* New York: Columbia University Press, 1982.

Olden, C. "Notes on the Development of Empathy," *Psychoanalytic Study of the Child.* Vol. 13 (1958):505-518.

Paine, R. "Pauperism in Great Cities: Its Four Chief Causes," *Proceedings, International Congress of Charities.* Chicago: 1895, Vol. I, Sec II, 23-52.

Paolino, T., and McCrady, B. *Marriage and Marital Therapy: Psychoanalytic, Behavioral, and Systems Theory Perspectives.* New York: Brunner/Mazel, 1978.

Papajohn, J., and Spiegel, J. *Transactions in Families.* San Francisco: Jossey Bass, 1975.

Parad, H. (ed.) *Ego Psychology and Dynamic Casework.* New York: FSAA, 1958.

Parad, H., and Miller, R. (eds.) *Ego-Oriented Casework: Problems and Perspectives.* New York: FSAA, 1963.

Perlman, H. Social Casework: *A Problem-solving Process.* Chicago: University of Chicago Press, 1957.

———. "Intake and Some Role Considerations," *Social Casework,* 41 (April 1960):171-177.

———. *Relationship: The Heart of Helping People.* Chicago: University of Chicago Press, 1979.

Piaget, J. *The Moral Judgment of the Child.* New York: The Free Press, 1948.

———. *The Child and Reality: Problems of Genetic Psychology.* New York: Grossman Publishers, 1973.

Pinderhughes, E. "The Effect of Ethnicity Upon the Psychological Task of Separation-Individuation: A Comparison of Four Ethnic Groups." Paper presented at the 56th *Annual Meeting of the American Orthopsychiatric Association.* City: April, 1979.

Polansky, N. *Ego Psychology and Communication: Theory for the Interview.* New York: Atherton Press, 1971.

——. *Integrated Ego Psychology.* New York: Aldine Publishing Co., 1982.

Rapaport, L. "Crisis Intervention as a Mode of Brief Treatment." *Theories of Social Casework.* Edited by R. Roberts and R. Nee. Chicago: University of Chicago Press, 1970, 265-311.

Redlich, F., Hollingshead, A. and Bellis, E. "Social Class Differences in Attitudes Toward Psychiatry," *The American Journal of Orthopsychiatry,* Vol. XXV, No. 1 (1955):60-70.

Reid, W., and Shyne, A. *Brief and Extended Casework.* New York: Columbia University Press, 1969.

Reid, W., and Epstein, L. *Task-Centered Casework.* New York: Columbia University Press, 1972.

Reynolds, B. "An Experiment in Short Contact Interviewing," *Smith College Studies in Social Work,* Vol. III, No. 1, 1932.

Richmond, M. *Social Diagnosis.* New York: Russell Sage Foundation, 1917.

——. *What is Social Casework: An Introductory Description.* New York: Russell Sage Foundation, 1922.

Roberts, R., and Nee, R. (Editors) *Theories of Social Casework:* Chicago: University of Chicago Press, 1957.

Robinson, V. *A Changing Psychology in Social Casework.* Cahpel Hill: University of North Carolina Press, 1930.

Rogers, C. "Characteristics of a Helping Relationship." Special Supplement, *Canada's Mental Health,* March, 1962, 18 pp.

Satir, V. *Conjoint Family Therapy.* Palo Alto: Science and Behavior Books, 1964.

Schofield, W. *Psychotherapy: The Purchase of Friendship.* Englewood Cliffs: Prentice-Hall, 1964.

Schubert, M. *Interviewing in Social Work Practice.* New York: Council on Social Work Education, 1971.

Schwartz, A. *The Behavior Therapies: Theory and Application.* New York: The Free Press, 1981.

Simon, B. *Relationship Between Theory and Practice in Social Casework.* New York: NASW, 1960.

Sloane, Staples, F., Crestol, A., Yorkston, N. and Whipple, K., *Psychotherapy versus Behavior Therapy.* Cambridge: Harvard University Press, 1975.

Smalley, R. "The Functional Approach to Casework Practice," *Theories of Social Casework,* Edited by R. Roberts and R. Nee. Chicago: University of Chicago Press, 1970, 77-128.

Smith, Z. "Country Help for City Charities," *Lend a Hand.* (III) 1888, 640-646.

Spiegel, J. "The Resolution of Role Conflict Within the Family," *A Modern Introduction to the Family,* edited by N. Bell and E. Vogel. New York: The Free Press, 1968, 391-411.

Spitz, R. *The First Year of Life.* New York: International Universities Press, 1965.

Strean, H. *Clinical Social Work: Theory and Practice.* New York: The Free Press, 1978.

Strupp, H. *Patients View Their Psychotherapy.* Baltimore: John Hopkins Press, 1969.

Strupp, H. *Psychotherapy: Clinical, Research, and Theoretical Issues.* New York: Jason Aronson, 1973.

Sze, W. *Human Life Cycle.* New York: Jason Aronson, 1975.

Truax, C., and Carkhuff, R. *Toward Effective Counseling and Psychotherapy: Training and Practice.* Chicago: Aldine Publishing Co., 1967.

Turner, F. *Differential Diagnosis and Treatment in Social Work.* (2nd Edition) New York: The Free Press, 1976.

————. *Psychosocial Therapy: A Social Work Perspective.* New York: The Free Press, 1978.

Turner, F. (Editor) *Social Work Treatment: Interlocking Theoretical Approaches.* New York: The Free Press, 1979.

Upham, F. *Ego Analyis in the Helping Professions.* New York: FSAA, 1973.

Vincent, C. "Family Spongea: The Adaptive Function," *Journal of Marriage and the Family,* Vol. 28, No. 1 (February 1966):29-36.

Watzlawick, P., Beavin, J. and Jackson, D. *Pragmatics of Human Communication: A Study of Interactional Patterns, Pathologies and Paradoxes.* New York: W. W. Norton & Company, 1967.

Weismann, M., and Paykel, E. *The Depressed Woman:* Chicago: University of Chicago Press, 1974.

Wheelis, A. "How People Change," *Commentary,* Vol. 47, No. 5 (May 1969):56-66.

Winnicott, D. "Transitional Objects and Transitional Phenomena: A Study of the First Not-me Possession," *International Journal of Psychoanalysis,* Vol. 34 (1953):1-25.

Wodarski, J. *The Role of Research in Clinical Practice:* Baltimore: University Park Press, 1981.

Yahraes, H. *Childhood Environment and Mental Health: A Conversation with Dr. Jerome Kagan.* Rockville: National Institute of Mental Health.

INDEX